ON TO
JAVA ₂

Patrick Henry Winston
Massachusetts Institute of Technology

Sundar Narasimhan
Ascent Technology, Incorporated

Addison
Wesley

Boston San Francisco New York
London Toronto Sydney Tokyo Singapore Madrid
Mexico City Munich Paris Cape Town Hong Kong Montreal

Library of Congress Cataloging-in-Publication Data

Winston, Patrick Henry
   On to Java / Patrick Henry Winston. Sundar Narasimhan.
      p.   cm.
   ISBN 0-201-72593-2 (pbk.)
   1. Java (Computer program language).   I. Title.
   QA76.73.J38 W56 2001
   005.13'3—dc21

                                                    20010022156

Reproduced by Addison-Wesley from PostScript files supplied by the author.

1 2 3 4 5 6 7 8 9 10-MA-030201

CONTENTS

ACKNOWLEDGMENTS

The cover of this book was designed by Chiai Takahashi, with counsel from Paul Keel.

Lyn Dupré was the developmental editor. She has a special gift for rooting out problems and suggesting improvements. The errors in this book were introduced—by authors who never stop writing—after Ms. Dupré finished her work.

If you write technical material, you should read Ms. Dupré's book *Bugs in Writing: A Guide to Debugging Your Prose (revised edition)*, (Addison-Wesley, 1998).

1 HOW THIS BOOK TEACHES YOU THE JAVA PROGRAMMING LANGUAGE

1   The purpose of this book is to help you learn the essentials of Java™ programming. In this chapter, you learn about Java's history, Java's special features, and this book's organization.

2   Java was designed for writing programs that run on computers embedded in consumer-electronics appliances, such as microwave ovens and television sets. Accordingly, the design choices made by the developers of Java reflect the expectation that the language would be used to implement small, distributed, and necessarily robust programs.

3   Java has captured the interest and attention of programmers because certain features—conceived in the expectation that programmers would use Java to build programs for consumer electronics—happen to make Java the ideal language for building programs for use on computers connected to the Internet:

- Java programs run on a wide variety of hardware platforms.

- Java programs can be loaded dynamically via a network.

- Java provides features that facilitate robust behavior.

In addition, Java has features that make it an excellent language even for applications that have nothing to do with networks:

- Java is a thoroughly object-oriented language.

- Java programs can work on multiple tasks simultaneously.

- Java programs automatically recycle memory.

4   To make Java programs **portable,** so that they will run on a variety of hardware platforms, the Java **compiler** translates the programs into **byte code.** Such translated programs are said to have been **compiled** into byte code.

Programs translated into byte code seem to be written in the instruction set of a typical computer, but byte code is neutral in that it does not employ the instruction set of any particular computer. Instead, byte code is executed by a program that pretends that it is a computer based on the byte-code instruction set. Such a program is called a **byte-code interpreter.** A byte-code interpreter intended to execute the byte code produced by the Java compiler is called a Java **virtual machine.**

Once a Java virtual machine has been implemented for a particular computer, that computer will run any compiled Java program. Or, said the other way around, any Java application will run on every machine for which a Java virtual machine has been implemented.

Java is a trademark of Sun Microsystems Computer Corporation.

5 You might think that byte-code interpretation must mean slow execution, relative to, say, C or C++ programs that are compiled directly into the native instruction set of a particular machine.

Fortunately, however, a full-capability Java virtual machine can translate byte code into the native instruction set of the computer through a process called **just-in-time compilation**. Accordingly, Java programs can run nearly as fast as programs written in older, less portable programming languages.

6 The Java virtual machine helps you to find errors, because the Java virtual machine performs **runtime checks** that complement the **compile-time checks** performed by all compilers. For example, when programs are about to access array elements that do not exist, the Java virtual machine displays an informative message and halts, thus catching a common programming error before a hard-to-debug crash occurs.

7 Because Java is **object oriented**, programs consist of **class definitions**.

In Java, some class definitions establish the characteristics of generic program elements, such as vectors. Other class definitions—the ones that you define yourself—establish the characteristics of application-specific categories, such as railroad cars, stocks, foods, movies, or whatever else happens to come up naturally in your application. Once a class is defined, you can create **class instances** that describe the particular properties of the individuals that belong to it.

When you design a program around classes and class instances, you are said to practice **object-oriented programming**. In contrast, when you design programs around procedures, you are said to practice **procedure-oriented programming**.

8 In this book, you learn more about what *object oriented* means and why many programmers prefer object-oriented languages. For now, it suffices for you to know that Java is a thoroughly object-oriented programming language; in contrast, most programming languages, such as C, are procedure-oriented, and other programming languages, such as C++, are half-procedure-oriented, half-object-oriented hybrids.

9 When you run a Java program, it fetches each class definition only when needed. Thus, Java is said to **load classes dynamically** or **on demand**.

Certain Java programs are intended to be used in cooperation with a **web browser** such as Netscape Navigator™, which contains a Java virtual machine capable of loading Java classes dynamically via a **local-area network** or via the Internet.

10 Java applications loaded by web browsers are based on **applet** classes. *Applet* is a word that means *little application*; however, some applications loaded by web browsers are large

11 Distributing software via web browsers is wonderfully effective: No programs have to be downloaded and manually installed, and, better still, no disks need to be packaged for sale and no update or bug-fix disks need to be mailed.

Netscape Navigator is a trademark of Netscape Communications Corporation.

12 Another distinguishing feature of Java is that Java allows you to create **multiple threads**. Each thread is like a separate program in that a thread seems to run at the same time as other threads; in contrast, however, the threads in one program share the same memory.

By exploiting the thread feature, you can write programs in which one thread is working through complex statistical formulas, another thread is fetching data from a file, still another thread is transmitting data over a network, and yet another thread is updating a display. All these threads share your computer's time. Because no thread ever has to wait for another thread to finish a task, you can write programs that exhibit an extraordinarily responsive look and feel.

13 Java increases your productivity by providing automatic memory recycling. When you use a language such as C++, you have to remember to free the memory allocated to program elements, such as class instances, once you are finished with them. Failing to free memory produces a **memory leak** that may exhaust all the memory available to your program, leading either to erratic behavior or to a total program crash.

Java frees memory automatically, by performing **automatic garbage collection**, so you never need worry about memory leaks or waste time looking for one. Thus, you are more productive, and less likely to be driven crazy via tedious, mind-numbing debugging.

Most programming languages do not offer garbage collection, even though languages such as Lisp and Smalltalk established the great value of garbage collection decades ago.

14 In addition to automatic garbage collection, the Java virtual machine provides a variety of other features that facilitate **secure behavior**. For example, no Java program, run via a web browser, can open, read, or write files on your computer; it is therefore difficult for someone to corrupt or hobble your software, either deliberately or inadvertently.

15 For many programmers, Java is easy to learn because Java's syntax is largely based on that of the popular C and C++ programming languages.

Although Java programs resemble C and C++ programs when viewed at a distance, the Java programming language excludes many of the characteristics of C and C++ believed by Java's designers to harm program readability and robustness. For example, Java programmers do not think in terms of pointers and they do not overload operators.

16 To get you up and running in Java quickly, the chapters in this book generally supply you with the most useful approach to each programming need, be it to display characters on your screen, to define a new method, or to read information from a file.

17 To help you aquire the knowledge you need quickly, this book is divided into chapters that generally focus on one question, which is plainly announced in the title of the chapter. Accordingly, you see titles such as the following:

- How to Compile and Run a Simple Program
- How to Define Constructor Instance Methods
- How to Benefit from Data Abstraction

- How to Define Abstract Classes and Abstract Methods

- How to Design Classes and Class Hierarchies

- How to Modularize Programs Using Compilation Units and Packages

- How to Enforce Requirements and to Document Programs Using Interfaces

- How to Use the Model-View Approach to Interface Design

- How to Access Applets from Web Browsers

- How to Use Threads to Implement Dynamic Applets

- How to Use Resource Locators to Access Files

- How to Collect Information Using Servlets

18 So that you are encouraged to develop a personal library of solutions to standard programming problems, this book introduces many useful, productivity-increasing, general-purpose, templatelike patterns that you can fill in to achieve particular-purpose goals. These templatelike patterns are often called **programming idioms**.

You learn about programming idioms because learning to program involves more than learning to use rules of program composition, just as learning to speak a human language involves more than learning to use vocabulary words.

19 So that you can deepen your understanding of the art of **good programming practice**, this book emphasizes the value of powerful ideas, such as procedure abstraction and data abstraction; introduces key mechanisms, such as the interface mechanism for imposing requirements and encouraging documentation; and explains important principles, such as the explicit-representation principle, no-duplication principle, lookup principle, and need-to-know principle.

20 In this book, single-idea segments, analogous to slides, are arranged in chapters that are analogous to slide shows. There are several segment varieties: **mainline segments** explain essential ideas; **sidetrip segments** introduce interesting, but skippable, ideas; **practice segments** provide opportunities to experiment with new ideas; and **highlights segments** summarize important points.

21 The book develops a simple, yet realistic Java program, which you see in many versions as your understanding of the language increases. In its ultimate version, the program reads from a file that contains information about movies, computes an overall rating for a selected movie, displays the rating on a meter, and shows an advertising poster, if one is available. The program runs either as a standalone application or as an applet meant to be used via a network viewer. The applet version presents the following appearance:

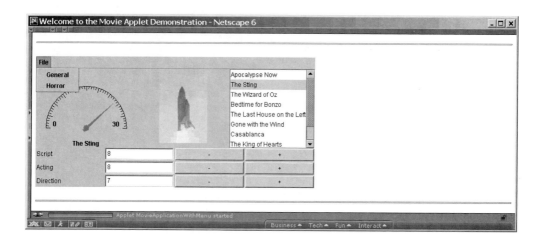

- Its features make Java ideally suited for writing network-oriented programs.

- Java is an object-oriented programming language. When you use an object-oriented programming language, your programs consist of class definitions.

- Java class definitions and the programs associated with classes are compiled into byte code, which facilitates program portability.

- Java class definitions and the programs associated with them can be loaded dynamically via a network.

- Java's compiler detects errors at compile time; the Java virtual machine detects errors at run time.

- Java programs can be multithreaded, thereby enabling them to perform many tasks simultaneously.

- Java programs collect garbage automatically, relieving you of tedious programming and frustrating debugging, thereby increasing your productivity.

- Java has syntactical similarities with the C and C++ languages.

- This book introduces and emphasizes powerful ideas, key mechanisms, and important principles.

2 HOW TO COMPILE AND EXECUTE A SIMPLE PROGRAM

23 In this chapter, you learn how to compile and execute a simple program that computes the overall rating of a movie from ratings provided for the movie's script, acting, and direction. You also review standard terminology used throughout the rest of this book.

24 When you work with Java, you work either within a vendor-specific **development environment** or within a general-purpose **editor**, with which you write your program, and a **compiler**, with which you translate your program into a form with which your Java virtual machine can work.

If you try to learn Java using a vendor-specific development environment, you learn a great deal about the vendor-specific development environment, but not enough about Java itself. Accordingly, this book introduces Java in the expectation that you will use a traditional editor and compiler.

25 In its original form, your program is **text** or **source code**. Once translated, the source code becomes **byte code**. You use the Java virtual machine to **execute** your program, or, said another way, you **run** your program.

26 You generally go around two key loops many times as you search for bugs.

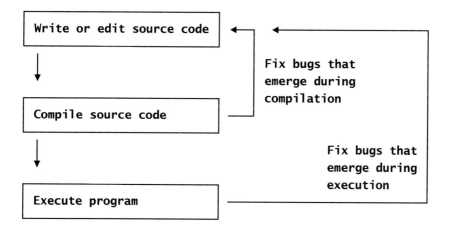

27 All Java programs contain one or more **class definitions**, each of which may contain various **method definitions**.

In particular, every standalone Java program must contain a class definition that defines a method named main. When you start a Java program, the Java virtual machine performs the computations specified in the main method, thereby executing your program.

28
SIDE TRIP Applets developed exclusively for use in web browsers do not contain a main method, because they are not standalone programs; web browsers execute applets using mechanisms explained in Chapter 43.

29 Java's methods take the place of the **functions** or **procedures** that programmers talk about

^{SIDE TRIP} when they work with other languages. Methods are much like functions and procedures, except that each method definition must be embedded in a class definition.

30 Suppose, for example, that you want to compute the overall rating of a movie, given integers that specify individual ratings for the script, acting, and direction. For the moment, assume each individual rating contributes equally to the total rating. In Java, your program will contain a simple summing expression:

```
6 + 9 + 8
```

31 To arrange for your arithmetic expression to be evaluated, you define `main`, inside a class definition, such that the arithmetic expression appears in that method.

```
public static void main (String argv[]) {
  6 + 9 + 8;
}
```

To understand the `main` definition, you need to zoom in to look at it piece by piece. Then, to use the `main` definition, you embed it in a class definition, as you learn, in Segment 35.

32 **Keywords** are words to which Java attributes special meanings. Three such keywords appear in the example.

Keywords

```
public static void main (String argv[]) {
  6 + 9 + 8;
}
```

- The keyword `public` indicates how accessible the `main` method is to be. You learn more about the `public` keyword in Chapter 15.

- The keyword `static` indicates that the `main` method is a **class method**, rather than an **instance method**. You learn about this distinction in Chapter 10.

- The keyword `void` indicates that the `main` method returns no value. You learn more about the `void` keyword in Chapter 5

You should accept the use of the three keywords as ritual for now. You will come to understand the ritual as you study the language.

33 Following the method name, `main`, you see a **parameter specification** surrounded by parentheses.

```
public static void main (String argv[]) {
  6 + 9 + 8;
}
```

Again, you can think of the parameter specification as a matter to be understood later: You learn about parameter specifications in general in Chapter 5, and about the parameter specification for main methods in Chapter 29.

For now, just accept the parameter specification as ritual that you will understand later in your learning process.

34 Finally, you come to the method's **body**. In general, a method's body consists of matched braces surrounding a sequence of one or more **statements**, which tell the Java compiler what computations to perform. In the example, the body exhibits only one statement:

```
public static void main (String argv[]) {
  6 + 9 + 8;                              ◄─── Body statement
}
```

The statement, like most Java statements, consists of an **expression**, 6 + 9 + 8, and the **statement terminator**, a semicolon, ;.

35 At this point, you are ready to embed the main method in a class definition. Because you are defining a demonstration program, you name the class Demonstrate.

You must store the definition of the Demonstrate class in a **source file**. The source file's **file name** must be Demonstrate, the name of the class contained in the file, and the source file's **extension** must be java.

36 Most Java programmers, by convention, start each class name with an uppercase letter. You should adhere to this convention; otherwise, other programmers may have difficulty understanding your.

37 The definition of the Demonstrate class begins with two keywords: public and class.

Keywords

```
public class Demonstrate {
  ...
}
```

- The keyword public indicates how accessible the Demonstrate class is to be.

- The keyword class indicates that a class is about to be defined.

38 Following the name of the class, `Demonstrate`, you come to the **body** of the class definition. In the example, the body contains a single method definition—the one for the `main` method—which computes the rating of a movie, given ratings for the movie's script, acting, and direction.

```
public class Demonstrate {
 public static void main (String argv[]) {
  6 + 9 + 8;
 }
}
```

39 The semicolon, ;, the parentheses, (), and the braces, {}, act as punctuation. Occasionally, such markers, in such contexts, are called **punctuators**.

40 Note that the sample program is catatonic: It accepts no input data and produces no output result. And, because the program does nothing with the arithmetic it performs, discriminating Java compilers refuse to compile it.

41 To relieve programs of their catatonia, you can include **display statements** that tell the Java compiler that you want information to be displayed, as in the following revised program, which, when executed, displays The rating of the movie is 23:

```
public class Demonstrate {
 public static void main (String argv[]) {
  System.out.print("The rating of the movie is ");
  System.out.println(6 + 9 + 8);
 }
}
```

The revised program introduces several new concepts. Accordingly, you need to zoom in, and to look at it piece by piece.

42 The **display methods**, `print` and `println`, display information delimited by parentheses. Whenever you use `println` instead of `print`, Java not only displays information, but also terminates the line on which the information is displayed.

43 In Java, whenever quotation marks delimit a sequence of characters, those characters are the contents of a **string**. In the sample program, there are two **display statements**, the first of which displays a string.

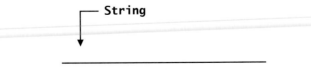

```
System.out.print("The rating of the movie is ");
```

44 In the second instance, the display method displays the result produced by an arithmetic expression:

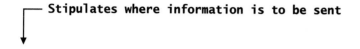

Arithmetic expression

```
System.out.println(6 + 9 + 8);
```

45 The System.out part of the display statement stipulates that the information is to be shown on your computer's display:

Stipulates where information is to be sent

```
System.out.print("The rating of the movie is ");
```

46 Said with more precision, print and println are display methods that are defined to
SIDE TRIP work on instances of the PrintStream class. System.out is an expression that produces the particular instance of the PrintStream class associated with your display. You learn about the syntax involved in Chapter 9, and you learn about the PrintStream class in Chapter 33.

47 A value that appears explicitly in a program is said to be a **literal**. Explicit numbers, such as 6, are integer literals. Explicit strings, such as "The rating of the movie is ", are string literals.

48 Spaces, tabs, line feeds, and carriage returns are said to be **whitespace characters**. Java is **blank insensitive**: It treats all sequences of whitespace characters—other than those in strings—as though there were just a single space. Thus, the following are equivalent:

```
public class Demonstrate {
 public static void main (String argv[]) {
  System.out.print("The rating of the movie is ");
  System.out.println(6 + 9 + 8);
 }
}

public class Demonstrate
{
public static void main (String argv[])

{
        System.out.print("The rating of the movie is ");
        System.out.println(6 + 9 + 8);
}

}
```

Neither of these layout options is "better" or "official." In fact, many experienced Java programmers argue heatedly about how to arrange methods to maximize transparency and to be most pleasing to the eye. In this book, the methods are written in a style that both uses paper efficiently and lies within the envelope of common practice.

49 Java is **case sensitive**; if you write `Main` or `MAIN` when you mean `main`, Java cannot understand your intent.

50 At this point, you have seen sample uses of just one Java operator: the addition operator. In general, an **operator** is a built-in method that works on inputs supplied to it according to the conventions of arithmetic; such methods are interspersed among their inputs, and those inputs are called **operands**.

51 To initiate compilation on a Windows system, you open a **window**. Next, you type the following, assuming that your class definition is in a source file named `Demonstrate.java`:

```
javac Demonstrate.java
```

Such a line is called a **command line**. The example command line has two parts:

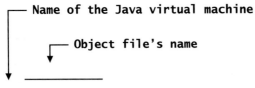

```
javac Demonstrate.java
```

The Java compiler places the resulting byte code in a file named `Demonstrate.class`.

52 Once the Java compiler has placed the resulting byte code in `Demonstrate.class`, you can execute the `main` program defined inside the class definition by typing another command line:

> ┌─ Name of the Java virtual machine
>
> ┌─ Object file's name

```
java Demonstrate
```

53 Although the sample program communicates with you by way of output data displayed on your screen, it does not receive any input data after it has been compiled. Instead, it works with data that were supplied as the program was written. Such data are said to be **wired in** or **hard coded**. You learn to work with data in a data file in Chapter 27.

54 In this book, you see many templatelike, general-purpose program patterns—sometimes called programming idioms—that you can fill in to suit your own specific purpose. In these patterns, each place to be filled in is identified by a description of the item to be inserted, such as this phrase .

When you fill in a pattern, replacing descriptions with specific instances of the general categories described, you are said to **instantiate** the pattern.

55
PRACTICE
Write a program that computes and displays the volume of Earth.

56
HIGHLIGHTS

- When you work with Java, you write source code, the Java compiler translates source code into byte code, and the Java virtual machine executes that byte code.

- Java programs consist of class definitions. If a program is to be a standalone program, one of the class definitions must contain a definition for a method named `main`. When you execute a standalone Java program, the Java virtual machine performs the computations specified in that `main` method.

- Java methods contain computation-specifying expressions embedded in statement sequences.

- Many expressions involve built-in operators, such as the addition operator, +. Operators do their work on operands.

- To test simple programs, you often use data that you supply when you write the program. Such data are said to be wired in.

- If you want to display data, **then** use a display statement:

  `System.out.print(expression whose value is to be displayed);`

- If you want not only to display data, but also to terminate a line, **then** use `println` instead of `print`.

3 HOW TO DECLARE VARIABLES

57 In this chapter, you learn how to declare variables in Java. You also learn more of the terminology used throughout the rest of this book.

58 A Java **identifier** is a name consisting of letters and digits, the first of which must be a letter. The underscore, _, and the dollar sign, $, count as letters.

Most Java programmers do not use the underscore when they run words together to produce long identifiers. Instead, they initiate the first word with a lowercase character and each interior word with an uppercase character, as in movieRating. You should adhere to this convention; otherwise, other programmers will find your programs difficult to understand.

59 A **variable** is a chunk of computer memory that contains a **value**. The **name** of a variable is an identifier that refers to the variable.

A variable's **data type** determines the size of the chunk and the way that the bits in the chunk are interpreted. If the data type of a variable is int, the variable holds a 32-bit signed **integer**. If the data type of a variable is double, the variable holds a 64-bit signed floating-point number.

As a program runs, a variable's value may change, but a variable's data type never changes. Thus, the value of a variable named script, with type int, could be 8 at one time and 9 at another, but the value of script could never be a number with type double, such as 8.5.

60 Because every variable is typed, the Java compiler can **allocate** a memory chunk of the right size for each variable, once and for all, taking advantage of the fact that the value of the variable always will fit within the allocated memory chunk.

61 When you tell the Java compiler the type of a variable, you are said to **declare** the variable. Thus, the following program fragment exhibits three variable declarations. All three variables are declared to be integer variables, because each is preceded by the data-type–declaring int keyword:

```java
public class Demonstrate {
 public static void main (String argv[]) {
  int script;
  int acting;
  int direction;
  ...
 }
}
```

62 You can combine several separate variable declarations into one, more concise variable declaration if each variable has the same data type. In the following program fragment, for example, all three variables are declared to be integer variables in a single declaration:

```
public class Demonstrate {
 public static void main (String argv[]) {
  int script, acting, direction;
  ...
 }
}
```

Note the obligatory, variable-separating commas.

63 Storing a value in the memory chunk allocated for a variable is called **variable assignment**. Accordingly, whenever Java places a value in such a memory chunk, the variable is said to be **assigned a value**, and the value is said to be **assigned to the variable**.

64 You can **initialize** a variable in the same statement in which the variable is declared:

```
public class Demonstrate {
 public static void main (String argv[]) {
  int script = 6;
  int acting = 9;
  int direction = 8;
  ...
 }
}
```

You can combine several declarations, with initializations, into one concise statement, as in the following example:

```
public class Demonstrate {
 public static void main (String argv[]) {
  int script = 6, acting = 9, direction = 8;
  ...
 }
}
```

Again, note the obligatory commas.

65 All Java variables have a **default value** until they are initialized or assigned. Thus, no Java variable is ever without a value. The default value of a number is 0.

Java expects you to assign a value to every variable, even though Java supplies default values. If Java can determine that you do not assign a value to a variable before you use that variable's value, Java will refuse to compile your program.

66 For the moment, the sample programs use test data that are wired in by way of initialized variables. Later on, in Chapter 27, you learn how to use test data that you provide via a file. Still later, in Chapter 49, you learn how to provide data via a text field in a graphical user interface.

67 To change the value of a variable, you use the **assignment operator**, =. Three assignment statements appear in the following program:

```
public class Demonstrate {
 public static void main (String argv[]) {
  int result, script = 6, acting = 9, direction = 8;
  result = script;
  result = result + acting;
  result = result + direction;
  System.out.print("The rating of the movie is ");
  System.out.println(result);
 }
}
```

Of course, this program is a bit awkward—the only reason to split the computation into three separate statements is to demonstrate that a variable can be assigned and then reassigned.

68 Your variable-declaration statements do not need to lie before all other statements. Accordingly, most programmers prefer to declare each variable close to its first use, as in the following example:

```
public class Demonstrate {
 public static void main (String argv[]) {
  int result, script = 6;
  result = script;
  int acting = 9;
  result = result + acting;
  int direction = 8;
  result = result + direction;
  System.out.print("The rating of the movie is ");
  System.out.println(result);
 }
}
```

69 For storing integers, Java provides a range of data-type possibilities, including `byte`, `short`, `int`, and `long`. Java compiler implementers are required to use a standard number of bytes for each:

Type	Bytes	Stores
byte	1	integer
short	2	integer
int	4	integer
long	8	integer

70 The char data type ordinarily is used for storing characters; however, because character codes can be viewed as integers, char also is viewed as one of the **integral data types**, as are byte, short, int, and long. Java uses 2 bytes for the char data type, so as to accommodate the characters in not only English, but also many of the world's other languages, such as Bengali, Kannada, and Telugu.

71 The byte, short, int, and long data types carry a sign, so as to accommodate negative numbers. The char data type has no sign.

72 For storing floating-point numbers, Java provides two data types, float and double. Again, Java compiler writers are required to use a standard number of bytes for each:

Type	Bytes	Stores
float	4	floating-point number
double	8	floating-point number

73
SIDE TRIP
Implementers of compilers for C and C++ are allowed to use as many bytes as they like for the integer and floating-point types, as long as they honor certain relative-length constraints. Flexibility interferes with portability, however, so Java requires compiler implementers to use the standard number of bytes for each data type.

74 For most integers, the byte and short integer types are a little small, and long is unnecessarily large, so the int data type, lying between, is popular. For most floating-point numbers, the float floating-point type is a little small, so the double data type, being twice as big, is popular. Accordingly, all the programs in the rest of this book use int for all integers and double for all floating-point numbers.

75
SIDE TRIP
Experienced programmers occasionally use byte, short, or float when either maximizing execution speed or minimizing program size are of prime importance.

76 All the integral and floating-point types are said to be **primitive types**, as is the boolean type, which you learn about in Chapter 21, and the character type, which you learn more about in Chapter 31. All other types are called **reference types**. The reference types include strings, arrays, and types you define yourself; you begin to learn about them in Chapter 9,

77 You can include **comments** in Java programs in two ways. First, whenever the Java compiler encounters two adjacent forward slashes, //, anywhere in a line, the Java compiler ignores both slashes and the remainder of the line on which the slashes appear:

```
// Short comment
```

Second, whenever Java encounters a slash followed immediately by an asterisk, /*, Java ignores both of those characters and all other characters up to and including the next asterisk followed immediately by a slash, */.

```
/*
Long comment
that just goes on
and on
*/
```

If you wish to test how a program works when you remove certain lines of source code, you can hide those lines in a comment, instead of deleting them.

78
SIDE TRIP In Java documentation, you often see comments that begin with a slash and two asterisks, and continue with a column of asterisks down the left side:

```
/**
 * A documentation comment
 * with a left column filled
 * with asterisks
 */
```

Such comments are designed to be noted and processed by programs that prepare documentation for display in web browsers.

79
SIDE TRIP Many programmers develop a personal style for writing comments, decorating them with asterisks or other distinctive characters, so as to make their comments attractive and easy to find.

80 Note that you cannot place a /* · · · */ comment inside another /* · · · */ comment. If you try to do so, you find that the inner comment's terminator, */, terminates the outer comment, and your Java compiler cannot compile your program:

```
/*   ◄──────────────────────────┐
                                 │
First part of outer comment      │
                                 │    Delimiter, */, of inner
/*   ◄── Commented out           │    comment terminates delimiter,
                                 │    /*, of outer comment
Inner comment                    │
                                 │
*/ ──────────────────────────────┘

Second part of outer comment

*/   ◄── Dangles
```

81
PRACTICE Write a program that computes the volume of Earth. Wire in the radius of Earth using a variable, r.

82
HIGHLIGHTS
- A variable is an identifier that names a chunk of memory.

CHAPTER 3 | **19**

- The integral data types are `char`, `byte`, `short`, `int`, and `long`.

- The floating-point data types are `float` and `double`.

- Integral, floating-point, and boolean data types are said to be primitive data types.

- If you wish to write a one-line comment, **then** introduce that comment with `//`.

- If you wish to write a multiline comment, **then** delimit that comment `/* ··· */`.

- If you wish to introduce a variable, **then** you must declare the data type of that variable in a variable declaration:

  `data type` `variable name` `;`

- If you wish to provide an initial assignment for a variable, **then** you can include that initial assignment in the declaration statement:

  `data type` `variable name` `=` `initial-value expression` `;`

- If you wish to assign a variable after that variable is declared, **then** use an assignment statement:

  `variable name` `=` `new-value expression` `;`

4 HOW TO WRITE ARITHMETIC EXPRESSIONS

83 So far, you have seen sample expressions involving the addition operator, +. In this chapter, you learn about other arithmetic operators, and about the way that Java handles operator precedence and associativity.

84 You arrange for basic arithmetic calculations using the +, -, *, and / operators for **addition**, **subtraction**, **multiplication**, and **division**:

```
6 + 3            // Add, evaluating to 9
6 - 3            // Subtract, evaluating to 3
6 * 3            // Multiply, evaluating to 18
6 / 3            // Divide, evaluating to 2
6 + y            // Add, evaluating to 6 plus y's value
x - 3            // Subtract, evaluating to x's value minus 3
x * y            // Multiply, evaluating to x's value times y's value
x / y            // Divide, evaluating to x's value divided by y's value
```

85 When an integer denominator does not divide evenly into an integer numerator, the division operator rounds the result toward zero, producing another integer. The **modulus operator**, %, produces the integer remainder:

```
5 / 3            // Divide, evaluating to 1
-5 / 3           // Divide, evaluating to -1
5 % 3            // Divide, evaluating to the remainder, 2
-5 % 3           // Divide, evaluating to the remainder, -2
```

Of course, when Java divides floating-point numbers, it produces a floating-point result:

```
5.0 / 3.0        // Divide, evaluating to 1.66667
```

86 Arithmetic expressions can contain one operator, but they can also contain no operators or more than one operator:

```
6                // Literal expression
x                // Variable expression
6 + 3 + 2        // Produces 11
6 - 3 - 2        // Produces 1
6 * 3 * 2        // Produces 36
6 / 3 / 2        // Produces 1
```

87 Java follows standard practice with respect to the syntax rules that dictate how the Java compiler crystallizes operands around operators. In the following, for example, the Java compiler takes 6 + 3 * 2 to be equivalent to 6 + (3 * 2), rather than to (6 + 3) * 2, because multiplication has **precedence** higher than addition:

```
6 + 3 * 2          // Equivalent to 12, rather than to 18
```

88 When an expression contains two operators of equal precedence, such as multiplication and division, the Java compiler handles the expression as shown in the following examples:

```
6 / 3 * 2          // Equivalent to (6 / 3) * 2 = 4,
                   // rather than to 6 / (3 * 2) = 1
6 * 3 / 2          // Equivalent to (6 * 3) / 2 = 9,
                   // rather than to 6 * (3 / 2) = 6
```

Thus, in Java, the multiplication and division operators are said to **associate** from left to right. Most operators associate from left to right, but certain operators do not, as shown in Segment 95 and in the table provided in Appendix A.

89 Of course, you can always deploy parentheses around subexpressions whenever the Java compiler's interpretation of the entire expression is not the interpretation that you want:

```
6 + 3 * 2          // Value is 12, rather than 18
(6 + 3) * 2        // Value is 18, rather than 12
```

You can also use parentheses to make your intentions clear. In the following, for example, the parentheses are not required, but many programmers insert them anyway, just to make the meaning of the expression absolutely clear:

```
6 + 3 * 2          // Value is clearly 12
6 + (3 * 2)        // Value is even more clearly 12
```

Inserting such parentheses is a good idea, especially when you are working with large expressions.

90 Most operators are **binary operators**; that is, they have two operands. In Java, those two operands are found on the immediate left and immediate right of the operator. Some operators, such as the **negation operator**, -, and **unary plus operator**, +, have just one operand, found on the immediate right of the operator. Such operators are **unary operators**.

You can always determine whether the - and + denote unary or binary operators by looking to see whether there is any literal, variable, or subexpression, to the immediate left. If there is, then - denotes subtraction and + denotes addition; otherwise, - denotes negation and + is handled as though it were not there at all.

91 The precedence of the negation operator, -, is higher than that of +, -, *, or /:

```
- 6 * 3 / 2        // Equivalent to ((- 6) * 3) / 2 = -9
```

92 When an arithmetic expression contains values that have a mixture of data types, it is called a **mixed expression**. When Java evaluates a mixed expression, it first uses the given values to produce a set of values that have identical types. Then, Java performs the prescribed arithmetic.

Thus, when given a mixed expression that multiplies a floating-point number by an integer, Java first produces a floating-point number from the integer, and then multiplies.

93 If you want to tell Java explicitly to convert a value from one type to another, rather than relying on automatic conversion, you **cast** the expression. To cast, you prefix the expression with the name of the desired type in parentheses.

If, for example, i is an `int` and d is a `double`, you can cast i to a `double` and d to an `int` as follows:

```
(double) i        // A double expression
(int) d           // An int expression
```

Note that the original types of the i and d variables remain undisturbed: i remains an `int` variable, and d remains a `double` variable.

94 The assignment operator, =, like all operators in Java, produces a value. By convention, the value produced is the same as the value assigned. Thus, the value of the expression y = 5 is 5.

Because assignment expressions produce values, assignment expressions can appear as subexpressions nested inside larger expressions.

In the following assignment expression, for example, the assignment expression, y = 5, which assigns a value to y, appears inside a larger assignment expression, which assigns a value to x:

```
x = (y = 5)
```

95 The assignment operator, =, in contrast to all the other binary operators that you have seen so far, associates from right to left. Accordingly, the expression x = y = 5 is equivalent to the expression x = (y = 5).

Fortunately, x = y = 5 *does not* mean (x = y) = 5, because the value of an assignment statement, such as x = y, is *not* a variable name. Thus, (x = y) = 5 makes no sense, and, if the assignment operator were to associate left to right, x = y = 5 would make no sense either.

96 The precedences and associativity of the operators that you have learned about so far, along with others about which you learn later, are listed in Appendix A.

97

- Java offers negation, unary plus, addition, subtraction, multiplication, division, modulus, and assignment operators.

- Java follows standard precedence and associativity rules.

- The assignment operator, =, has precedence lower than that of the arithmetic operators.

- **If** the standard precedence and associativity rules do not produce the result you want, **then** use parentheses to create subexpressions.

5 HOW TO DEFINE SIMPLE METHODS

98 In this chapter, you learn how to define Java methods other than the required `main` method. In the process, you learn how to work with arguments, parameters, and returned values.

99 If you propose to compute the ratings of many movies, you certainly should define a rating-computing method, perhaps named `movieRating`, to do the work. Once you have defined the `movieRating` method, you can have the `main` method **call** the `movieRating` method as in the following example:

```java
public class Demonstrate {
 // Definition of movieRating ...
 public static void main (String argv[]) {
  System.out.print("The rating of the movie is ");
  System.out.println(movieRating(6, 9, 8));
 }
}
```

In the example, the `movieRating` method has three **arguments**: 6, 9, and 8. As illustrated, Java requires method arguments to be separated by commas.

100 Whenever a call to the `movieRating` method appears, the Java compiler must arrange for the following to be done:

- Determine which `movieRating` method you have in mind.

- Evaluate the argument expressions.

- Assign argument-expression values to the **parameters** of the method—say, s, a, and d.

- Evaluate the expression s + a + d.

- Return the value of s + a + d for use in other computations.

101 You define the `movieRating` method as follows:

```java
public class Demonstrate {
 // Definition of main ...
 public static int movieRating (int s, int a, int d) {
  return s + a + d;
 }
}
```

102 Here is what each part of the method definition does:

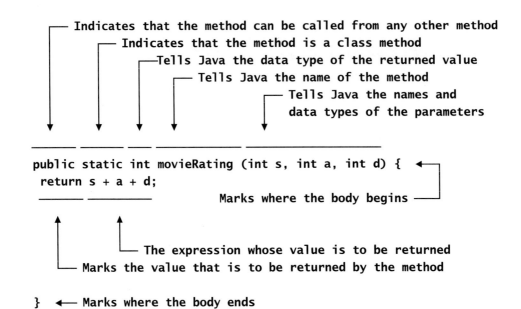

Indicates that the method can be called from any other method
Indicates that the method is a class method
Tells Java the data type of the returned value
Tells Java the name of the method
Tells Java the names and
data types of the parameters

```
public static int movieRating (int s, int a, int d) {
  return s + a + d;
                           Marks where the body begins
```

The expression whose value is to be returned
Marks the value that is to be returned by the method

`}` ◄— Marks where the body ends

103 A method's **parameters** are just variables that are initialized with argument values each time that the method is called. You can assign parameters to new values, just as you can other variables, but many programmers consider such assignment to be bad programming practice.

104 Note that you must specify data types for parameters and returned values when you define a Java method:

- You specify the data type of each parameter in each method at the place where you introduce the parameter.

- You specify the data type of the value returned by each method in every Java program at the place where you name the method to be defined.

105 Finally, you use keywords to indicate what sort of method you are defining:

- The `static` keyword indicates that the `movieRating` method is a class method. If you were to leave out the `static` keyword, you would define an instance method, as described in Chapter 10.

- The `public` keyword indicates that any method, defined in any class, can call the `movieRating` method. If you were to use the `protected` or `private` keywords instead, you would indicate that access to the `movieRating` method is restricted, as described in Chapter 15.

106 In the following example, the definition of the `movieRating` method appears in a complete program containing wired-in test data, which produces a resulting value of 23 when the program is executed.

```
public class Demonstrate {
 public static void main (String argv[]) {
  int script = 6, acting = 9, direction = 8;
  System.out.print("The rating of the movie is ");
  System.out.println(movieRating(script, acting, direction));
 }
 public static int movieRating (int s, int a, int d) {
  return s + a + d;
 }
}
────────────────────── Result ──────────────────────
The rating of the movie is 23
```

107 Most Java programmers, by convention, start each method name with a lowercase letter. Then, they capitalize each interior word in the method name. You should adhere to this convention; otherwise, other programmers will find your programs difficult to understand.

108 You must specify the data type of each parameter individually, because data types in parameter declarations, unlike data types in variable declarations, do not propagate across commas. Thus, the following is wrong:

┌─ BUG: Data type does not propagate
│
↓
─────────────

```
public static int movieRating (int s, a, d) {
 ...
}
```

109
SIDE TRIP
The Java compiler does not require Java programs to be ordered such that each method's definition appears before calls to that method appear. Thus, movieRating does not need to be defined before main is defined, just because main contains a call to movieRating.

In this respect, Java is much easier to work with than is C or C++, both of which require that you define functions—their analogs of methods—before you use those functions.

110
SIDE TRIP
You never can leave out the specification of a method's return value data type. In this respect, Java differs from C and C++, which allow you to leave out the return-value data type if that type happens to be int.

111 Some methods *do not* return values used in other computations. Instead, they are executed for some other purpose, such as to display a value.

Accordingly, Java allows you to use the void keyword as though void were a data type for return values. When Java sees void used as though void were a return-value data type, Java knows that nothing is to be returned.

112 For example, in the following variation on the program in Segment 106, display is handled in the displayMovieRating method, so there is no value to be returned. Accordingly, void appears instead of a data-type name in the definition of displayMovieRating, and displayMovieRating contains no **return statement**—that is, no statement containing the return keyword:

```
public class Demonstrate {
 public static void main (String argv[]) {
  int script = 6, acting = 9, direction = 8;
  displayMovieRating(script, acting, direction);
 }
 public static void displayMovieRating (int s, int a, int d) {
  System.out.print("The rating of the movie is ");
  System.out.println(s + a + d);
 }
}
```
———————————— Result ————————————
```
The rating of the movie is 23
```

113 Because displayMovieRating has no return statement, it is said to **fall off its end**, returning nothing; that behavior is allowed for only those methods that have a void return type.

Picky programmers think that defining a method that can fall off its end is inelegant. Those programmers write empty return statements, as in the following slightly amended version of displayMovieRating:

```
public class Demonstrate {
 public static void main (String argv[]) {
  int script = 6, acting = 9, direction = 8;
  displayMovieRating(script, acting, direction);
 }
 public static void displayMovieRating (int s, int a, int d) {
  System.out.print("The rating of the movie is ");
  System.out.println(s + a + d);
  return;
 }
}
```

114 You do not need to define a method called in the main method in the same class in which you define that main method. For example, you can define movieRating in the Movie class in the Movie.java file:

```
// Movie class defined in Movie.java
public class Movie {
 public static int movieRating (int s, int a, int d) {
  return s + a + d;
 }
}
```

Then, you can define `main` in the `Demonstrate` class in the `Demonstrate.java` file:

```
// Demonstrate class defined in Demonstrate.java
public class Demonstrate {
 public static void main (String argv[]) {
  int script = 6, acting = 9, direction = 8;
  System.out.print("The rating of the movie is ");
  System.out.println(Movie.movieRating(script, acting, direction));
 }
}
```

115
SIDE TRIP You can define more than one class in the same file, as you learn in Chapter 35. For now, however, you are to assume that you define each class in a file dedicated to that class.

116 As shown in Segment 114, if you define `movieRating` in a class that is different from the one in which `movieRating` is called, you must preface the name of the method, `movieRating`, by the name of the class in which that method is defined, and you must join the two names by a dot.

The class name appears because Java allows you to define `movieRating` methods in more than one class. Thus, you must always specify which particular `movieRating` method you have in mind.

117 You might, for example, define not only the `Movie` class, but also the `JamesBondMovie` class, in which the `movieRating` method reflects, say, a belief that 10 should be used instead of the value of the script parameter, s, when rating James Bond movies:

```
public class JamesBondMovie {
 public static int movieRating (int s, int a, int d) {
  return 10 + a + d;
 }
}
```

118 Once you have defined and compiled both the `Movie` class and the `JamesBondMovie` class, you can use both:

```
public class Demonstrate {
 public static void main (String argv[]) {
  int script = 6, acting = 9, direction = 8;
  System.out.print("The ordinary rating of the movie is ");
  System.out.println(Movie.movieRating(script, acting, direction));
  System.out.print("The James Bond movie rating of the movie is ");
  System.out.println(
    JamesBondMovie.movieRating(script, acting, direction)
  );
 }
}
```
───────────────────── Result ─────────────────────
```
The ordinary rating of the movie is 23
The James Bond movie rating of the movie is 27
```
───

119 Whenever there is more than one definition for a method, the method name is said to be **overloaded**. The use of the word *overloaded* is unfortunate, because *overloaded* usually suggests imminent breakdown, as in *the overloaded circuit blew a fuse*. In Java, no suggestion of imminent breakdown is intended, however. Rather, the ability to handle method overloading is a powerful feature of the language.

Because Java allows method overloading, Java is said to be a **polymorphic** language.

120 Java also allows you to define multiple methods with the same name in the same class, as long as each version has a different arrangement of parameter data types. Each arrangement of return and parameter data types is called a **method signature**.

You can, for example, define one displayMovieRating method that handles integers, and another displayMovieRating method that handles floating-point numbers. Then, you can put both methods to work in the same program:

```
public class Demonstrate {
 public static void main (String argv[]) {
  int intScript = 6, intActing = 9, intDirection = 8;
  double doubleScript = 6.0, doubleActing = 9.0, doubleDirection = 8.0;
  displayMovieRating(intScript, intActing, intDirection);
  displayMovieRating(doubleScript, doubleActing, doubleDirection);
 }
 // First, define displayMovieRating with integers:
 public static void displayMovieRating (int s, int a, int d) {
  System.out.print("The integer rating of the movie is ");
  System.out.println(s + a + d);
  return;
 }
```

```
// Next, define displayMovieRating with floating-point numbers:
public static void displayMovieRating (double s, double a, double d) {
  System.out.print("The floating-point rating of the movie is ");
  System.out.println(s + a + d);
  return;
 }
}
```

───────────────────── Result ─────────────────────

```
The integer rating of the movie is 23
The floating-point rating of the movie is 23.0
```

121 The + operator, which normally means *add*, has an entirely different meaning when one of the operands is a string. In such situations, the + operator converts the other operand into a string, if that operand is not already a string, and **concatenates** the two strings, producing a third string.

Because + has two fundamentally different meanings, + is said to be an **overloaded operator**.

122 You frequently see the + operator, viewed as the **concatenation operator**, in print statements. Such use of the + operator often enables compact display statements.

For example, you can certainly write an expression such as the following:

```
System.out.print("The rating of the movie is ");
System.out.println(s + a + d);
```

Alternatively, you can combine the two statements into one, using concatenation to bring the information together:

```
System.out.print("The rating of the movie is " + (s + a + d));
```

Note that the parentheses around the summed variables are essential. If they are absent, Java assumes that you want to concatenate the first string with the value of s, transformed into a string, then a, then d; Java does concatenation, but does no addition.

123
SIDE TRIP Although Java allows you to define your own overloaded methods, you cannot define your own overloaded operators. In this respect, Java differs from C++, which allows you to overload both method and operators.

Java itself comes with overloaded operators, however. The use of the + operator for concatenation is a conspicuous example. The use of the + operator for adding together all sorts of arithmetic types is a less conspicuous example.

124
SIDE TRIP Java offers a variety of powerful built-in class methods for the Math class. The following illustrates:

```
public class Demonstrate {
 public static void main (String argv[]) {
   System.out.println("Natural logarithm of 10:    " + Math.log(10));
   System.out.println("Absolute value of -10:      " + Math.abs(-10));
   System.out.println("Maximum of 2 and 3:         " + Math.max(2, 3));
   System.out.println("5th power of 6:             " + Math.pow(6, 5));
   System.out.println("Square root of 7:           " + Math.sqrt(7));
   System.out.println("Sin of 8 radians:           " + Math.sin(8));
   System.out.println("Random number (0.0 to 1.0): " + Math.random());
 }
}
```

———————————————— Result ————————————————
```
Natural logarithm of 10:    2.302585092994046
Absolute value of -10:      10
Maximum of 2 and 3:         3
5th power of 6:             7776.0
Square root of 7:           2.6457513110645907
Sin of 8 radians:           0.9893582466233818
Random number (0.0 to 1.0): 0.8520107471627543
```

125
PRACTICE
Write a program that computes the volume of any planet in cubic meters. Have the volume computation performed by a method named sphereVolume. Arrange to provide the radius by wiring a value into the main method.

126
PRACTICE
The energy of a moving mass is given by the formula $1/2mv^2$. Write a program that determines the ratio of energies of a car moving at two specified velocities. Write and use a method named square in your solution. Use your program to determine the ratio of energies for one car moving at 80 miles per hour and another moving at 55 miles per hour. Use numbers of type double throughout.

127
HIGHLIGHTS

- Whenever a method is called, that method's arguments are evaluated, and copies of the resulting values are assigned to the method's parameters. Then, the statements in the method's body are evaluated. When a return statement is evaluated, the argument of the return expression is evaluated, and that value becomes the value of the method call.

- Every method in Java is defined inside a class definition.

- You can define many identically named methods, with identical patterns of parameter data types, as long as each of them appears in a different class.

- You can define many identically named methods in the same class, as long as each of them has a unique pattern of parameter data types.

- If you want to define a public class method, in a public class, **then** instantiate the following pattern:

32

```
public class class name {
 public static return type method name
  (data type 1 parameter 1,
   ...,
    data type 1 parameter 1) {
   declaration 1
   ...
   declaration m
   statement 1
   ...
   statement n
 }
}
```

- If you want to define a method that does not return a value, **then** supply void in place of an ordinary data-type declaration.

- If you want to call a class method from another class, **then** specify both the class and the method name, joining them by a period:

```
class name . method name (ordinary arguments)
```

6 HOW TO UNDERSTAND VARIABLE SCOPE AND EXTENT

128   In this chapter, you learn where a parameter or variable can be evaluated or assigned.

129   It is important to know that the parameter values established when a method is entered are available only inside the method. It is as though Java builds an isolating fence to protect any other uses of the same parameter name outside of the method.

Consider movieRating, for example:

```
public class Movie {
 // Define movieRating:
 public static int movieRating (int s, int a, int d) {
  return s + a + d;
 }
}
```

When movieRating is used, any existing values for other variables that happen to be named s, a, and d are ignored:

movieRating fence	The values of s, a, and d
The value of s, a, and d inside this fence are isolated from the values outside movieRating method computes the value of s + a + d using the values inside this fence	outside the fence, if any, are not affected by the values inside

130   The reason Java acts as though it builds an isolating fence around each method's parameters is that Java reserves a chunk of memory for each parameter every time that the method is called. Java copies argument values into those reserved chunks:

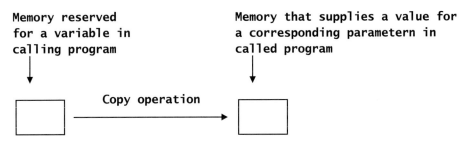

Memory reserved for a variable in calling program

Memory that supplies a value for a corresponding parametern in called program

Copy operation

In the movieRating example, a new chunk of memory is reserved for each of the integer parameters, s, a, and d. Argument values are copied into those chunks.

131 Because Java generally reserves new chunks of memory for parameters of primitive type, into which values are copied, Java's parameters are said to be **call-by-value parameters**, and Java is said to be a **call-by-value language**.

132
SIDE TRIP
One alternative to call-by-value parameters, characteristic of some languages, is provided by **call-by-reference parameters**. If a parameter is a call-by-reference parameter and the corresponding argument is a variable, then the parameter shares the same chunk of memory with the argument variable:

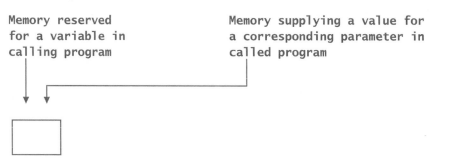

```
Memory reserved              Memory supplying a value for
for a variable in            a corresponding parameter in
calling program              called program
```

If a parameter is a call-by-reference parameter and the corresponding argument is a variable, a parameter reassignment inside the called program propagates outside to the calling program.

133 The following program defines movieRating, albeit awkwardly, to illustrate the limited availability of parameter values:

```java
public class Demonstrate {
 // First, define adder:
 public static int adder () {
  return s + a + d;                             // BUG!
 }
 // Next, define movieRating:
 public static int movieRating (int s, int a, int d) {
  return adder();                               // BUG!
 }
 // Then, define main:
 public static void main (String argv[]) {
  int script = 6, acting = 9, direction = 8, result;
  result = movieRating(script, acting, direction);
  System.out.print("The rating of the movie is ");
  System.out.println(s + a + d);                // BUG!
 }
}
```

In this program, movieRating asks adder—a method with no parameters—to perform the computation of s + a + d. However, the Java compiler cannot compile adder, because values for the s, a, and d parameters of the movieRating method are not available in expressions that lie outside of the definition of movieRating, and thus, they are not available in the adder method.

Moreover, Java cannot compile the second print statement in the `main` method, because values for the `s`, `a`, and `d` parameters of the `movieRating` method are not available in expressions that lie outside of the definition of `movieRating`, and thus, they are not available in the `main` method.

134 A **block** is a sequence of statements surrounded by braces. Accordingly, the body of a method is a block, as is any other sequence of statements surrounded by braces.

You see examples of blocks that are not method bodies in Chapter 22, because blocks are used liberally inside Java's `if` and `if–else` statements.

135 Variables that are declared inside blocks are said to be **local variables**. Local-variable values are available only in the statements that appear inside the block in which the local variable is declared.

A **parameter** is treated as though it were a local variable declared inside a method body. Accordingly, a parameter is really a local variable that happens to be initialized with an argument value.

136 Parameters and local variables are said to have **local scope**, because both parameters and local variables can be evaluated and assigned only in the statements that appear in the block in which those parameters and local variables are declared.

Parameters and local variables are said to have **dynamic extent**, because the memory allocated for parameters and local variables is reallocated as soon as the corresponding block's execution is complete.

137
HIGHLIGHTS

- A local variable is a variable that is declared inside a block, such as a block that constitutes a method body.

- Java isolates parameters and local variables, enabling you to reuse their names. The values of a method's parameters and local variables are not available in expressions that appear outside of the method's definition.

7 HOW TO BENEFIT FROM PROCEDURE ABSTRACTION

138   In this chapter, you learn about the procedure-abstraction concept, by which you increase your efficiency and make your programs easier to maintain.

139   When you move computational detail into a method, you are said to be doing **procedure abstraction**, and you are said to be hiding the details of how a computation is done behind a **procedure-abstraction barrier**.

The key virtue of procedure abstraction is that *you make it easy to reuse your programs*. Instead of copying particular lines of program, you—or another programmer—arrange to call a previously defined method.

140   A second virtue of procedure abstraction is that *you push details out of sight and out of mind*, making your programs easier to understand and enabling you to concentrate on high-level steps.

141   A third virtue of procedure abstraction is that *you can debug your programs easily*. By dividing a program into small, independently debuggable pieces, you exploit the powerful **divide-and-conquer** problem-solving heuristic.

142   A fourth virtue of procedure abstraction is that *you can augment repetitive computationseasily*. For example, in Segment 114, you have seen the movieRating method defined as follows:

```
public class Movie {
 // Define movieRating:
 public static int movieRating (int s, int a, int d) {
   return s + a + d;
 }
}
```

You can easily add a line that displays the rating every time that the rating is computed:

```
public class Movie {
 // Define movieRating:
 public static int movieRating (int s, int a, int d) {
   System.out.print("The rating of the movie is " + (s + a + d));
   return s + a + d;
 }
}
```

Thus, you do not need to bother to find all the places where a rating is computed, because you need to change only the movieRating method's definition.

143   A fifth virtue of procedure abstraction is that *you easily can improve how a computation is done*. You might decide, for example, that it is wasteful for your movieRating method

to add up the ratings for the script, acting, and direction twice. Accordingly, you decide to do the computation just once, assigning the value to a variable:

```
public class Movie {
 // Define movieRating:
 public static int movieRating (int s, int a, int d) {
  int result = s + a + d;
  System.out.print("The rating of the movie is " + result);
  return result;
 }
}
```

Again, you do not need to bother to find all the places where the rating is computed via the movieRating method; you need to change only the movieRating method's definition.

144 A sixth virtue of procedure abstraction is that *you can easily change the way that a computation is done*. If you decide to combine ratings by multiplying, rather than by adding, you can redefine movieRating easily.

```
public class Movie {
 // Define movieRating:
 public static int movieRating (int s, int a, int d) {
  int result = s * a * d;
  System.out.print("The rating of the movie is " + result);
  return result;
 }
}
```

145
PRACTICE Write a method, named convert, that converts Celsius temperature to Fahrenheit, by transforming an integer argument into twice that integer plus 30.

Next, arrange for your method to display the result every time that it is called.

Next, amend your method such that it performs temperature conversion only once.

Finally, improve your method by having it add 40 to the argument, multiply by 9/5, and subtract 40.

For each change, comment on the corresponding benefit provided by method abstraction.

146
HIGHLIGHTS

- Procedure abstraction hides the details of computations inside methods, thus moving those details behind an abstraction barrier.

- You should practice procedure abstraction to take advantage of the following benefits:

  - Your programs become easier to reuse.

  - Your programs become easier to understand.

- Your programs become easier to debug.

- Your programs become easier to augment.

- Your programs become easier to improve.

- Your programs become easier to adapt.

8 HOW TO DECLARE CLASS VARIABLES

147   In this chapter, you learn about class variables. Such variables are particularly useful when you need a variable with values that are broadly accessible.

148   Suppose that you want to adjust your way of calculating movie ratings by introducing weights. You could insert those weights into the movie-rating method directly:

```
public class Movie {
 // Define movieRating:
 public static int movieRating (int s, int a, int d) {
  return 6 * s + 13 * a + 11 * d;
 }
}
```

Such direct insertion is not a good idea, however. Sprinkling numbers throughout a program creates problems, as a program grows, because you easily can forget where such numbers are located.

A safer approach is to use variables. You cannot use local variables, however, because local variables exist only during the execution of their corresponding blocks.

149   You have learned that classes act as repositories for class methods. They also act as repositories for **class variables**:

A class definition

```
┌─────────────────────────────┐
│                             │
│  Class methods              │
│                             │
│  Class variables            │
│                             │
│                             │
│        .                    │
│        .                    │
│        .                    │
│                             │
│                             │
└─────────────────────────────┘
```

In contrast to local variables, class variables continue to exist throughout a program's execution; their life is not limited to the execution of a block.

150   You tell Java about class variables in much the same way that you tell Java about local variables, but there are important differences. First, you declare the class variables inside the body of the class definition, but not inside the body of any method definition. Second, you mark class-variable declarations with the `static` keyword, to distinguish them from instance variables, which you learn about in Chapter 9.

The following, for example, declares wScript, a class variable meant to capture a weight.

```
public class Movie {
 public static int wScript;
```

```
            ↑      ↑      ↑
            |      |      └── Variable name
            |      └── Variable type
            └── Class-variable marker
 // Rest of class definition ...
}
```

And just as you can initialize local variables, you also can initialize class variables:

```
public class Movie {
 // Define class variables:
 public static int wScript = 6;
 ...
}                            ↑
                            └── Initial value
```

151 You can combine several class-variable declarations, as is done in the following example. There, several class variables are declared and initialized for use instead of literal numbers in the movieRating method:

```
public class Movie {
 // Define class variables:
 public static int wScript = 6, wActing = 13, wDirection = 11;
 // Define movieRating:
 public static int movieRating (int s, int a, int d) {
  return wScript * s + wActing * a + wDirection * d;
 }
}
```

In the example, variable names provide access to the class-variable values, because the variables and the method in which they appear are defined in the same class.

152 With the Movie class and movieRating method defined as in Segment 151, you produce the following result with the Demonstrate program:

```
public class Demonstrate {
 public static void main (String argv[]) {
  int script = 6, acting = 9, direction = 8;
  System.out.print("The rating of the movie is ");
  System.out.println(Movie.movieRating(script, acting, direction));
 }
}
```
———————————————————— Result ————————————————
```
The rating of the movie is 241
```

153 The class variables in Segment 151 are public class variables because they are marked by the keyword `public`.

To access a public class variable that is defined in a class different from that of the method that uses that variable, you must use the class name, a period, and the variable name, just as you would to access a class method in a different class. For example, to access the value of the `wScript` variable in the `Demonstrate` class, you write the following expression:

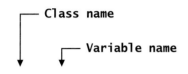

```
Movie.wScript
```

Java programmers think in terms of selecting the value from a **field** in the appropriate class. Accordingly, the period is called the **field-selection operator**.

154 You need not use a class name and field-selection operator to access a class variable in methods defined in the same class, except in places in which there is a parameter or local variable that happens to have the same name as the variable. Such parameters or local variables are said to **shadow**, or to **override**, the corresponding class variables.

You can change the value of a class variable in all the methods defined in the same class, without using the class's name, except in places in which there is a parameter or local variable that happens to have the same name. If there is such a parameter or local variable, you can still change a class variable's value by using the class's name in the assignment statement. For example, if you want to change the value of the class variable that serves as a weight for script ratings, you can write the following assignment statement:

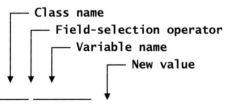

```
Movie.wScript = 7;
```

The change affects all subsequent evaluations of the class variable.

155 If you intend never to change a class variable, such as `wScript`, you should inform Java that no change will be made by including the keyword `final` in the variable declaration. The `final` keyword indicates that the variable is not variable at all; once that variable is initialized, the value never changes, so such a variable is really a **constant**:

```
                          ┌─ The variables are all constants
                          ↓
public static final int wScript = 6, wActing = 13, wDirection = 11;
```

Constants also are called **final variables**. Note that they must be initialized, because no value can be assigned later.

156 In general, a **declaration** is a program element that provides a compiler with essential information or useful advice. For example, when you introduce a local variable or parameter, you are said to *declare* it, because you tell the compiler its type. On the other hand, no memory is set aside for local variables or parameters at compile time, because neither local variable memory nor parameter memory exists until the method is called.

In contrast, a **definition** causes a compiler to set aside memory at compile time. For example, when you introduce a class variable, you both *declare* and *define* the variable, because you inform the compiler about the variable's type and you cause the compiler to set aside memory for the variable at compile time.

Generally, when a variable is both declared and defined, you say, as a shorthand phrase, that it is defined; otherwise, it is declared.

157 Public class variables defined in public classes can be evaluated and assigned at any point in a program, so public class variables are said to have **universal scope**.

The memory set aside for a class variable is never reallocated, so class variables are said to have **static extent**; that explains why `static` is the keyword used to mark class variables.

158 Class variables provide you with a way to collect together the values, such as weights, that determine a program's behavior. Such collection makes those elements easy to find, and thus makes your program easy to understand.

159
SIDE TRIP
Java's class variables take the place of the **global variables** used in other languages. Class variables are much like global variables, except that each class variable is associated with a class.

160
SIDE TRIP
Java offers two useful built-in final class variables for the `Math` class. The following illustrates:

```
public class Demonstrate {
 // First, define displayMovieRating with integers:
 public static void main (String argv[]) {
  System.out.println("Value of pi: " + Math.PI);
  System.out.println("Value of e:  " + Math.E);
 }
}
```
———————————————— Result ————————————————
```
Value of pi: 3.141592653589793
Value of e:  2.718281828459045
```

161
PRACTICE
Amend the temperature-conversion method that you were asked to write in Segment 145 such that, each time that it is called, it reports the total number of times that it has been called.

- If you need a variable with a value that is accessible everywhere, **then** define a public class variable by instantiating the following pattern:

  `public static` `data type` `variable name` `;`

- If you want to access the value of a public class variable, **then** instantiate one of the following patterns:

  `···` `class name` `.` `variable name` `···`
  `class name` `.` `variable name` `=` `new-value expression` `;`

- If you want a variable to be a constant, **then** add the keyword `final` to the variable declaration, **and** be sure to initialize the variable in the declaration statement.

  `public static final` `data type` `variable name`
  `=` `new-value expression` `;`

9 HOW TO CREATE CLASS INSTANCES

163 To remember the characteristics of a particular movie, you may think naturally in terms of the quality of the script, of the acting, and of the direction. To describe the characteristics of a particular symphony, you may think naturally in terms of the quality of the music, of the musician's performances, and of the conducting.

If you express quality on a numeric scale, then the numbers that describe a particular movie or symphony constitute a natural bundle—a bundle of three numbers for each individual that belongs to the movie category, or of three for each individual that belongs to the symphony category.

In this chapter, you learn that one of Java's great virtues is that Java offers you the means to describe, construct, and manipulate bundles of descriptive data items that mirror real-world individuals and categories. These special mechanisms distinguish object-oriented programming from traditional programming.

164 Once you have defined a class, you can create any number of **class instances** that belong to that class, each of which corresponds to an individual that belongs to the corresponding category.

When you define the Movie class, for example, you indicate that all movies are associated with numbers that express the quality of the script, the acting, and the direction. Then, you can construct movie instances with particular numbers for the script, the acting, and the direction. Thus, the employment of classes enables you to create information bundles in your programs that describe naturally occurring individuals. The class acts as a factory for class-instance production:

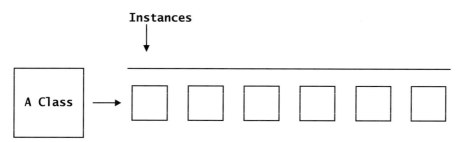

165 The variables that appear in particular class instances are called **instance variables**, as distinguished from **class variables**. There are as many sets of instance variables as there are class instances belonging to a class; there is just one set of class variables for an entire class.

Thus, in the following diagram, the Movie class definition contains descriptions of instance variables, whereas the descriptions of particular Movie instances contain instance-variable values:

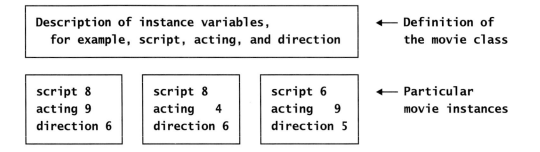

```
Description of instance variables,        ← Definition of
    for example, script, acting, and direction    the movie class


script 8        script 8        script 6        ← Particular
acting 9        acting   4      acting   9          movie instances
direction 6     direction 6     direction 5
```

166 With the introduction of instance variables, you now know of three elements that can appear in class definitions:

A class definition

Class methods

Class variables

Instance variables

.
.
.

167 In this book, you often see a `Movie` instance referred to as a movie. In general, you may refer to a class instance by the name of the class, set in all lowercase letters, as long as the context makes the meaning clear.

168 All classes and class instances are said to be **objects**, as are instances of the `Object` class, which you learn about in Segment 253. Usually, however, when you see the word *object*, it generally refers to a class instance, rather than a class. Usually, context identifies exceptions.

In the rest of this book, we avoid the ambiguity of the word *object* by using the word *class* and the phrase *class instance* (or more concisely, *instance*), when referring to classes and class instances. We reserve the word *object* for instances of the `Object` class.

169 The following is a Java definition of the `Movie` class in which instance variables are declared; evidently, the chunks of memory that describe movies hold values for three integers: script, acting, and direction:

```
public class Movie {
 // First, define instance variables:
 public int script, acting, direction;
 // Remainder of class definition ...
}
```

This definition indicates, via the absence of the `static` keyword, that the variables are instance variables, rather than class variables.

Furthermore, the definition of the `Movie` class indicates, via the `public` keyword, that all the instance variables describing a `Movie` instance will be available, and changeable, from anywhere in your program. You learn about other kinds of instance variables in Chapter 15.

170 In Segment 156, you learned that a **declaration** is a program element that provides a compiler with information or advice, whereas a definition causes the compiler to allocate storage. Class definitions in which only instance variables appear may not cause storage to be allocated. Accordingly, purists prefer to use the phrase **class declaration** unless storage actually is allocated. Nevertheless, the declaration–definition distinction tends to be blurred when programmers talk about classes, and the phrase **class definition** tends to be used whether or not storage is allocated.

171 In other programming languages, instance variables are called **member variables, fields,** or **slots.** The virtue of terms such as *slot* is that they encourage you to think of class definitions as patterns and of class instances as filled-in patterns. Bowing to convention, however, this book uses the term *instance variable* throughout.

172 Once the `Movie` class is defined, you can introduce a variable with `Movie` as the variable's data type:

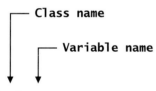

```
Movie m;
```

The syntax is the same as that you use when you introduce a variable with, say, `int` or `double` as the data type.

173 To create a `Movie` instance, you deploy the `new` keyword, with the class name and a pair of parentheses, as shown in the following expression:

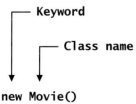

```
new Movie()
```

You will learn why you need the parentheses in Segment 216; for now, just accept the parentheses as ritual to be understood later.

174 Just as you can combine variable declaration and initialization for a variable that has integral or floating-point type, you also can combine declaration and initialization of a variable with a class as its type:

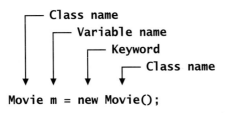

```
Movie m = new Movie();
```

175 Once you have created a variable and have assigned an instance of the `Movie` class to it, you can refer to the instance's `script`, `acting`, and `direction` instance variables. To refer to an instance variable, you join the name of the `Movie` variable, via the field-selection operator, to the name of the instance variable in which you are interested. Thus, `m.script` produces the value of the `script` instance variable of the `Movie` instance assigned to the variable named `m`.

Once you know how to refer to a `Movie` instance's instance variables, you are free to assign values to those instance variables, as well as to retrieve previously assigned values:

```
··· m.script ···   ◄── Retrieve a value from the script instance variable
m.script = 3;       ◄── Assign a new value to the script instance variable
```

176 In the following definition of the `Movie` class, three instance variables appear, along with the `movieRating` class method:

```
public class Movie {
  public int script, acting, direction;
  public static int movieRating (int s, int a, int d) {
    return s + a + d;
  }
}
```

177 In the following definition of the `Demonstrate` class, a `Movie` instance is created, values are assigned to the instance variables, and the `Movie` instance's rating is computed by a class method named `movieRating`. The field-selection operator appears frequently:

```
public class Demonstrate {
 public static void main (String argv[]) {
  Movie m = new Movie();
  m.script = 8; m.acting = 9; m.direction = 6;
  System.out.print("The rating of the movie is ");
  System.out.println(
   Movie.movieRating(m.script, m.acting, m.direction)
  );
 }
}
```

178 Instead of handing three integer arguments to movieRating, you can write a rating method
that takes just one argument, which you declare to be a Movie instance. Of course, you
need to change the body: instead of s, a, and d parameters, the body must refer to the
Movie instance's script, acting, and direction instance variables:

```
public class Movie {
 public int script, acting, direction;
 public static int rating (Movie m) {
  return m.script + m.acting + m.direction;
 }
}
```

Because the method defined in this segment works only on those arguments that are movies,
there is no need to call the method movieRating—the method cannot be called on any
argument that is not a movie.

179 With rating defined to operate on Movie instances—instead of on script, acting, and
direction values—you can rewrite the program in Segment 177 as follows:

```
public class Demonstrate {
 public static void main (String argv[]) {
  Movie m = new Movie();
  m.script = 8; m.acting = 9; m.direction = 6;
  System.out.print("The rating of the movie is ");
  System.out.println(Movie.rating(m));
 }
}
```

180 The **arithmetic** types are like atoms in ordinary chemistry: You cannot take apart particular
integral and floating-point values. Accordingly, those data types are said to be among
primitive types. The primitive types also include the boolean type, which you learn about
in Chapter 21.

In contrast to primitive types, class instances, which you learned about in this chapter, are
like molecules in ordinary chemistry: you can take apart particular instances. Such data
types are called **reference types**.

181 The **default value** of a reference variable is null—a value that indicates that there is no class instance assigned to the variable.

182 The Movie and Demonstrate classes are not the only classes that you have encountered in this book. You have, for example, encountered many strings. Each string is actually an instance of the String class. By the convention mentioned in Segment 167, a String instance is also known, simply, as a **string**.

183 If a variable or parameter is of primitive type, then you can think of it as a label for a chunk of memory that holds a value.

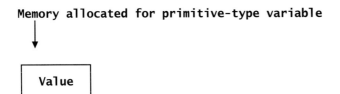

If, however, a variable or parameter is of reference type, then you can think of it as a label for a chunk of memory that holds the address of a chunk of memory that holds an instance. That is, a *reference-type variable* is a label for a chunk of memory that *refers to* another chunk of memory.

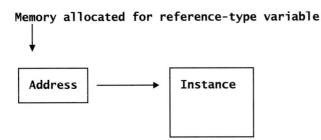

You need to understand a nuance of the primitive–reference distinction described in the following segments.

184 In Chapter 6, you learned that Java is a **call-by-value** language: Memory is allocated for each parameter when a method is called, so parameter reassignments inside a method are prevented from propagating outside the method.

When an argument is a reference-type variable, the memory allocated for the parameter holds a copy of the address of the argument. Both addresses point to the same place:

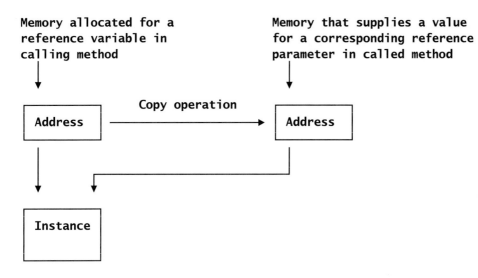

Memory allocated for a
reference variable in
calling method

Memory that supplies a value
for a corresponding reference
parameter in called method

Copy operation

Address

Address

Instance

Because the address is copied, a parameter reassignment inside a method cannot propagate outside the method.

185 Now, suppose that you hand a class instance to a method as an argument, and then, inside that method, you use the corresponding parameter to reassign an instance variable. Then, because the argument and the parameter share the same chunk of memory for the class instance, and hence for the instance variables, the change survives the method call.

186 You might wonder what happens to the memory that is allocated for a class instance when that class instance is no longer accessible. Such no-longer-accessible instances are created, for example, when variables are reassigned:

```
...
movie m;               ←— Declaration
...
m = new movie();       ←— Assignment
...
m = new movie();       ←— Reassignment; first class instance abandoned
...
```

The answer is that Java has built-in mechanisms that find the memory allocated for abandoned class instances. Inasmuch as those class instances cannot enter into any further computations, Java returns the memory to the **free-storage list**, making that memory available for the creation of new, useful class instances.

The process of returning abandoned memory to the free-storage list is called **garbage collection**.

187 Because Java has automatic garbage collection, there are no mechanisms for manual memory reclamation. Automatic garbage collection banishes the tedium of manual memory
SIDE TRIP reclamation and eliminates the memory leaks that plague C++ programmers.

188

PRACTICE Using what you have learned about defining classes, such as the `Movie` class, devise a class, `BoxCar`, for railroad box cars. Include instance variables for the height, width, and length of individual box cars.

189

PRACTICE Devise a `volume` class method for the `BoxCar` class.

190

HIGHLIGHTS

- Java classes correspond to categories; Java class instances correspond to individuals.

- Class definitions generally include instance variables, also known as member variables, slots, or fields.

- If you want to define a class with public instance variables, **then** instantiate the following pattern:

```
public class class name {
  ...
 public instance-variable type  instance-variable name ;
  ...
}
```

- If you want to declare a variable such that the value of the variable can be a class instance, **then** instantiate the following pattern:

```
class name  variable name ;
```

- If you want to create a new class instance, **and** you want to assign that new class instance to a variable, **then** instantiate the following pattern:

```
variable name  = new class name ();
```

- If you want to declare a variable, initialized with a class instance, **then** instantiate the following pattern:

```
class name  variable name  = new class name ();
```

- If you wish to access an instance-variable value, **then** instantiate one of the following patterns:

```
... variable name . instance-variable name  ...
variable name . instance-variable name  = new-value expression ;
```

10 HOW TO DEFINE INSTANCE METHODS

191 In this chapter, you learn how you can define methods that are called in a special way, with a class-instance argument supplied via the field-selection operator, rather than via the usual list-of-arguments mechanism.

192 In the program in Segment 178, you saw the `rating` method defined as follows for `Movie` instances:

```
public static int rating (Movie m) {
  return m.script + m.acting + m.direction;
}
```

You can transform `rating` from a **class method** into an **instance method**. Each instance method has one special argument, called the **target**:

- The special argument's value is a class instance. The class instance's class definition includes the definition of the instance method.

- The special argument does not appear in parentheses with other, ordinary arguments. Instead, the special argument is joined, via the field-selection operator, to the name of the instance method, in a manner reminiscent of instance-variable references.

193 Suppose, for example, that you want the `rating` instance method—the one that is to be defined for the `Movie` class in Segment 194—to work on a `Movie` instance named by a variable, m, you write the following:

```
m.rating()
```

Note that the `rating` instance method, as defined in this segment, happens to have no ordinary arguments.

194 In instance methods, all references to instance variables refer to the particular instance variables that belong to the target instance.

Thus, you define `rating` as an instance method as follows:

```
public class Movie {
  public int script, acting, direction;
  public int rating () {
    return script + acting + direction;
  }
}
```

When this `rating` instance method is called on a particular Movie target, the `script`, `acting`, and `direction` variables that appear in the definition of `rating` automatically refer to the `script`, `acting`, and `direction` instance variables that are associated with that target:

```
public class Demonstrate {
 public static void main (String argv[]) {
  Movie m = new Movie();
  m.script = 8; m.acting = 9; m.direction = 6;
  System.out.println("The rating of the movie is " + m.rating());
 }
}
```
———————————————— Result ————————————
```
The rating of the movie is 23
```

195 Note the contrast between the definition of a rating instance method and that of a rating class method:

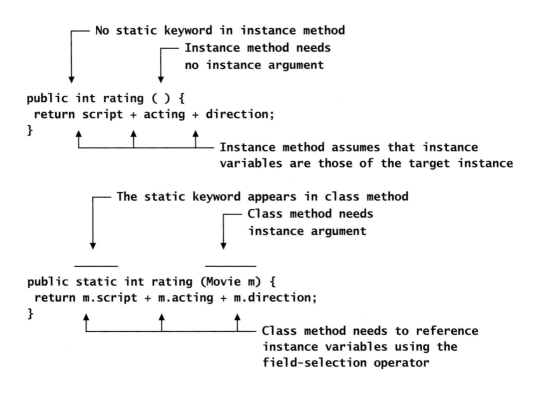

196 Also, note the difference in the way that instance methods and class methods are called:

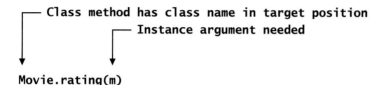

Class method has class name in target position

Instance argument needed

```
Movie.rating(m)
```

197 Now you can write the program with one version of `rating` defined as an instance method of the Movie class, as in Segment 194, and another version defined as an instance method of the Symphony class:

```
public class Symphony {
  public int music, playing, conducting;
  public int rating () {
    return music + playing + conducting;
  }
}
```

Java picks the method defined in the class of the target instance, as shown in the following example:

```
public class Demonstrate {
  public static void main (String argv[]) {
    Movie m = new Movie();
    m.script = 8; m.acting = 9; m.direction = 6;
    Symphony s = new Symphony();
    s.music = 7; s.playing = 8; s.conducting = 5;
    System.out.println("The rating of the movie is " + m.rating());
    System.out.println("The rating of the symphony is " + s.rating());
  }
}
——————————————————— Result ———————————————————
The rating of the movie is 23
The rating of the symphony is 20
```

198 When an instance method is called, the target argument's value is assigned to a special parameter, `this`. Thus, the `this` parameter's value is the target class instance. Accordingly, you can write, say, the Movie `rating` instance method in two ways. One way—the way introduced in Segment 194—exploits the convention that instance variables refer to the target instance:

```
public class Movie {
  public int script, acting, direction;
  public int rating () {
    return script + acting + direction;
  }
}
```

Another way to define `rating` uses the `this` parameter, thus referring to the target instance explicitly:

```
public class Movie {
 public int script, acting, direction;
 public int rating () {
  return this.script + this.acting + this.direction;
 }
}
```

Some programmers use `this` liberally, arguing that liberal use of `this` makes programs easier to understand. In this book, we use `this` only when necessary, believing that liberal use of `this` makes programs bulky.

199

The value of the `this` parameter is a copy of the address of an instance; it is not a copy of the instance itself. Consequently, when you reassign an instance variable inside an instance method, you change the value of the instance variable in the target instance.

Thus, if the value of `m` is a movie, and you call an instance method with `m` as the target, and the instance method changes the value of an instance variable, then you see the instance-variable change in the movie assigned to `m`.

200 Instance methods can have ordinary arguments, in addition to the target instance. You might, for example, have an instance method named `scaledRating` that multiplies the rating of its target instance by a scale factor supplied as an ordinary argument:

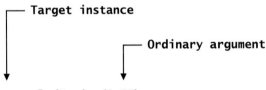

```
m.scaledRating(0.75)
```

The definition of a `scaledRating` instance method is similar to that of a `rating` instance method. The only difference is the addition of an ordinary parameter, `scaleFactor`:

```
public class Movie {
 // First, define instance variables:
 public int script, acting, direction;
 // Define rating:
 public int rating (double scaleFactor) {
  return (int) (scaleFactor * (script + acting + direction));
 }
}
```

The following shows the new version in action:

```
public class Demonstrate {
 // Define main:
 public static void main (String argv[]) {
  Movie m = new Movie();
  m.script = 8; m.acting = 9; m.direction = 6;
  System.out.println("The rating of the movie is " + m.rating(0.75));
 }
}
```
———————————————— Result ————————————
The rating of the movie is 17

201 With the introduction of instance methods, you have seen all of the four elements that can appear in class definitions:

A class definition

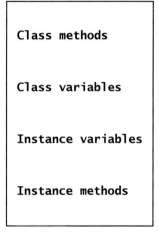

Class methods

Class variables

Instance variables

Instance methods

202
PRACTICE Convert into an instance method the volume method for the BoxCar instances, which you were asked to define in Segment 189.

203
HIGHLIGHTS

- If you want to define a public instance method, in a public class, **then** instantiate the following pattern:

```
public class class name {
 public return type method name
  (data type 1 parameter 1,
   ...,
    data type 1 parameter 1) {
   declaration 1
   ...
   declaration m
   statement 1
   ...
   statement n
  }
}
```

- If you want to call an instance method, **then** specify both the target instance and the method name, joining them by the field-selection operator:

```
target instance . method name (ordinary arguments)
```

- If you want to refer to the target explicitly, **then** use the `this` parameter.

11 HOW TO DEFINE CONSTRUCTORS

204 In this chapter, you learn about constructor methods, which are special methods that are called when you create class instances.

205 In Chapter 9, you saw how to create an instance in one statement and to initialize that instance's instance variables in others. The following illustrates instance creation and initialization for a Movie variable, m:

```
Movie m = new Movie();
m.script = 8; m.acting = 9; m.direction = 6;
```

As the new Movie instance is created, zeros are assigned to all the arithmetic instance variables. Then, three statements reassign those instance variables.

206 Java allows you to initialize instance variables in the same way that you initialize local variables and class variables. For example, you could, pessimistically, arrange for the instance variables in every Movie instance to have an initial value of 3:

```
public class Movie {
 public int script = 3, acting = 3, direction = 3;
 public int rating () {
  return script + acting + direction;
 }
}
```

If you have not initialized an instance variable, that variable will have the **default value** prescribed for its type. The default value of a variable with arithmetic type is 0.

207 Java also allows you to define special methods, called **constructors**, that are called automatically whenever a new class instance is created. You can use such constructors to assign values to the instance variables in class instances, instead of supplying initializing values in variable-declaration statements.

208 In class definitions, constructor methods stand apart from other instance methods in two ways:

- Constructor-method names are the same as the name of the class.

- Constructor methods return new class instances; no return type is specified explicitly.

209 To define a zero-parameter constructor for the Movie class, you would write the following:

```
        ┌─ No return type specified
        │  ┌─ Constructor name is the same as class name
     ┌──┘  │
     │     │
     ▼     ▼
public Movie() {
 ...
}
```

210   In the following program, the Movie class definition includes a constructor method that assigns the value 5 to all the instance variables in Movie instances; 5 is intended to represent typical ratings for an average movie:

```
public class Movie {
 public int script, acting, direction;
 public Movie() {
   script = 5; acting = 5; direction = 5;
 }
 public int rating () {
   return script + acting + direction;
 }
}
```

211   Because it uses the new definition of the Movie class introduced in Segment 210, the following main method does not need to assign values to the instance variables:

```
public class Demonstrate {
 // Define main:
 public static void main (String argv[]) {
   Movie m = new Movie();
   System.out.println("The rating of the movie is " + m.rating());
 }
}
```
────────────────── Result ──────────────────
```
The rating of the movie is 15
```
──

212   Now, suppose that you want to provide values for the script, acting, and direction instance variables when you create certain Movie instances. You should define a constructor with three parameters:

```
public class Movie {
 public int script, acting, direction;
 public Movie() {
   script = 5; acting = 5; direction = 5;
 }
```

```
public Movie(int s, int a, int d) {
  script = s; acting = a; direction = d;
}
public int rating () {
  return script + acting + direction;
}
}
```

Note that the constructor for three parameters, like the one for zero parameters, is named for the class in which it appears.

213 To tell Java to use the three-parameter constructor, blocking the involvement of the zero-parameter constructor, you modify the Movie creation statement:

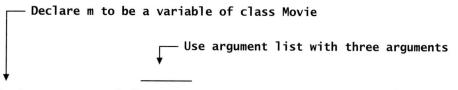

Declare m to be a variable of class Movie

Use argument list with three arguments

```
Movie m = new Movie(8, 9, 6);
```

The arguments dictate that initialization is to be done with the three-parameter constructor; it is *not* to be done with the zero-parameter constructor.

214 The following program uses both the zero-parameter constructor and the three-parameter constructor:

```
public class Demonstrate {
  // Define main:
  public static void main (String argv[]) {
    Movie m1 = new Movie();
    Movie m2 = new Movie(8, 9, 6);
    System.out.println("The first movie rating is " + m1.rating());
    System.out.println("The second movie rating is " + m2.rating());
  }
}
```
———————————— Result ————————————
```
The first movie rating is 15
The second movie rating is 23
```

215 If you do not define any constructors, Java defines a do-nothing **default constructor** for you. The default constructor is a **zero-parameter constructor**.

216 Now you can understand how the instance-creation expression shown in Segment 173 works, and why it has parentheses:

```
new Movie()
```

The parentheses, with no arguments, indicates that a zero-parameter constructor is to be called. In Segment 173, no constructors are defined, so the do-nothing default constructor, supplied by Java, is called.

217 All instance variables are initialized before any constructor is called. Thus, an initial value supplied by a constructor for an instance variable dominates an initial value supplied in an instance-variable–definition statement.

218
SIDE TRIP
You must include a definition for your own zero-parameter constructor in a class definition under the following condition: You define a constructor with parameters *and* you create instances using a constructor with no arguments.

The rationale is as follows: If you have not defined a zero-parameter constructor, then the lack of arguments suggests that you have forgotten to include arguments for the parameter-bearing constructor that you have defined.

219
PRACTICE
Devise a zero-parameter constructor and a three-parameter constructor for the BoxCar class that you were asked to design in Segment 188. The three-parameter constructor is to receive height, width, and length values. Assume reasonable default dimensions for the zero-parameter constructor.

220
HIGHLIGHTS

- Constructors perform computations, such as instance-variable assignment, that you want to occur when your program creates an instance.

- Each constructor is named for the class in which it is defined. All constructors return class instances.

- In the absence of any constructors defined by you, Java creates a default constructor, which has no parameters.

- If you want to define a zero-parameter constructor to displace the default constructor, **then** instantiate the following pattern:

```
public class name () {
  ...
}
```

- If you want to define a constructor with parameters, **then** instantiate the following pattern:

```
public class name (parameter specifications) {
  ...
}
```

- When you create instances, the number and types of the arguments that you supply determine which constructor is called.

12 HOW TO DEFINE GETTER AND SETTER METHODS

221 In this chapter, you learn that getter and setter instance methods help you to work with instance-variable values.

222 You know that you can refer to an instance-variable value directly by using the field-selection operator. For example, suppose that you have defined the `Attraction` class with a `minutes` instance variable that records the duration of an entertainment attraction in minutes. You can refer to the value of that instance variable in a particular attraction, x:

```
x.minutes
```

Alternatively, you can refer to an instance-variable value indirectly by defining an instance method that returns the instance-variable value. In the following `Attraction` class definition, for example, an instance method named `getMinutes` returns the value of the `minutes` instance variable:

```
public class Attraction {
  // First, define instance variable:
  public int minutes;
  // Define zero-parameter constructor:
  public Attraction () {minutes = 75;}
  // Define one-parameter constructor:
  public Attraction (int m) {minutes = m;}
  // Define getter:
  public int getMinutes () {
    return minutes;
  }
}
```

With `getMinutes` defined, you have another way to refer to the value of the `minutes` instance variable of a particular attraction, x:

```
x.getMinutes()
```

223 A **getter** is a method that extracts information from an instance.

One reason that you may wish to use a getter, rather than accessing an instance variable directly, is that you can include additional computation in a getter. For example, if you are concerned about how often your program accesses the `minutes` instance variable, you can add a statement to the `getMinutes` getter that announces each access:

```
public class Attraction {
 public int minutes;
 public Attraction () {minutes = 75;}
 public Attraction (int m) {minutes = m;}
 // Define getter:
 public int getMinutes () {
  System.out.println("Accessing a value ...");
  return minutes;
 }
}
```

224 Analogously, you do not need to assign an instance-variable value directly. Instead, you can assign an instance-variable value indirectly by defining an instance method that does the actual value assigning.

In general a **setter** is a method that inserts information into an instance. Setters are also known as **mutators**.

In the following Attraction class definition, for example, a setter named setMinutes assigns a value to the minutes instance variable:

```
public class Attraction {
 public int minutes;
 public Attraction () {minutes = 75;}
 public Attraction (int m) {minutes = m;}
 // Define getter:
 public int getMinutes () {
  return minutes;
 }
 // Define setter:
 public void setMinutes (int m) {
  minutes = m;
 }
}
```

With setMinutes defined, you have another way to assign a value to the minutes instance variable of a particular attraction, x:

```
x.setMinutes(4)
```

225 Because the only purpose of setMinutes, as defined in Segment 224, is to assign a value to a instance variable, setMinutes is marked void, indicating that no value is to be returned. If you prefer, you can write setMinutes such that it returns the previous value or the new value.

226 One reason that you may wish to use a setter, rather than assigning a value to an instance variable directly, is that you can include additional computation in a setter. In Segment 223, you saw how to add a statement to the getMinutes getter that announces each access. The following provides the same enhancement to the setMinutes setter:

```
public class Attraction {
 public int minutes;
 public Attraction () {minutes = 75;}
 public Attraction (int m) {minutes = m;}
 // Define getter:
 public int getMinutes () {
  return minutes;
 }
 // Define setter:
 public void setMinutes (int m) {
  System.out.println("Assigning a value ...");
  minutes = m;
 }
}
```

227 Setters are especially valuable when you need to coordinate instance-variable changes with display changes. You learn about such coordination in Chapter 41.

228 You may also wish to use getters and setters to provide access to **imaginary instance variables** that exist only in the sense that their values can be computed from instance variables that do exist. For example, you can create getHours and setHours, which seem to refer to the contents of an imaginary hours instance variable, of type double, but which actually work with the contents of the minutes instance variable:

```
public class Attraction {
 public int minutes;
 public Attraction () {minutes = 75;}
 public Attraction (int m) {minutes = m;}
 // Define getters:
 public int getMinutes () {return minutes;}
 public double getHours () {
  return minutes / 60.0;
 }
 // Define setters:
 public void setMinutes (int m) {minutes = m;}
 public void setHours (double h) {
  minutes = (int)(h * 60);
 }
}
```

229 The names of the getMinutes, setMinutes, getHours, and setHours methods, with the get and set prefixes, makes it clear that the methods are getters and setters, but the use of get and set is a convention, rather than a language-enforced imperative. You should follow the convention, however, because certain Java programming environments expect getters and setters to have names that begin with get and set.

230 Constructor methods are part of the Java language, whereas getter and setter methods are not. You should understand, however, that the use of getter and setter methods, as explained in this chapter, is recommended by many expert programmers, regardless of the programming language that you happen to use. You learn why in Chapter 13.

PRACTICE

231 Write getters and setters for the BoxCar class that you were asked to design in Segment 188.

HIGHLIGHTS

232

- Getter and setter instance methods provide an indirect route to instance-variable access and assignment.

- You can define getter and setter instance methods for imaginary instance variables.

- If you want to refer to an instance-variable value using a getter, **then** instantiate the following pattern:

    `instance` . `getter method` ()

- If you want to assign an instance-variable value using a setter, **then** instantiate the following pattern:

    `instance` . `setter method` (`new-value expression`)

13 HOW TO BENEFIT FROM DATA ABSTRACTION

233 You now know how to use constructor, getter, and setter methods. Moreover, you have seen how getters and setters make it easy to add computation at the point where values are accessed and assigned, and how getters and setters can be defined for imaginary instance variables. In this chapter, you learn how constructors, getters, and setters help you to practice data abstraction, thereby increasing your efficiency and making your programs easier to maintain.

234 Suppose that you develop a big program around an Attraction class definition that includes getters and setters for the minutes instance variable, as well as for an imaginary hours instance variable.

Next, suppose that you discover that your program accesses to hours more often than to minutes. If speed is a great concern, you should arrange to store a number representing hours, rather than a number representing minutes, to reduce the number of multiplications and divisions performed.

If you work with the instance variables in attractions using constructors, getters, and setters only, you need to change what happens in only the constructor, getter, and setter instance methods:

```java
public class Attraction {
 // First, define instance variable:
 public double hours;
 // Define zero-parameter constructor:
 public Attraction () {hours = 1.25;}
 // Define one-parameter constructor, presumed to take minutes:
 public Attraction (double m) {hours = m / 60.0;}
 // Define getters:
 public int getMinutes () {
  return (int)(hours * 60);}
 public double getHours () {
  return hours;
 }
 // Define setters:
 public void setMinutes (int m) {
  hours = m / 60.0;
 }
 public void setHours (double h) {
  hours = h;
 }
}
```

235 Suppose, for example, that your program contains statements that read the minutes or hours of a particular attraction, x. If you work with getters, you need to make no change

to that statement to accommodate the switch from a minutes-based class definition to an hours-based class definition:

```
··· x.getMinutes() ··· ——→ ··· x.getMinutes() ···
··· x.getHours() ···    ——→ ··· x.getHours() ···
```

On the other hand, if you do not work with the instance variables in attractions that use constructors, getters, and setters only, then you have to go through your entire program, modifying myriad statements:

```
··· x.minutes ···           ——→ ··· (int)(x.hours * 60) ···
··· (x.minutes / 60.0) ··· ——→ ··· x.hours ···
```

Thus, constructors, getters, and setters isolate you from the effects of your efficiency-motivated switch from a minutes-based class definition to an hours-based class definition.

236 In general, constructors, getters, and setters isolate you from the details of how a class is implemented. Once you have written those instance methods, you can forget about how they access and assign values; none of the details, such as whether you have a minutes or an hours instance variable, clutter the programs that use attractions.

237 Collectively, constructors, getters, and setters sometimes are called **access methods**. When you move representation detail into a set of access methods, you are said to be practicing **data abstraction**, and you are said to be hiding the details of how data are represented behind a **data-abstraction barrier**.

Good programmers carefully design into their programs appropriate access methods so as to create data-abstraction barriers.

238 Because the virtues of data abstraction parallel those of procedure abstraction, the following discussion of the virtues of data abstraction is much like the previous discussion, in Chapter 7, of the virtues of procedure abstraction.

The key virtue of data abstraction is that *you make it easy to reuse your work*. You can develop a library of class definitions, and can transfer the entire library to another programmer with little difficulty.

239 A second virtue of data abstraction is that *you push details out of sight and out of mind*, making your methods easy to understand and enabling you to concentrate on high-level steps.

240 A third virtue of data abstraction is that *you can easily augment what a class provides*. You can, for example, add information-displaying statements to your getters and setters, as you saw in Segment 223 and Segment 226.

241 A fourth virtue of data abstraction is that *you can easily improve the way that data are stored*. In this chapter, you have seen an example in which there is an efficiency-motivated switch from a minutes-based class definition to an hours-based class definition.

242 Most good programmers provide getters and setters for some instance variables, but do not provide them for others. The choice is a matter of taste and style. Until you have developed your own taste and style, you should rely on the following heuristic: Whenever the detailed implementation of a class may change, provide instance-variable getters and setters to insulate your class-using methods from the potential change.

243
PRACTICE
Revise the getters and setters that you defined in Segment 231 for the BoxCar class, such that they display messages when used.

244
PRACTICE
Revise the getters and setters for the BoxCar class such that class variables are incremented when corresponding instance methods are called.

245
HIGHLIGHTS

- Constructors, getters, and setters are called access methods. When you move instance-variable accesses and assignments into access methods, you are practicing data abstraction.

- Data abstraction has many virtues, including the following:

  - Your programs become easier to reuse.

  - Your programs become easier to understand.

  - You can easily augment what a class provides.

  - You can easily improve the way that data are stored.

- If you anticipate that the detailed definition of a class may change, **then** you should provide access methods for the instance variables to isolate the effects of the potential changes.

14 HOW TO DEFINE CLASSES THAT INHERIT INSTANCE VARIABLES AND METHODS

246   In this chapter, you learn that you can tie together classes in hierarchies such that the instance variables declared in one class automatically appear in instances belonging to another, and such that the instance methods defined in one class automatically work with target instances that belong to another. Thus, you learn about the notion of inheritance. Object-oriented programming languages provide for classes, instances, and inheritance, whereas traditional programming languages do not.

247   So far, you have learned how you can define classes for two entertainment types: movies and symphonies. Now, suppose that you want to add information that is common to all entertainment types, such as an instance variable, `minutes`, that records duration.

One way to proceed is to start with the classes that you have already defined for movies and symphonies, adding a `minutes` instance variable to both classes. If you define movies and symphonies in this way, adding the `minutes` instance variable to the `Movie` and `Symphony` class definitions creates exact duplicates.

248   Maintaining multiple copies of instance variables and instance methods makes software development and maintenance difficult as you try to correct bugs, add features, improve performance, and change behavior. Adding multiple programmers and multiple years to the mix turns mere difficulty into certain failure.

Of course, with just two new `minutes` instance variables about which to worry, you could cope. In a more complex example, every kind of entertainment—from football to opera—would have a `minutes` instance variable, as well as a variety of other instance variables.

249   Fortunately, Java encourages you to cut down on duplication—thereby easing program developing, debugging, and maintenance—by allowing you to arrange class definitions in hierarchies that reflect natural category hierarchies.

Using Java, you can say, for example, that movies and symphonies are attractions. Then, you can declare a `minutes` instance variable in the `Attraction` class alone, because the `minutes` instance variable will appear in each `Movie` instance and `Symphony` instance, as though `minutes` had been declared in each.

250   Once you have decided in which classes instance variables and instance methods should be declared and defined, you can proceed to define the classes, and to link them up in a class hierarchy.

The following definition of the `Attraction` class contains the `minutes` instance variable and a zero-parameter constructor with a statement that announces its use:

```
public class Attraction {
 // Define instance variable:
 public int minutes;
 // Define zero-parameter constructor:
 public Attraction () {
  System.out.println("Calling zero-parameter Attraction constructor");
  minutes = 75;
 }
 public Attraction (int m) {minutes = m;}
}
```

251 To specify a class's superclass, you insert the keyword extends, and the name of the superclass, just after the name of the class in the class's definition.

For example, as you define the Movie class and the Symphony class, you specify that Attraction is the superclass by inserting the keyword extends, followed by Attraction, just after the class name:

```
public class Movie extends Attraction {
 // Define instance variables:
 public int script, acting, direction;
 // Define zero-parameter constructor:
 public Movie () {
  System.out.println("Calling zero-parameter Movie constructor");
  script = 5; acting = 5; direction = 5;
 }
 // Define three-parameter constructor:
 public Movie (int s, int a, int d) {
  script = s; acting = a; direction = d;
 }
 // Define rating:
 public int rating () {
  return script + acting + direction;
 }
}

public class Symphony extends Attraction {
 // Define instance variables:
 public int music, playing, conducting;
 // Define zero-parameter constructor:
 public Symphony () {
  System.out.println("Calling zero-parameter Symphony constructor");
  music = 5; playing = 5; conducting = 5;
 }
 // Define three-parameter constructor:
 public Symphony (int m, int p, int c) {
  music = m; playing = p; conducting = c;
 }
```

```
  // Define rating:
  public int rating () {
    return music + playing + conducting;
  }
}
```

252 Because the `Movie` class is directly under the `Attraction` class in the class hierarchy, with no other class in between, the `Movie` class is said to be the **direct subclass**, relative to the `Attraction` class, and the `Attraction` class is said to be the **direct superclass**, relative to the `Movie` class.

253 Because no direct superclass is specified for the `Attraction` class, the direct superclass of the `Attraction` class is taken to be the `Object` class—a class supplied by Java. Every class is a subclass of the `Object` class, but it is not necessarily a direct subclass.

254 You can, if you like, specify explicitly that a class is a direct subclass of the `Object` class. For example, you can define the `Attraction` class in either of two equivalent ways:

```
public class Attraction {
  ...
}

public class Attraction extends Object {
  ...
}
```

255 Whenever an instance variable or instance method is made available because of a subclass–superclass relationship, it is said to be **inherited**.

256 In addition to reducing duplication, there are other reasons for exploiting inheritance, such as the following:

- You may already have defined a fully debugged `Attraction` class. To prevent the gratuitous introduction of bugs, you would want to use that class definition as it stands, rather than, say, copying bits of the `Attraction` class definition into the `Movie` and `Symphony` class definitions.

- You may have decided to purchase code for the `Attraction` class from a vendor, because you anticipate using the elaborate capabilities advertised by that vendor. Because the vendor supplies you with compiled code only, you cannot access the source code, so you cannot copy bits of the vendor's `Attraction` class definition into your `Movie` and `Symphony` class definitions. You can only define new classes that inherit from your purchased classes.

257 Usually, it is a good idea to draw a **class-hierarchy diagram**, such as the following, to see how your classes fit together:

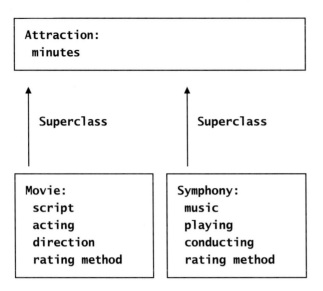

Such a class-hierarchy diagram helps you to see how to distribute instance variables and instance methods among the classes in the hierarchy.

258 Instances exhibit the instance variables of their class and all the public instance variables declared in that class's superclasses. Each `Movie` instance, for example, has its own copy of every instance variable declared in the `Movie` and `Attraction` classes.

Similarly, instances serve as targets for instance methods defined in their class and all the public instance methods defined in that class's superclasses. You can, for example, work on a `Movie` instance not only with instance methods defined in the `Movie` class, but also with those defined in the `Attraction` class.

259 As a general rule, you should place public instance variables and public instance methods in classes such that two criteria are satisfied:

- There is no needless duplication of a public instance variable or public instance method.

- Each public instance variable and public instance method is useful to instances of all the subclasses of the class in which the instance variable or instance method is defined.

For example, the `minutes` instance variable is in the `Attraction` class, because it is useful for all `Attraction` subclasses.

On the other hand, there are two `rating` instance methods, because the way that you compute the rating of a `Movie` instance is different from the way that you compute the rating of a `Symphony` instance. There is duplication, because there are two rating methods; however, there is no needless duplication.

260 In general, the first step taken by any constructor in any class, other than the Object class, is to call the zero-parameter constructor in the direct superclass.

Thus, when you create an instance, all the zero-parameter constructors in the instance's superclasses are called automatically, and each has the opportunity to contribute to the values of the instance variables associated with the new instance.

In Chapter 17, you learn how to arrange for a constructor to call a constructor other than the zero-parameter constructor.

261 In the following example, print statements in the zero-parameter constructors defined in Segment 250 and Segment 251 tell you when those zero-parameter constructors are executed:

```
public class Demonstrate {
 public static void main (String argv[]) {
  Movie m = new Movie();
  Symphony s = new Symphony();
 }
}
————————————————— Result —————————————————
Calling zero-parameter Attraction constructor
Calling zero-parameter Movie constructor
Calling zero-parameter Attraction constructor
Calling zero-parameter Symphony constructor
```

262 In Segment 117, you saw that you could define a completely independent JamesBondMovie class. Now, you can see that you can define a JamesBondMovie class that extends the Movie class. Once you have defined such a JamesBondMovie class, you can adjust for your particular attitude toward James Bond movies by defining a special rating method for the JamesBondMovie class:

```
public class JamesBondMovie extends Movie {
 // Define rating:
 public int rating () {
  return 10 + acting + direction;
 }
}
```

263 The following shows how instance variables and the rating instance method are distributed for movies:

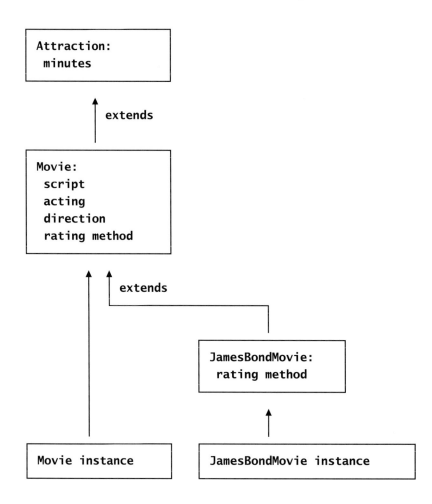

264　To decide which rating instance method to use on, say, a Movie instance, the Java compiler searches up from the Movie class, through the subclass–superclass chain, to find the first instance method named rating. For the Movie instance example, the only rating instance method that the Java compiler finds is the one in the Movie class.

On the other hand, the rating instance method selected by the Java compiler to work on JamesBondMovie instances is the one in the JamesBondMovie class, and the rating instance method in the Movie class is said to be **shadowed** or **overridden** by that lower-level instance method.

Thus, you see the following result when your program calls the rating method. For both the ordinary movie and the James Bond movie, the constructor in the Movie class assigns 5 to the script, acting, and direction instance variables.

```
public class Demonstrate {
 public static void main (String argv[]) {
  Movie m = new Movie();
  System.out.println("The movie rating is " + m.rating());
  JamesBondMovie jbm = new JamesBondMovie();
  System.out.println("The James Bond movie rating is " + jbm.rating());
 }
}
```
———————————————— Result ————————————————

Calling zero-parameter Attraction constructor
Calling zero-parameter Movie constructor
The movie rating is 15
Calling zero-parameter Attraction constructor
Calling zero-parameter Movie constructor
The James Bond movie rating is 20

---

265 Note the distinction between **overloading** and **shadowing** or **overriding**:

- **Overloading** occurs when Java can distinguish two procedures with the same name by examining the number or types of their parameters.

- **Shadowing** or **overriding** occurs when two procedures with the same name, the same number of parameters, and the same parameter types are defined in different classes, one of which is a superclass of the other.

266 *Shadowing* and *overriding* are synonyms. *Shadowing* is used in this book, rather than *overriding*, because similar-sounding terms, such as *overloading* and *overriding*, are easily confused.

267 The Attraction class must be defined before you define the Movie and Symphony classes. You cannot define a direct subclass class until its direct superclass has been defined.

268 The syntax of class definition allows you to specify only one superclass for any class. Accordingly, Java is said to exhibit **single inheritance**.

269
SIDE TRIP
Unlike Java, C++ allows multiple inheritance. Because multiple inheritance creates all sorts of complexities, without proportionate benefits, Javas designers decided to limit Java to single inheritance.

270
PRACTICE
Create a class, TankCar, for tank cars, patterned on the BoxCar class that you were asked to define in Segment 231. Include instance variables for the length and radius of each car. Include a volume instance method that makes use of the instance variables in the TankCar class.

271
PRACTICE
Define a RailroadCar class. Include instance variables for the weight and year of manufacture. Then, redefine the BoxCar and TankCar classes to make them extensions of the RailroadCar class.

- Class hierarchies reflect subclass–superclass relations among classes.

- You have several reasons to arrange classes in hierarchies:

  - To parallel natural categories

  - To prevent avoidable duplication and to simplify maintenance

  - To avoid introducing bugs into previously debugged code

  - To use purchased code

- When a subclass–superclass relation is direct, with no intervening classes, the subclass is called the direct subclass, and the superclass is called the direct superclass.

- A class inherits public instance variables and public instance methods from all its superclasses.

- When a subclass–superclass chain contains multiple instance methods with the same name, argument number, and argument types, the one closest to the class of the target instance in the subclass–superclass chain is the one executed. All others are shadowed.

- **If** you want to create a class hierarchy, **then** draw a diagram that reflects natural categories. Populate the classes in that class hierarchy with public instance variables and public instance methods such that there is no needless duplication of an instance variable or instance method, and such that each public instance variable and public instance method is useful to instances of every subclass.

- **If** you want to create a direct-subclass–direct-superclass relation, **then** instantiate the following pattern:

```
public class subclass name extends superclass name {
  ...
}
```

15 HOW TO ENFORCE ABSTRACTION USING PROTECTED AND PRIVATE VARIABLES AND METHODS

273   In Chapter 13, you learned that constructor, getter, and setter instance methods help you to benefit from data abstraction. In this chapter, you learn how to ensure that all instance-variable accesses and assignments are channeled through such instance methods.

274   Some benefits of data abstraction disappear if you write methods that include direct instance-variable accesses or assignments.

If, for example, you decide to switch from a minutes-based definition to an hours-based definition, then Java no longer can compile any expression that attempts to access the minutes instance variable directly. On the other hand, if you prevent direct access to the minutes instance variable, no one can accidentally come to rely on expressions that include such access.

275   You prevent direct instance-variable access by marking instance variables with the private keyword.

You can, for example, redefine the Attraction class as follows, with minutes marked with the private keyword, rather than with the public keyword:

```
public class Attraction {
 // First, define instance variable:
 private int minutes;
 // Define zero-parameter constructor:
 public Attraction () {minutes = 75;}
 // Define one-parameter constructor:
 public Attraction (int m) {minutes = m;}
 // Define getter:
 public int getMinutes () {return minutes;}
 // Define setter:
 public void setMinutes (int m) {minutes = m;}
}
```

With the Attraction class so redefined, attempts to access an attraction's instance-variable values from outside the Attraction class fail to compile:

```
x.minutes        ◄─ Access fails to compile;
                    the minutes instance variable is private
x.minutes = 6  ◄─ Assignment fails to compile;
                    the minutes instance variable is private
```

276   Note, however, that all instance methods in the Attraction class have access to private instance variables declared the Attraction class definition. Thus, attempts to access an

attraction's instance-variable values from outside the `Attraction` class, via public instance methods, are successful:

```
x.getMinutes()      ⟵ Access compiles;
                       getMinutes is a public method
x.setMinutes(6)     ⟵ Assignment compiles;
                       setMinutes is a public method
```

277 Public instance variables and public instance methods are said to constitute the class's **public interface**. Once you have marked the `minutes` instance variable `private`, instead of `public`, the only way to get at that `minutes` instance variable from methods defined outside the `Attraction` class is via the public getter and setter in the `Attraction` class's public interface.

278 You also can mark instance methods with the `private` keyword. Thus, instance methods are not necessarily part of the public interface, just as instance variables are not necessarily part of the public interface.

279 Most programmers put the public instance variables and methods first, on the aesthetic ground that what is *public* should be up front and open to view, whereas what is *private* should not be so up front and not so open to view.

```
public class Attraction {
  // Define zero-parameter constructor:
  public Attraction () {minutes = 75;}
  // Define one-parameter constructor:
  public Attraction (int m) {minutes = m;}
  // Define getter:
  public int getMinutes () {return minutes;}
  // Define setter:
  public void setMinutes (int m) {minutes = m;}
  // Define private variable:
  private int minutes;
}
```

280 Data abstraction and the notion of a public interface fit together as follows:

- Channeling instance-variable accesses and assignments through access methods isolates you from the details of class implementation.

- When you define private instance variables, you force all instance-variable accesses and assignments to go through the constructors, getters, setters, and other instance methods in the public interface, thus providing a means to ensure that you practice data abstraction.

281 If you decide that an assignment of the `minutes` instance variable never changes once the `Attraction` instance is constructed, you can reflect that decision by removing the

setter, `setMinutes`. Then, only the constructor can assign a value to the `minutes` instance variable:

```
public class Attraction {
  // Define zero-parameter constructor:
  public Attraction () {minutes = 75;}
  // Define one-parameter constructor:
  public Attraction (int m) {minutes = m;}
  // Define getter:
  public int getMinutes () {return minutes;}
  // No setter defined here ...
  // Define private variable:
  private int minutes;
}
```

Because `getMinutes` is defined publicly in the `Attraction` class, the value of the `minutes` instance variable is accessible via `getMinutes` everywhere. Once construction is complete, however, the `minutes` instance variable cannot be written everywhere, because there is no publicly defined setter.

282 Instead of defining public getters to expand access to private instance variables and methods, you can expand access, without providing totally public access, by marking the instance variables and methods with the `protected` keyword, rather than with the `public` or `private` keywords. Variables and methods so marked are said to be in the protected part of the class definition, which, by convention, generally is defined between the public and private parts of the class definition:

```
public class Attraction {
  // Define zero-parameter constructor:
  public Attraction () {minutes = 75;}
  // Define one-parameter constructor:
  public Attraction (int m) {minutes = m;}
  // Define getter:
  public int getMinutes () {return minutes;}
  // Define setter:
  public void setMinutes (int m) {minutes = m;}
  // Define protected variable:
  protected int minutes;
}
```

283 A particular class's protected instance variables and instance methods are accessible from instance methods defined in the same class or in any subclass of that class.

Thus, the protected `minutes` instance variable is available not only to methods defined in the `Attraction` class definition, but also to methods defined in the Movie and Symphony classes, because those classes are subclasses of the `Attraction` class.

If you mark the `minutes` instance variable with the `protected` keyword, all the instance methods defined in the Movie, Symphony, and `Attraction` classes can assign values to the `minutes` instance variable, as well as can obtain a value from it.

284
In Segment 36, you learn that a particular class's protected variables and methods also are accessible from instance methods defined in another class, as long as that other class belongs to the same **compilation unit** or **package**.

285 If you like, you can combine the virtues of `private` and `protected` placement. First, you return the `minutes` instance variables to the private part of the `Attraction` class definition, to prevent accidental writing by instance methods defined outside the `Attraction` class. Second, you provide access to the `minutes` instance variable's value through a getter and setter defined in the protected part of the `Attraction` class definition:

```
public class Attraction {
 // Define zero-parameter constructor:
 public Attraction () {minutes = 75;}
 // Define one-parameter constructor:
 public Attraction (int m) {minutes = m;}
 // Define protected methods:
 // Define getter:
 protected int getMinutes () {return minutes;}
 // Define setter:
 protected void setMinutes (int m) {minutes = m;}
 // Define private variable:
 private int minutes;
}
```

Because the instance variable is in the private part of the `Attraction` class definition, it is accessible to only those instance methods that are defined in the `Attraction` class. Because the getter and setter are in the protected part of the `Attraction` class definition, they are also accessible to instance methods defined in subclasses of the `Attraction` class.

286 You learn more about how you can exploit Java's private, protected, and public machinery in Chapter 36, after you have learned about Java's package machinery in Chapter 35.

287
Revise the BoxCar class that you were asked to define in Segment 231 such that the instance variables are protected from access, except via getters and setters.

288
Describe and explain what happens when you run the following program:

```
public class Demonstrate {
 public static void main (String argv[]) {
  new Test();
 }
}
class Test {
 public Test () {
  System.out.println("Creating a Test instance");
 }
}
```

Then, describe and explain what happens when you mark the zero-parameter constructor with the `private` keyword.

- Inadvertent instance-variable accesses and assignments destroy data abstraction.

- You can prevent inadvertent direct access to instance variables by making such instance variables private. Thus, the public–private dichotomy helps to ensure that you can benefit from data abstraction.

- The public instance variables and public instance methods constitute the class's public interface.

- If you want to provide universal access to instance variables and methods, **then** mark them with the `public` keyword.

- If you want to limit access to instance variables and methods to the class in which they are introduced and to subclasses of the class in which they are introduced, **then** mark them with the `protected` keyword.

- If you want to limit access to instance variables and methods to the class in which they are introduced, **then** mark them with the `private` keyword.

16 HOW TO WRITE CONSTRUCTORS THAT CALL OTHER CONSTRUCTORS

290 In Chapter 11, you learned that constructors are instance methods that you use to construct class instances. In this chapter, you learn how to arrange for one class's constructor to call another class's constructor explicitly.

291 Suppose that you want to define for the Movie class a constructor that takes four arguments: the familiar script, acting, and direction values, plus the length of the movie in minutes. You want to use the constructor to create new Movie instances as follows:

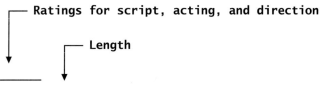

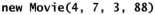

new Movie(4, 7, 3, 88)

The fourth argument establishes the value of the minutes instance variable inherited from the Attraction class.

292 You could, of course, define the required four-parameter constructor as follows, duplicating the assignment statements of the three-parameter constructor and adding a statement that assigns the minutes instance variable:

```
public class Movie extends Attraction {
 public int script, acting, direction;
 public Movie () {script = 5; acting = 5; direction = 5;}
 public Movie (int s, int a, int d) {
  script = s; acting = a; direction = d;     ←          Duplicates
 }
 public Movie (int s, int a, int d, int m) {
  script = s; acting = a; direction = d;   ←
  minutes = m;
 }
 public int rating () {return script + acting + direction;}
}
```

293 In a small class definition, it does no particular harm for a four-parameter constructor to duplicate the assignment statements of a three-parameter constructor; in general, however, you should avoid duplicating any program fragment on the ground that, when you debug or improve the duplicated program fragment, you must make identical changes in more than one place, which is difficult for the author of a program to do without error, and is completely impracticable for someone else to attempt.

Accordingly, you need a way for the four-parameter constructor not only to do its own unique work, but also to call the three-parameter constructor.

294 Ordinarily, the first action of a constructor is to call the zero-parameter constructor in the direct superclass. Thus, both of the constructors in the Movie class, as now defined, call the zero-parameter constructor in the Attraction class:

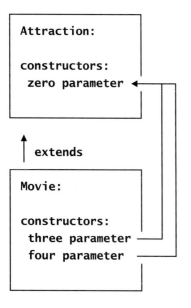

295 Whenever you want a constructor to hand arguments to another constructor in the same class, you modify the calling constructor's definition by adding a statement consisting of the this keyword followed by an argument list. That added statement must be the first statement in the calling constructor. For example, you modify the four-parameter constructor to call the three-parameter constructor as follows:

```
public class Movie extends Attraction {
  public int script, acting, direction;
  public Movie () {script = 5; acting = 5; direction = 5;}
  public Movie (int s, int a, int d) {
    script = s; acting = a; direction = d;
  }
  public Movie (int s, int a, int d, int m) {
    this(s, a, d);
    minutes = m;
  }
  public int rating () {return script + acting + direction;}
}
```

Call to three-parameter constructor

296 As you learned in Segment 198, in any instance method, this can be viewed as a special parameter, not listed with the other parameters, whose value is the instance method's target. Thus, a constructor-calling expression—such as this(s, a, d)—can be viewed as a method call with a target but no name; that call, by convention, means a call to a constructor.

297 The altered four-parameter constructor calls only the three-parameter constructor. Thus, the four-parameter constructor leaves it to the three-parameter constructor to call the zero-parameter constructor in the Attraction class.

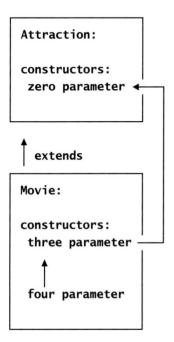

298 Now, suppose that you want to define constructors for the Movie class and for the Symphony class that assign only the minutes instance variable. You could, of course, define the constructors as follows:

```
public class Movie extends Attraction {
  ...
  public Movie (int m) {minutes = m;}          ◄─────────┐
  ...                                                     │
}                                                         │
                                                          │  Duplicates
public class Symphony extends Attraction {                │
  ...                                                     │
  public Symphony (int m) {minutes = m;}     ◄───────────┘
  ...
}
```

299 You should avoid duplication, however, even in simple methods—and the Movie and Symphony constructors shown in Segment 298 are duplicates.

Fortunately, you have already defined a suitable one-argument, `minutes`-assigning constructor in the `Attraction` class:

```
public class Attraction {
 private int minutes;
 public int getMinutes() {return minutes;}
 public void setMinutes(int m) {minutes = m;}
 public Attraction () {minutes = 75;}
 public Attraction (int m) {minutes = m;}
}
```

300 You can arrange for the one-parameter constructors in the `Movie` and `Symphony` classes to call the one-parameter `Attraction` constructor, shown, for example, in Segment 299. Ordinarily, all constructors call only the zero-parameter constructor in the direct superclass.

Whenever you want a constructor to hand one or more arguments to another constructor in the direct superclass, you modify the constructor's definition by adding, as the first statement in that constructor, a statement consisting of the `super` keyword followed by an argument list.

301 Thus, to modify the one-parameter constructors in the `Movie` class and the `Symphony` class, such that they call the one-parameter constructor in the `Attraction` class, you add `super` constructor calls to both:

```
public class Movie extends Attraction {
 ...
 public Movie (int m) {
  super(m);        ←——————————— Call to one-parameter constructor
 }                              in Attraction class
 ...
}

public class Symphony extends Attraction {
 ...
 public Symphony (int m) {
  super(m);        ←——————————— Call to one-parameter constructor
 }                              in Attraction class
 ...
}
```

302 Now, the one-parameter constructors in the `Movie` and `Symphony` classes call the one-parameter constructor in the `Attraction` class:

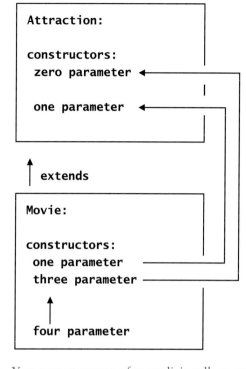

Attraction:

constructors:
  zero parameter
  one parameter

extends

Movie:

constructors:
  one parameter
  three parameter

  four parameter

303
SIDE TRIP You cannot arrange for explicit calls to more than one constructor. In this respect, Java differs from C++.

304
PRACTICE Redefine the zero-parameter constructor that you were asked to define for the BoxCar class in Segment 219, such that it calls the three-parameter constructor.

305
HIGHLIGHTS

- If you want a constructor to call another constructor in the same class, **then** instantiate the following pattern:

```
public class name ( parameter specification ) {
  this( arguments for called constructor );
  ...
}
```

- If you want a constructor to call another constructor in the direct superclass, **then** instantiate the following pattern:

```
public class name ( parameter specification ) {
  super( arguments for called constructor );
  ...
}
```

17 HOW TO WRITE METHODS THAT CALL OTHER METHODS

306 From what you have learned so far, you supply an instance method with a class instance by providing the class instance as the target: You write the name of the class instance, followed by the field-selection operator, followed by the name of the instance method.

In this chapter, you learn how to pass along an instance from a directly called instance method to an indirectly called instance method.

307 Suppose that you want to write an attraction-analysis program that displays a report containing each attraction's category, rating, and length:

```
Movie with rating 14 lasts 88 minutes
Symphony with rating 22 lasts 62 minutes
```

308 To do the work, you define the `describe` instance method in both the `Movie` class and the `Symphony` class.

At first glance, the following definition of `describe` in the `Movie` class, might seem likely to fail, because there is no target for either the `rating` method or the `getMinutes` method. By convention, however, because the target and the field-selection operator are absent, the `rating` and `getMinutes` methods are handed the same class-instance target as that handed to `describe`. Thus, `rating` and `getMinutes` have **implicit targets**.

```
public class Movie extends Attraction {
 // Rest of Movie definition ...
 // Define rating:
 public int rating () {
  return script + acting + direction;
 }
 // Define describe
 public void describe () {
  System.out.println(
   "Movie with rating "
   + rating() + " lasts "
   + getMinutes() + " minutes"
  );
 }
}
```

309 The following diagram shows how the various instance variables and methods fit together. The `getMinutes` method is defined in only the `Attraction` class. The `rating` and `describe` methods are defined in the `Movie` and `Symphony` classes:

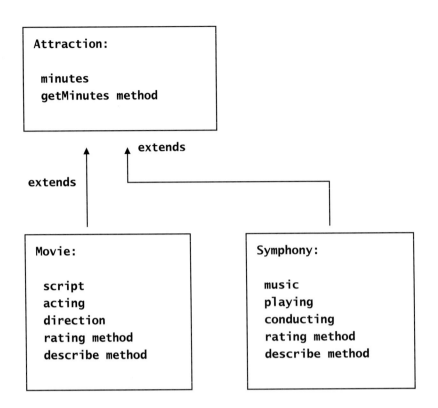

310 Because getMinutes is defined in the Attraction class, but is not defined in the Movie class, the getMinutes method defined in the Attraction class is called whenever the getMinutes method is called with a movie target.

311 Now, you can use describe in a demonstration program:

```
public class Demonstrate {
 public static void main(String argv[]) {
  Movie m;
  m = new Movie(4, 7, 3, 88);
  m.describe();
  Symphony s = new Symphony(10, 9, 3, 66);
  s.describe();
 }
}
```

——————————— Result ———————————
```
Movie with rating 14 lasts 88 minutes
Symphony with rating 22 lasts 66 minutes
```

312 As you learned in Segment 295, this can be viewed as a special instance-method parameter whose value is the instance method's target. If you wish, you can use this as an explicit target. Thus, you can redefine the Movie class's describe method as follows:

```
public class Movie extends Attraction {
 // Rest of Movie definition ...
 // Define rating:
 public int rating () {
   return script + acting + direction;
 }
 // Define describe
 public void describe () {
   System.out.println(
     "Movie with rating "
     + this.rating() + " lasts "
     + this.getMinutes() + " minutes"
   );
 }
}
```

Thus, the real result of leaving out an explicit target is that Java takes the target to be the value of the this parameter.

313 Similarly, you can use super, introduced in Segment 300, as a method target, if you want Java to ignore the method defined in the target's class, using instead a method defined in a superclass of the target.

For example, you can divide into two parts the work previously handled by the describe method defined in the Movie class. One part of the work is handled by a newly defined describe method in the Attraction class:

```
public class Attraction {
 private int minutes;
 public int getMinutes() {return minutes;}
 public void setMinutes(int m) {minutes = m;}
 public Attraction () {minutes = 75;}
 public Attraction (int m) {minutes = m;}
 // Define describe
 public void describe () {
   System.out.println(
     " and lasts "
     + this.getMinutes() + " minutes"
   );
 }
}
```

And the other part of the work is handled by a redefined describe method in the Movie class:

```
public class Movie extends Attraction {
 // Rest of Movie definition ...
 // Define rating:
 public int rating () {
  return script + acting + direction;
 }
 // Define describe
 public void describe () {
  System.out.print("Movie with rating " + this.rating());
   super.describe();
 }
}
```

314 The Movie class's describe method, as defined in Segment 313, calls describe with super as its target. That call uses the describe method defined in the Attraction class.

In general, if you write a call to a method with a super target, Java ignores the definition of that method in the target's class, if any; instead, Java uses the first method with the same name defined in the chain of classes leading upward in the class hierarchy from the target's superclass.

315 In Segment 295 and Segment 300, you learned that you can use this and super in a constructor, **without** field selection operators and method names, to call constructors. When so used, the this or super call must be the first call in the constructor. When super is used, the constructor called is the one defined in the direct superclass.

In this chapter, you learned that you can use this and super in methods, **with** field selection operators and method names, to call methods. Such calls can appear anywhere. When super is used, the method called is the first one encountered in the subclass–superclass chain.

316 By way of summary, the following are complete definitions of the Attraction, Movie, and Symphony classes that serve from here through Chapter 37. They include all that has been developed so far, plus two additional instance variables, title and poster, which are used in Chapter 31:

```
public abstract class Attraction {
 // First, define instance variables:
 public int minutes;
 public String title, poster;
 // Define constructors:
 public Attraction () {minutes = 75;}
 public Attraction (int m) {minutes = m;}
```

```java
 // Define getters and setters:
 public int getMinutes () {return minutes;}
 public void setMinutes (int m) {minutes = m;}
 // Define rating as an abstract method:
 public abstract int rating () ;
 // Define category as an abstract method:
 public abstract String category () ;
 // Define describe:
 public void describe () {
  System.out.println(
   category() + " with rating "
   + rating() + " lasts "
   + getMinutes() + " minutes"
  );
 }
}


public class Movie extends Attraction {
 // First, define instance variables:
 public int script, acting, direction;
 // Define zero-parameter constructor:
 public Movie () {script = 5; acting = 5; direction = 5;}
 // Define one-parameter constructor:
 public Movie (int m) {super(m);}
 // Define three-parameter constructor:
 public Movie (int s, int a, int d) {
  script = s; acting = a; direction = d;
 }
 // Define four-parameter constructor:
 public Movie (int s, int a, int d, int m) {
  this(s, a, d);
  minutes = m;
 }
 // Define rating:
 public int rating () {return script + acting + direction;}
 // Define category:
 public String category () {return "Movie";}
}


public class Symphony extends Attraction {
 // First, define instance variables:
 public int music, playing, conducting;
 // Define zero-parameter constructor:
 public Symphony () {music = 5; playing = 5; conducting = 5;}
 // Define one-parameter constructor:
 public Symphony (int m) {super(m);}
```

```
// Define three-parameter constructor:
public Symphony (int s, int a, int d) {
 music = s; playing = a; conducting = d;
}
// Define four-parameter constructor:
public Symphony (int s, int a, int d, int m) {
 this(s, a, d);
 minutes = m;
}
// Define rating:
public int rating () {return music + playing + conducting;}
// Define category:
public String category () {return "Symphony";}
}
```

317

PRACTICE Adapt the program that was shown in Segment 313 such that you enable the display of information about BoxCar and TankCar instances, rather than about Movie and Symphony instances.

318

HIGHLIGHTS

- If you want to call an instance method from inside another instance method, **and** the called instance method is to work on the same target instance that you handed to the calling method, **then** instantiate the following pattern:

  instance method (ordinary arguments)

- If you prefer to use an explicit target, **then** exploit the assignment of the this parameter:

  this. instance method (ordinary arguments)

- If you want Java to ignore a method defined in the target's class, using a method defined in a superclass instead, **then** use the super parameter:

  super. instance method (ordinary arguments)

18 HOW TO DESIGN CLASSES AND CLASS HIERARCHIES

319   At this point, you have learned how to **define** classes and class hierarchies. In this chapter, you learn how to **design** classes and class hierarchies by observing several principles of representation design.

320   The **explicit-representation principle**: Whenever there is a natural category with which your program needs to work, there should be a class in your program that corresponds to that category.

In the attraction domain, for example, there are natural categories corresponding to movies and symphonies.

321   The **no-duplication principle**: Instance variables and instance methods should be distributed among class definitions to ensure that there is no needless duplication. Otherwise, duplicate copies are bound to become gratuitously different.

For example, in Segment 316, the `minutes` instance variable and the `getMinutes` method are declared and defined in the `Attraction` class, rather than in the `Movie` and `Symphony` classes, making that instance variable and that method more generally available.

322   The **look-it-up principle**: A program should look up a frequently needed answer, rather than computing that answer, whenever practicable.

For example, in Segment 316, a `minutes` instance variable was declared in the `Attraction` class, whereas an `hours` instance variable could have been declared. The right choice depends on whether you are more likely to be interested in minutes or in hours.

323   The **need-to-know principle**: Generally, when you design classes to be used by other programmers, your classes will contain more instance variables and methods than you expect to be accessed by the methods written by those other programmers.

By restricting access to instance variables and methods in public interfaces, you can revise and improve the other instance variables and methods without worrying about whether other programmers have already come to depend on them.

For example, when you define an `Attraction` class, you might choose to make the `minutes` instance variable private, requiring all access to be through public access methods. Your rationale would be that you could change later to an hours-based definition without fear that anyone would have come to depend on direct access to the `minutes` instance variable. Instead, all users of the `Attraction` class would have to use the `getMinutes` and `setMinutes` methods in the public interface, which you easily could redefine to work with an `hours` instance variable.

324   The **is-a versus has-a principle**: You learned in Chapter 9 that instances mirror real-world individuals and classes mirror real-world categories. Accordingly, when you decide to implement a class, you are building a **model** of an aspect of the real world.

Many programmers new to object-oriented programming find it difficult to decide between implementing a new class and installing a new instance variable, because the **subclass–superclass relation** is easily confused with the **part–whole relation**.

Generally, if you find yourself using the phrase *an X is a Y* when describing the relation between two classes, then the first class is a subclass of the second. On the other hand, if you find yourself using *X has a Y*, then instances of the second class appear as parts of instances of the first class.

For example, a human is an animal. Accordingly, the **is-a rule** dictates that if you define a Human class, that class should be a subclass of the Animal class. Similarly, a box car is a railroad car, and the BoxCar class should be a subclass of the RailroadCar class.

On the other hand, humans have arms and legs, so the **has-a rule** dictates that the Human class should have Arm and Leg instance variables. Similarly, a box car has a box, and the BoxCar class therefore should have a Box instance variable.

325 Deciding between a subclass–superclass relation and a part–whole relation is not always straightforward. For example, you may decide to model a piano as an instrument that has a keyboard, or you may decide to model a piano as a keyboard instrument. If you follow the has-a rule, you implement the Piano class with a Keyboard instance variable; if you follow the is-a rule, you implement the Piano class as a subclass of the KeyboardInstrument class.

The rule you should follow is the one that seems to make the most sense in light of the aspects of the real world that you are modeling. If your program is to deal with many types of keyboard instruments, then defining a KeyboardInstrument class probably is the better choice. If your program is to deal with only pianos, then defining a Keyboard instance variable probably is the better choice.

Thus, there is no universal right answer to the decision between modeling with the subclass–superclass relation and the part–whole relation.

326
PRACTICE Design a class hierarchy for a dozen houses and buildings. At the highest level, place an instance variable named squareFeet and age and locationMultiplier. Write an instance method, appraise, for the classes in your hierarchy. Include classes such as Bungalow, Mansion, Skyscraper, and Warehouse.

327
PRACTICE Design a class hierarchy for a dozen occupations. At the highest level, place an instance variable named yearsOfExperience and locationMultiplier. Write an instance method, estimatedSalary, for the classes in your hierarchy. Include classes such as Physician, Lawyer, Engineer, Athlete, Ornithologist, Astrologer, and Editor.

328
HIGHLIGHTS

- Programs should obey the explicit-representation principle, with classes included to reflect natural categories.

- Programs should obey the no-duplication principle, with instance methods situated among class definitions to facilitate sharing.

- Programs should obey the look-it-up principle, with class definitions including instance variables for stable, frequently requested information.

- Programs should obey the need-to-know principle, with public interfaces designed to restrict instance-variable and instance-method access, thus facilitating the improvement and maintenance of nonpublic program elements.

- **If** you find yourself using the phrase *an X is a Y* when describing the relation between two classes, **then** the X class is a subclass of the Y class.

- **If** you find yourself using *X has a Y* when describing the relation between two classes, **then** instances of the Y class appear as parts of instances of the X class.

19 HOW TO ENFORCE REQUIREMENTS USING ABSTRACT CLASSES AND ABSTRACT METHODS

329   Abstract classes are like ordinary classes in that they serve as collection points for variables and methods needed in subclasses. In contrast to an ordinary class, however, an abstract class allows you to declare methods without defining them. Such methods must be defined in any ordinary class that directly extends the abstract class.

In this chapter, you learn what abstract classes are and how they impose method-definition requirements. In this chapter and in Chapter 20, you learn that the ability to impose method-definition requirements plays an important role in promoting good programming practice.

330   Suppose that you want to insist that both the `Movie` class and the `Sympony` class have a `rating` method. If both use the same rating method, then you can define it in the `Attraction` class, enabling its use in all subclasses.

If the two classes use different rating methods, then your good-faith intention to define `rating` in both the `Movie` and `Symphony` subclasses may be derailed, especially if someone else is in charge of those classes. Fortunately, Java provides a mechanism that turns good-faith intentions into ironclad requirements.

331   To ensure that the `rating` method is defined in both the `Movie` and `Symphony` subclasses of the `Attraction` class, you perform two steps.

First, you mark the `Attraction` class with the `abstract` keyword:

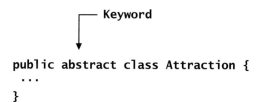

```
public abstract class Attraction {
  ...
}
```

Second, you define the `rating` method, again marking that method with the `abstract` keyword, but now inserting a semicolon where you would ordinarily expect the definition's body:

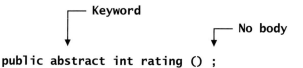

```
public abstract int rating () ;
```

332   Once you have defined an abstract method, Java forces you to define nonabstract methods accessible to all nonabstract subclasses of the abstract class.

For example, because both the Movie class and the Symphony class are subclasses of the Attraction class, both must have rating methods. On the other hand, if the Movie class were to have subclasses, no rating method would be required in those subclasses, because they would inherit the nonabstract rating method from the Movie class.

333 In general, the abstract-method declarations in an abstract class specify both return types and parameter types. Such specifications are called **method signatures**, which you first learned about in Segment 120.

334 When an abstract-method signature includes parameters, the various parameter names are not constrained to be the same parameter names used in the definitions that appear in subclasses. Thus, an abstract-method signature may use numberIndicatingScriptQuality as a parameter name, as an aid to documentation:

```
public abstract int setScript (int numberIndicatingScriptQuality) ;
```

The corresponding implementation may use s as the corresponding parameter name:

```
public int setScript (int s) {
  script = s;
}
```

335 Once you have told Java that a class is abstract, any attempt to create an instance of that class produces a complaint:

```
        ┌─ Attempt to create an instance of an abstract class
        │    fails to compile
        ▼
  ───────────────
  new Attraction()
```

Thus, the purposes of the class are strictly to define inheritable, shared variables and methods and to impose requirements via abstract methods.

```
public abstract class Attraction {
  public int minutes;
  public Attraction () {minutes = 75;}          Shared
  public Attraction (int m) {minutes = m;}
  public int getMinutes () {return minutes;}
  public void setMinutes (int m) {minutes = m;}
  public abstract int rating () ;          ◀── Required
}
```

336 Note that you can define abstract methods only in abstract classes. The rationale is that, if a class is not abstract, you can create instances of that class, and you should be able to call any instance method of the class on those instances.

337 When you impose a method-definition requirement by declaring an abstract method, you shift to the Java compiler a requirement-managing responsibility that otherwise would require your own, human attention. Because good programming practice dictates that method-definition requirements should be thought through and managed carefully, good programmers often exploit the abstract-class–abstract-method mechanism.

338 Although you cannot create an instance of an abstract class, you can declare a variable that is typed by an abstract class:

```
...
Attraction x;
...
```

The value of such a variable can be either a Movie instance or a Symphony instance, because the value of a variable declared for a particular class can be an instance of any subclass:

```
...
x = new Movie();
...
x = new Symphony();
...
```

339 With the abstract rating method installed in the abstract Attraction class, you can use it with an Attraction variable that has a value that is a Movie instance or Symphony instance; the rating is computed by the methods defined in the Movie or Symphony class:

```
public class Demonstrate {
 public static void main (String argv[]) {
   // Movie instance assigned to x:
   Attraction x = new Movie (7, 7, 7);
   System.out.println("The movie's rating is " + x.rating());
   // Symphony instance assigned to x:
   x = new Symphony (7, 7, 7);
   System.out.println("The symphony's rating is " + x.rating());
 }
}
———————————————— Result ————————————————
The movie's rating is 21
The symphony's rating is 21
```

340 Note that, should you declare a variable to be an Attraction variable, assigned to a Movie instance, you can call only the ordinary or abstract methods that appear in the Attraction class. Thus, even if both the Movie class and the Symphony class define, say, a method named profit, the following will not compile:

```
public class Demonstrate {
 public static void main (String argv[]) {
  // Movie instance assigned to x:
  Attraction x = new Movie (7, 7, 7);
  System.out.println("The movie's profit is " + x.profit());
  // Symphony instance assigned to x:
  x = new Symphony (7, 7, 7);
  System.out.println("The symphony's profit is " + x.profit());
 }
}
```

341 In general, you can assign a subclass instance to a superclass variable. You cannot, however, call any of the subclass's methods with that superclass variable as the target. Only the methods defined or declared in the superclass, and its superclasses, are available.

342 On the other hand, because each Java instance retains all its data, even if it is viewed as an instance of a superclass, you can cast an `Attraction` variable, assigned to a `Movie` instance, to the `Movie` class, and then use any method that can be applied to a `Movie` instance. Thus, the following will compile, if the `profit` method is defined in both the Movie and Symphony classes.

```
public class Demonstrate {
 public static void main (String argv[]) {
  // Movie instance assigned to x:
  Attraction x = new Movie (5, 7, 7);
  System.out.println("The movie's profit is " + ((Movie)x).profit());
  // Symphony instance assigned to x:
  x = new Symphony (7, 5, 5);
  System.out.println("The symphony's profit is "
                     + ((Symphony)x).profit()
                    );
 }
}
```

343 You can mark a class with the `final` keyword, making that class a **final class**. Such classes cannot be extended. Thus, abstract classes can have no instances, and final classes can have no subclasses.

344 All classes form an inverted tree with the `Object` class at the root. Final classes appear only as leaves.

Abstract classes generally lie high in the tree, because they generally declare instance variables and declare or define instance methods that you intend to share among multiple subclasses.

No class can be both abstract and final.

345 In the following illustration, all arrows represent subclass–superclass relations:

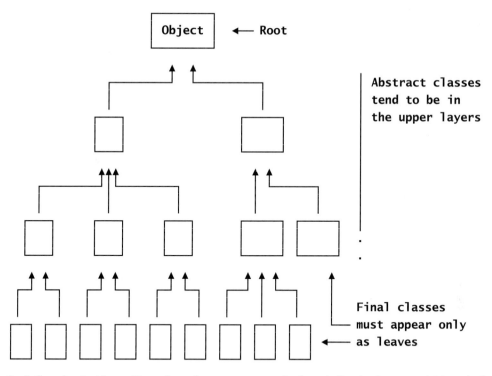

Object ← Root

Abstract classes tend to be in the upper layers

Final classes must appear only as leaves

346
PRACTICE Redefine the RailroadCar class that you were asked to define in Segment 271 such that you make the class abstract. Be sure to include an abstract volume method.

347
HIGHLIGHTS

- **If** no instances are to be created for a particular class, **then** you should tell Java that the class is an abstract class by instantiating the following pattern:

  ```
  public abstract class class name {
    ...
  }
  ```

- **If** you want every subclass of an abstract class to define a particular method, **then** you should define an abstract method in the abstract class by instantiating the following pattern:

  ```
  public abstract return type method name
    (parameter specifications) ;
  ```

- You can use abstract class names as variable or parameter type declarations.

20 HOW TO ENFORCE REQUIREMENTS AND TO DOCUMENT PROGRAMS USING INTERFACES

348 In Chapter 19, you learned how to use abstract classes to impose method-definition requirements on subclasses. In this chapter, you learn how to use Java's **interface mechanism** to establish method-definition requirements on a class without relying on inheritance from an abstract class.

A principle of good programming practice is that you should think about what you want your programs to do before you proceed to write them. Because establishing requirements forces you to think about what you want your programs to do, liberal use of Java's interface mechanism is good programming practice.

In this chapter, you also learn that Java's interface mechanism help teams of programmers to work together effectively, and you learn that interfaces offer splendid locations for program documentation.

Thus, Java's interface mechanism, reflectively used, can make you a much better programmer.

349 Suppose that you have begun to think about a movie application, but you have not yet written any portion of that movie application. Following the principle that you should think first and hack later, you start off with a design phase, during which you think about what classes and methods you will need in your movie application.

In particular, suppose that you decide that there shall be a Movie class, that class shall have a rating method, and that rating method shall have no ordinary arguments and shall return an integer.

350 To ensure that a rating method honoring your design decisions is defined in the Movie class, you perform steps that run parallel to the steps layed out in Segment 331:

First, you define an **interface** called, say, RatingInterface, substituting the interface keyword for the class keyword that you would expect in a class definition:

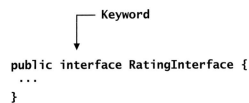

Keyword

```
public interface RatingInterface {
  ...
}
```

Second, you define the rating method in the body of the interface, as though you were defining that rating method in an abstract class, marking that method with the abstract keyword, and inserting a semicolon where you would ordinarily expect the definition's body.

Keyword

No body

```
public abstract int rating () ;
```

Third, you define the Movie and Symphony classes to **implement** the RatingInterface interface, using the implements keyword, as well as to extend an appropriate superclass:

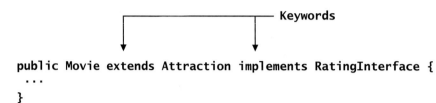

Keywords

```
public Movie extends Attraction implements RatingInterface {
 ...
}
```

351 A class definition that implements an interface must define all the methods specified in that interface. In this respect, an interface is like an abstract class.

An interface differs from an abstract class, however, in the following respects:

- An interface only imposes definition requirements; it does not supply definitions.

- A class extends exactly one superclass; a class can implement an unlimited number of interfaces.

352 Thus, the purpose of the interface is strictly to impose requirements via that interface's abstract methods. Note that there are no method implementations:

```
public interface RatingInterface {
 public abstract int rating () ;          ← Required
}
```

353 As you learned in Segment 333, abstract-method definitions specify both return types and parameter types, and such specifications are called **method signatures**.

When an abstract-method signature includes parameters, the parameter names are not constrained to be the same in the definitions that appear in subclasses.

354 Now you can be sure that your definition of the Movie class defines the rating method by insisting that the Movie class implements the RatingInterface interface.

Suppose that after a month passes, you have forgotten your decisions. The interface will still insist that the Movie class define a rating method, with your previously specified return value type and argument types. If you hand off to another programmer the job of Movie-class implementation, the interface will still insist that the Movie class define the specified rating method. In both situations, the interface retains a deployable memory of your design decisions.

355 Interfaces provide specifications not only for you, but also for all implementers who use them.

For example, suppose that you have completed your movie application, and it works fine. Some time later, another programmer claims to have a definition of the Movie class that is somehow better, perhaps because its methods compute faster. Further, the other programmer claims that his Movie class can be dropped into your application, substituting for your Movie class, with no other changes to your application.

Naturally, you would like to be able to use the other Movie definition without fear. Also, you would not want to require the other programmer to implement his Movie class in any particular way, because that might handicap his creativity or force rework.

Fortunately, if you have defined the specification-retaining RatingInterface interface, and the other programmer's Movie class implements that interface, you can be sure that his class does, in fact, have a rating method that has return type and argument types the same as those of your rating method.

Thus, RatingInterface is a specification not only for you, but also for all implementers who which to define Movie classes.

356 Interface method signatures specify types and arguments, but they do not specify all the requirements that you might like to specify. For example, you might wish to specify that a method:

- Runs in less than 1 microsecond
- Uses a linear-time algorithm
- Reads no information from a file
- Returns the square root of the argument value

357 Although interfaces provide no mechanism for enforcing method specifications, other than method signatures, you are free to deposit descriptive comments in an interface.

Interfaces tend to be excellent places for descriptive comments for two reasons:

- Interfaces, unlike class definitions, are not cluttered by code.
- Programmers, by convention, look to interfaces for method and class documentation.

358 The interface mechanism is an enormously important aid to good programming practice.

- Interfaces allow you to shift to the Java compiler a requirement-managing responsibility that otherwise would engage your own, human attention.
- Interfaces encourage you to document your classes by acting, by convention, as documentation centers.

359 Because a class can extend only one direct superclass, Java is said to allow only single inheritance, and to disallow multiple inheritance. If Java did allow multiple inheritance, then you could impose requirements on a class by having that class inherit directly from several abstract classes.

Java does allow a class to implement multiple interfaces, however. Thus, from the perspective of method-definition requirements, you can view Java's interface mechanism as an alternative to multiple inheritance.

360 The designers of Java deliberately did not provide for multiple inheritance, because multi-
SIDE TRIP ple inheritance introduces problems. For example, if multiple branches in an inheritance hierarchy provide an instance method or instance-variable value, then language designers have to decide which branch dominates the others. C++ resolves the problem by complaining about ambiguity at compile time. Other languages, such as Lisp, resolve the problem by using an elaborate ordering mechanism called topological sorting.

361 You can declare a variable that is typed by an interface:

```
...
RatingInterface x;
...
```

The value of such a variable can be an instance of any class that implements the interface. For example, if both the Movie class and the Symphony class implement the RatingInterface interface, you can write the following:

```
...
x = new Movie();
...
x = new Symphony();
...
```

362 With a rating method installed in the Movie class and the Symphony class, both of which implement the RatingInterface interface, you can use the rating method with either a Movie instance or Symphony instance assigned to a RatingInterface variable; the rating is computed by the methods defined in the Movie or Symphony class:

```
public class Demonstrate {
  public static void main (String argv[]) {
    // Movie instance assigned to x:
    RatingInterface x = new Movie (5, 7, 7);
    System.out.println("The movie's rating is " + x.rating());
    // Symphony instance assigned to x:
    x = new Symphony (7, 5, 5);
    System.out.println("The symphony's rating is " + x.rating());
  }
}
```

363 Note, that should you declare a variable using an interface, then you can call only those methods that appear in that interface. Thus, even if both the Movie class and the Symphony class define, say, a method named profit, the following will not compile:

```
public class Demonstrate {
 public static void main (String argv[]) {
  // Movie instance assigned to x:
  RatingInterface x = new Movie (5, 7, 7);
  System.out.println("The movie's profit is " + x.profit());
  // Symphony instance assigned to x:
  x = new Symphony (7, 5, 5);
  System.out.println("The symphony's profit is " + x.profit());
 }
}
```

364 In general, you can declare an interface variable. You cannot, however, call any of a class's methods that are not specified in the interface.

Thus, you can use an interface not only to require definitions for methods specified in the interface, but also to prevent deployment of methods that are not specified in the interface.

365 On the other hand, because each Java instance retains all its data, even if the instance is viewed as an implementer of an interface, you can cast a `RatingInterface` variable, bound to a `Movie` instance, to the `Movie` class, and then use any method that can be applied to a `Movie` instance. Thus, the following will compile, if the `profit` method is defined in both the `Movie` and `Symphony` classes.

```
public class Demonstrate {
 public static void main (String argv[]) {
  // Movie instance assigned to x:
  RatingInterface x = new Movie (5, 7, 7);
  System.out.println("The movie's profit is " + ((Movie)x).profit());
  // Symphony instance assigned to x:
  x = new Symphony (7, 5, 5);
  System.out.println("The symphony's profit is "
                        + ((Symphony)x).profit()
                        );
 }
}
```

366
SIDE TRIP

Note that the word *interface* is used in Java in two ways. In this chapter, a Java **interface** imposes requirements; in Chapter 15, a Java class's **public interface** is the set of methods and variables that are universally accessible.

367
PRACTICE

Define a `RailroadCarInterface` as a substitute for the requirement-imposing abstract class that you were asked to define in Segment 346. Be sure to include an abstract `volume` method.

368
HIGHLIGHTS

- If you want to require a class to implement certain methods, **and** those requirements are not appropriate for an abstract class in the ordinary inheritance chain, **then** you should define an interface.

- If you want to define a public interface, **then** instantiate the following pattern:

  ```
  public interface interface name {
   ...
  }
  ```

- If you want every implementer of an interface to define a particular method, **then** you should define an abstract method in the interface by instantiating the following pattern:

  ```
  public abstract return type method name
   ( parameter specifications ) ;
  ```

- If you want to impose requirements on a particular class using an interface, **then** instantiate the following pattern. You may add a superclass name before the `interface` keyword, marking the superclass name with the `extends` keyword. You may add additional interface names, separating them with commas:

  ```
  public class class name implements interface name {
   ...
  }
  ```

- No class can extend more than one superclass; any class can implement multiple interfaces.

- You can use interface names as variable or parameter type declarations.

21 HOW TO PERFORM TESTS USING PREDICATES

369 In this and the next several chapters, you set aside classes and class instances, temporarily, to learn how to do routine testing, branching, iterating, and recursing. You see that Java's mechanisms for accomplishing such tasks are not much different from those that you would find in just about any programming language.

In this chapter, you learn how to test numbers.

370 Operators and methods that return values representing true or false are called **predicates**. Java offers several operator predicates that test the relationship between pairs of numbers:

Predicate	Purpose
==	Are two numbers equal?
!=	Are two numbers not equal?
>	Is the first number greater than the second?
<	Is the first number less than the second?
>=	Is the first number greater than or equal to the second?
<=	Is the first number less than or equal to the second?

371 In general, the value returned by a predicate must be a **Boolean value**; that is, in Java, the value must be either `true` or `false`.

The value of the expression 6 != 3, in which the **inequality operator** appears, is `true`. The value of the expression 6 == 3, in which the **equality operator** appears, is `false`.

372 A common error is to write a single equal-to sign, =, the assignment operator, when you intend to check for equality. Be sure to remember that the equality predicate is written as a double equal-to sign, ==.

373 You now know that, whenever the character ! is followed immediately by the character =, the two characters together denote the inequality operator.

The ! character also can appear alone, in which case it denotes the **not operator**. The not operator is a unary operator that converts `true` into `false`, and vice versa. Thus, the value of `!false` is `true` and `!true` is `false`. Similarly, the value of `!(6 == 3)` is `true`, meaning that "it is true that '6 is equal to 3' is `false`." Also, the value of `!(6 != 3)` is `false`, meaning that "it is false that '6 is not equal to 3' is `true`."

374 You can declare variables to have **boolean type**. You can assign either of the **literal Boolean values**, `true` or `false`, to such variables. Note that, although the Reverend Boole no doubt spelled his name with an uppercase B, the `boolean` type is marked with a lowercase `boolean` keyword.

```
public class Demonstrate {
 public static void main (String argv[]) {
   boolean b;
   b = (2 + 2 == 4);
   System.out.println(b);
 }
}
```
———————————————— Result ————————————————
```
true
```

375 The `boolean` type is one of the **primitive types**, which you learned about in Segment 180. The **default value** of a Boolean variable is `false`.

376 Note that you do not need to perform a cast, of the sort you learned about in Segment 93, if you want a program to compare an integer with a floating-point number. Java will perform the cast automatically, as illustrated by the following program:

```
public class Demonstrate {
 public static void main (String argv[]) {
   int i = 50; double d = 50.0;
   System.out.println(i == d);
   System.out.println(i != d);
 }
}
```
———————————————— Result ————————————————
```
true
false
```

377 Occasionally, you need to work with predicates that work on class instances, rather than on numbers. For example, if you want to determine whether a particular instance is an instance of a particular class, you use the `instanceof` operator, which returns `true` if the instance is either a direct instance of the given class or a direct instance of a subclass of that class.

Suppose, for example, that the `JamesBondMovie` class extends the `Movie` class, which extends the `Attraction` class. Then, a James Bond movie is an instance of all three classes. An ordinary movie is an instance of the `Movie` class as well as of the `Attraction` class, but it is not an instance of the `JamesBondMovie` class:

```
public class Demonstrate {
 public static void main (String argv[]) {
  JamesBondMovie jbm = new JamesBondMovie();
  Movie m = new Movie(1, 1, 1);
  System.out.println(jbm instanceof Attraction);
  System.out.println(jbm instanceof Movie);
  System.out.println(jbm instanceof JamesBondMovie);
  System.out.println(m instanceof Attraction);
  System.out.println(m instanceof Movie);
  System.out.println(m instanceof JamesBondMovie);
 }
}
```

———————————— Result ————————————

```
true
true
true
true
true
false
```

378 If you want to determine whether two class instances are the same instance, you use `equals`, which is a method rather than an operator. Note that the `equals` method determines whether two instances are the same instance, rather than equivalent instances:

```
public class Demonstrate {
 public static void main (String argv[]) {
  Movie m1 = new Movie(3, 4, 5);
  Movie m2 = new Movie(3, 4, 5);
  Movie m3 = new Movie(4, 5, 6);
  System.out.println(m1.equals(m2));
  System.out.println(m2.equals(m3));
  m3 = m2 = m1;
  System.out.println(m1.equals(m2));
  System.out.println(m2.equals(m3));
 }
}
```
———————————— Result ————————————
```
false
false
true
true
```

379 In C and C++, true and false are just alternate names for 1 and 0. In Java, true and
SIDE TRIP false are distinct values; they are not 1 and 0.

380

SIDE TRIP In C and C++, you must perform an explicit cast if you want to compare numbers of different types.

381

PRACTICE The energy of a moving mass is given by the formula $1/2mv$ sup 2. Write a program that accepts the mass and velocity of two automobiles. If the energy of the first automobile is greater than that of the second, your program is to display `true`; otherwise, your program is to display `false`. Use `double` variables for all numbers.

382

HIGHLIGHTS

- A predicate is an operator or method that returns `true` or `false`, which are, collectively, the `boolean` values.

- The binary predicates include ==, !=. >, <, >=, and <=.

- The binary predicates also include `instanceof` and `equals` for instance-to-class membership and instance equality.

- If you want to turn `true` into `false`, or vice versa, **then** use the unary ! operator.

22 HOW TO WRITE CONDITIONAL STATEMENTS

383 In this chapter, you learn how to use conditional statements when the computation that you want to perform depends on the value of an expression involving a predicate.

384 A **Boolean expression** is an expression that produces a true or false result. Reduced to practice in Java, a Boolean expression is an expression that produces either `true` or `false`.

385 An `if` statement contains a Boolean expression, in parentheses, followed by an embedded statement:

```
if ( Boolean expression )
   embedded statement
```

If the Boolean expression of an `if` statement evaluates to `true`, Java executes the embedded statement; if the Boolean expression evaluates to `false`, Java skips the embedded statement.

386 Suppose, for example, that you want to write a program that displays a message that depends on the length of a movie in minutes. Specifically, if the length is greater than 90 minutes, you want your program to display `It is long!`, and if the length is less than 60 minutes, you want your program to display `It is short!`.

One solution is to write a program that uses `if` statements in which the embedded statements are display statements:

```
public class Demonstrate {
 public static void main (String argv[]) {
   int length = 95;
   if (length < 60)
     System.out.println("It is short!");
   if (length > 90)
     System.out.println("It is long!");
 }
}
—————————————— Result ——————————————
It is long!
```

387 The `if–else` statement is like the `if` statement, except that a second embedded statement follows `else`:

```
if ( Boolean expression )
   if-true statement
else
   if-false statement
```

The if-false statement is executed if the Boolean expression evaluates to `false`.

388 Either the if-true statement or the if-false statement may be embedded `if` statements. Accordingly, another solution to the duration-testing problem looks like this:

```
public class Demonstrate {
 public static void main (String argv[]) {
   int length = 95;
   if (length < 60)
     System.out.println("It is short!");
   else
     if (length > 90)
       System.out.println("It is long!");
 }
}
```
———————————— Result ————————————
```
It is long!
```

389 The layout of nested `if` statements is a matter of convention. Here is another common arrangement:

```
public class Demonstrate {
 public static void main (String argv[]) {
   int length = 95;
   if (length < 60)
     System.out.println("It is short!");
   else if (length > 90)
     System.out.println("It is long!");
 }
}
```
———————————— Result ————————————
```
It is long!
```

390 Suppose that you want more than one statement to be executed when a Boolean expression evaluates to `true`. You need only to combine the multiple statements, using braces, into a single **block**.

In the following `if-else` statement, for example, two display statements are executed whenever the value of `length` is greater than 90:

```
if (length > 90) {
 System.out.println("It is long!");
 System.out.println("It may try your patience");
}
```

391 In the following nested `if` statement, it is not immediately clear whether the question mark would be replaced by `"long"` or `"short"`:

```
if (length > 60)
 if (length < 90)
  System.out.println("It is normal!");
 else
  System.out.println("It is ?");
```

As the nested if statement is laid out on the page, it seems that "long" is the right answer. If the nested if statement were laid out another way, however, you might have the impression that "short" is the right answer:

```
if (length > 60)
 if (length < 90)
  System.out.println("It is normal!");
else System.out.println("It is ?");
```

Because Java pays no attention to layout, you need to know that Java assumes that each else belongs to the nearest if that is not already matched with an else. Thus, the question mark should be replaced by "long".

392 Although you can rely on the rule that an else statement belongs to the nearest unmatched if, it is better programming practice to use braces to avoid potential misreading.

In the following example, it is clear that the question mark should be replaced by "long", because the braces clearly group the else statement with the second if:

```
if (length > 60) {
 if (length < 90)
  System.out.println("It is normal!");
 else
  System.out.println("It is ?");
}
```

On the other hand, in the following example, it is clear that the question mark should be replaced by "short", because the braces clearly group the else statement with the first if:

```
if (length > 60) {
 if (length < 90)
  System.out.println("It is normal!");
}
else
 System.out.println("It is ?");
```

393 Many Java programmers use block-delimiting braces in every if statement that they write, even though the braces often surround just one statement. Such programmers argue that the habitual use of braces reduces errors later on when a program is modified. When braces are not used, it is easy to add a second embedded statement to an if statement or else statement, yet to forget that the modification requires the addition of braces.

394 An if—else statement may include an **empty statement**—one that consists of a semicolon only—in the if-true position. Thus, the following tests are equivalent:

```
if (length < 60) System.out.println("It is short!");

if (length >= 60) ; else System.out.println("It is short!");
```

395 So far, you have learned how to use if—else statements to execute one of two embedded computation-performing *statements*. You should also know about Java's **conditional operator**, which enables you to compute a value from one of two embedded, value-producing *expressions*.

The conditional operator sees frequent service in display statements, where it helps you to produce the proper singular–plural distinctions. Consider, for example, the following program, which displays a length change:

```
public class Demonstrate {
 public static void main (String argv[]) {
   int change = 1;
   if (change == 1) {
    System.out.print("The length has changed by ");
    System.out.print(change);
    System.out.println(" minute");
   }
   else {
    System.out.print("The length has changed by ");
    System.out.print(change);
    System.out.println(" minutes");
   }
 }
}
```
```
———————————————— Result ————————————————
The length has changed by 1 minute
```

The program works, but most experienced programmers would be unhappy because there are two separate display statements that are almost identical. Such duplication increases the chance that a bug will creep in during subsequent modification, as you modify one of the duplicates, but overlook another.

You can improve such a program by moving the variation—the part that produces either the word *minute* or the word *minutes*—into a value-producing expression inside a single display statement.

396 The following is the pattern for Java's value-producing conditional-operator expression:

`Boolean expression` ? `if-true expression` : `if-false expression`

In contrast to the operators that you have seen so far, the conditional operator consists of a combination of distributed characters, ? and :, separating three operands—the Boolean expression, the if-true expression, and the if-false expression. Thus, the conditional operator combination is said to be a **ternary operator.**

397 Java evaluates either the if-true expression or the if-false expression is evaluated; it does not evaluate both. Thus, any **side effects,** such as variable assignment or display, called for in the unevaluated expression, do not occur.

398 The value of the following expression is the string, `"minute"`, if the length change is 1 minute; otherwise, the value is the string, `"minutes"`:

```
Conditional    If-true      If-false
expression    expression   expression
     |            |            |
     v            v            v
 _____   _____   _____

change == 1 ? "minute" : "minutes"
```

You can, if you wish, employ parentheses to delineate the Boolean expression, but parentheses are not needed in the example, because the equality operator has precedence higher than that of the conditional operator.

399 Because a conditional-operator expression, unlike an `if` statement, produces a value, you can place it inside another expression. In the following, for example, a conditional-operator expression appears inside a display expression, solving the duplication problem encountered in Segment 395:

```
public class Demonstrate {
 public static void main (String argv[]) {
  int change = 1;
  System.out.print("The length has changed by ");
  System.out.print(change);
  System.out.println(change == 1 ? " minute" : " minutes");
 }
}
——————————————— Result ———————————————
The length has changed by 1 minute
```

400 Write a program that transforms a person's weight and height into one of three messages:
PRACTICE "The subject seems to be underweight," "The subject seems to be of normal weight," or "The subject seems to be overweight." Your program's input is three numbers: the person's weight in kilograms, the person's height in meters, and a gender code—0 for men and 1 for women. You may assume that a person's "ideal" weight is proportional to height, and that the overweight and underweight messages should not appear unless the person's weight differs from the ideal weight by more than 10 percent.

401 Write a program that displays a complete sentence that indicates the deviation from the
PRACTICE person's ideal weight, truncated to the nearest integer. Your program's input is three
numbers: weight in kilograms, height in meters, and a gender code. Be sure that, if the
deviation is just 1 kilogram, the word *kilogram* appears, rather than *kilograms*.

402
HIGHLIGHTS

- If you want to execute a statement only when a Boolean expression produces
  `true`, then use an `if` statement:

  `if (` `Boolean expression` `)` `statement`

- If you want to execute one statement when an expression evaluates to `true`, and
  another when the expression evaluates to `false`, then use an `if–else` statement:

  `if (` `Boolean expression` `)`
  `    ` `if-true statement`
  `else`
  `    ` `if-false statement`

- If you want to execute a group of statements in an `if` or `if–else` statement, **then**
  use braces to combine those statements into a single block.

- If you want to use nested `if–else` statements, **then** use braces to clarify your
  grouping intention.

- If you want the value of an expression to be the value of one of two embedded
  expressions, **and** you want the choice to be determined by the value of a Boolean
  expression, **then** instantiate the following pattern:

  `Boolean expression`
  `  ?` `if-true expression` `:` `if-false expression`

23 HOW TO COMBINE BOOLEAN EXPRESSIONS

403 In this chapter, you learn how to combine Boolean expressions to form a larger Boolean expression that contains multiple predicates.

404 The **and operator**, &&, returns `true` if *both* of its operands evaluate to `true`. The **or operator**, ||, returns `true` if *either* of its operands evaluates to `true`.

405 The following expression, for example, evaluates to `true` only if the value of the `length` variable is between 60 and 90:

```
60 < length && length < 90
```

Accordingly, the display statement embedded in the following `if` statement is evaluated only if the value of the `length` variable is inside the 60-to-90 range.

```
if (60 < length && length < 90)
 System.out.println("The length is normal.");
```

406 The evaluation of && and || expressions is complicated because certain subexpressions may not be evaluated at all.

In && expressions, the left-side operand is evaluated first: If the value of the left-side operand is `false`, then the right-side operand is ignored completely, and the value of the && expression is `false`.

Of course, if both operands evaluate to `true`, the value of the && expression is `true`.

In || expressions, the left-side operand also is evaluated first: If the left-side operand evaluates to `true`, nothing else is done, and the value of the || expression is `true`; if both operands evaluate to `false`, the value of the || expression is `false`.

407
SIDE TRIP

The & and | operators also combine Boolean expressions, returning `true` or `false`. But & and | differ from && and || in that & and | evaluate both arguments, no matter what.

Ordinarily, you would not use & and | on Boolean operands, because && and || are more efficient. You would use & and | on integral expressions, however, because, when provided integral operands, & and | perform logical **and** and **or** operations on the bits that constitute the integers. Neither & nor | is discussed further in this book, because understanding bit manipulation is not a prerequisite to understanding either basic Java programs or the special strengths of the language.

408
SIDE TRIP

Java specifies that Boolean operands are always evaluated from left to right. Other languages, such as C and C++, do not insist on left-to-right evaluation in general. In those languages, operators such as && and ||, about which you learned in this chapter, and ?:, about which you learned in Chapter 22, are exceptions to the general rule.

You might think that it would be possible to use a doulbe-ampersand expression instead of an `if` statement by exploiting the property that the right-side operand of an double-ampersand expression is evaluated only if the value of the left-side operand is `true`.

You cannot do so, however, because both the operands surrounding && and || operators must be Boolean expressions.

Do not think that this requirement is a handicap. Most good programmers object to the use of && and || operators to allow or prevent evaluation. They argue that, when an && or || operator is included in an expression, anyone (other than the original programmer) who looks at the expression, naturally expects the value produced by the expression to be used. If the value is not used, the person who looks at the program may wonder whether the original programmer left out a portion of the program unintentionally.

Write a method that transforms an athlete's pulse rate into one of three integers: if the rate is less than 60, the value returned by the method is to be -1; if the rate is more than 80, the value returned is to be 1; otherwise, the value returned is to be 0. Then, write another method that transforms an athlete's body fat as a percentage of weight into one of three integers: if the athlete's body-fat percentage is less than 10, the value returned is to be -1; if it is more than 20, the value returned is to be 1; otherwise, the value returned is to be 0.

Write a program that accepts two numbers—a pulse rate and a body-fat percentage—and displays "The athlete seems to be in great shape," if both the athlete's pulse rate and body fat are low.

- If you want to combine two predicate expressions, **and** the result is to be `true` if the values of *both* expressions are `true`, **then** use &&.

- If you want to combine two predicate expressions, **and** the result is to be `true` if the value of *either* expression is `true`, **then** use ||.

- Both && and || evaluate their left operand before they evaluate their right operand. The right operand is not evaluated if the value of the left operand of an && expression is `false`, or if the value of the left operand of a || expression is `true`.

24 HOW TO WRITE ITERATION STATEMENTS

413 In this chapter, you learn how to tell Java to repeat a computation by looping through that computation until a test has been satisfied.

414 Java's `while` statement consists of a Boolean expression, in parentheses, followed by an embedded statement or block:

```
while ( Boolean expression )
  embedded statement or block
```

The Boolean expression is evaluated; if it evaluates to `true`, the embedded statement or block is evaluated as well; otherwise, Java skips the embedded statement or block. In contrast to an `if` statement, however, the **test–evaluate loop** continues as long as the Boolean expression evaluates to `true`, so the computation is said to **iterate**.

415 For example, the following method fragment repeatedly decrements n by 1 until n is 0:

```
while (n != 0)
  n = n - 1;
```

Replacement of the single embedded statement, n = n - 1;, by an embedded block enables the `while` statement to do useful computation while counting down n to 0:

```
while (n != 0) {
  n = n - 1;
  ...
}
```

416 Many programmers prefer to use embedded blocks, instead of embedded statements, in `while` statements, even if a the embedded block contains just one statement.

The rationale is that, whenever you use an embedded statement instead of an embedded block, you run a small risk of forgetting to add braces later, should new requirements force you to switch from an embedded statement to an embedded block. Accordingly, in this book, you see mostly embedded blocks.

417 Now suppose, for example, that you want to compute the total number of viewers that a movie will have if the number doubles each month after the release date. Such a relationship cannot hold for a long time, but while it does hold, the total number of viewers after n months is proportional to $2 \sup n$; thus, you need to develop a method that computes the nth power of 2.

One way to do the computation is to count down a parameter, n, to 0, multiplying a variable, `result`, whose initial value is 1, by 2 each time that you decrement n:

```
public class Demonstrate {
 public static void main (String argv[]) {
  System.out.println(powerOf2(4));
 }
 public static int powerOf2 (int n) {
  int result = 1;              // Initial value is 1
  while (n != 0) {
    result = 2 * result;       // Multiplied by 2 n times
    n = n - 1;
  }
  return result;
 }
}
```

—————————————— Result ——————————————

16

418
SIDE TRIP
In C and C++, *true* is represented by any integer other than 0, and *false* is represented by 0. In such languages, the value of the Boolean expression n != 0 is false if and only if the value of n is 0.

Accordingly, the following while statement is legitimate in those languages, but is not accepted by Java:

```
while (n) {              // BUG! Will not work in Java!
  ...
}
```

419 The defect of many while loops is that the details that govern the looping appear in three places: the place where the counting variable is initialized, the place where it is tested, and the place where it is reassigned. Such distribution makes looping difficult to understand. Accordingly, you also need to know about the for statement:

```
for ( entry expression ;
      Boolean expression ;
      continuation expression )
   embedded statement or block
```

The entry expression is evaluated only once, when the for statement is entered. Once the entry expression is evaluated, the Boolean expression is evaluated, and, if the result is true, the embedded statement or block is evaluated, followed by the continuation expression. Then, the test–evaluate loop continues until the Boolean expression eventually evaluates to false.

420 Many programmers prefer to use only embedded blocks, instead of embedded statements, in for statements, for the same reasons that many programmers use only embedded blocks in while statements, as explained in Segment 416.

421 Specialized to counting down a counter variable, the for statement becomes the **counting loop:**

```
for ( counter initialization expression ;
      counter testing expression ;
      counter reassignment expression )
   embedded statement or block
```

422 Now, you can define the powerOf2 method using a for loop instead of a while loop. The initialization expression, counter = n, assigns the value of the parameter n to counter. Then, as long as the value of counter is not 0, the value of result, whose initial value is 1, is multiplied by 2, and the value of counter is decremented by 1:

```
public class Demonstrate {
 public static void main (String argv[]) {
  System.out.println(powerOf2(4));
 }
 public static int powerOf2 (int n) {
  int counter, result = 1;
  for (counter = n; counter != 0; counter = counter - 1) {
    result = 2 * result;
  }
  return result;
 }
}
```

423 Conveniently, you can both declare and initialize the counter variable in the for statement itself, thus producing a more compact for loop:

```
public class Demonstrate {
 public static void main (String argv[]) {
  System.out.println(powerOf2(4));
 }
 public static int powerOf2 (int n) {
  int result = 1;
  for (int counter = n; counter != 0; counter = counter - 1) {
    result = 2 * result;
  }
  return result;
 }
}
```

424 An **augmented assignment operator** reassigns a variable to a value that it computes—via addition, subtraction, multiplication, or division—from a combination of the variable's current value and an expression's value . The following diagram illustrates how an assignment that uses an augmented assignment operator differs from an ordinary assignment:

variable name = variable name operator expression

variable name operator = expression

For example, you can rewrite `result = result * 2` as follows:

`result *= 2`

Even though this shorthand gives you a perfectly valid way to multiply and reassign, you may choose to write `result = result * 2`, which you see throughout this book, on the ground that `result = result * 2` stands out more clearly as a reassignment operation.

425
SIDE TRIP
Although augmented assignment operators are not used further in this book, you should know that an expression written with an augmented assignment operator may execute faster than the corresponding expression written without the augmented assignment operator. In Chapter 28, for example, you learn about Java arrays. In particular, you learn that you can reassign an array element to twice its former value as follows:

array name [index-producing expression]
= array name [index-producing expression] * 2

Alternatively, using an augmented assignment operator, you can write the reassignment expression as follows:

array name [index-producing expression] *= 2

Plainly, if the index-producing expression is complex, the augmented assignment operator offers one way to increase speed, to keep size down, and to avoid a maintenance headache should the expression require modification, because the index-producing expression is written only once and is evaluated only once.

426
In principle, you could rewrite `counter = counter - 1`, using an augmented assignment operator, as `counter -= 1`. You are not likely to see such expressions, however, because Java offers a still more-concise shorthand for adding 1 to a variable or for subtracting 1 from a variable. To use the shorthand, you drop the equal-to sign altogether, as well as the 1, and prefix the variable with the **increment operator**, ++, or the **decrement operator**, --. Thus, you can replace `counter = counter - 1` by the following expression:

`--counter`

427
Using Java's shorthand notations for variable reassignment, you can write the `powerOf2` method as follows:

```
public class Demonstrate {
 public static void main (String argv[]) {
  System.out.println(powerOf2(4));
 }
 public static int powerOf2 (int n) {
  int result = 1;
  for (int counter = n; counter != 0; --counter) {
   result = 2 * result;
  }
  return result;
 }
}
```

428 You can embed expressions involving the increment operator, ++, or the decrement operator, --, in larger expressions, such as the following:

++x + x

In such an expression, the increment operator, ++, is said not only to produce a value, but also to have the **side effect** of incrementing x.

Note that the Java language prescribes that operands are evaluated in left-to-right order. Thus, in the expression ++x + x, the left-side operand, ++x, is evaluated before the right-side operand, x.

429

SIDE TRIP

C and C++ do not prescribe the order in which operands are evaluated for many operators, including the + operator. In those languages, the use of side-effect operators, such as ++ and --, can lead to mysterious portability problems.

Other mysterious problems occur because a C or C++ compiler is free to compile certain expressions for left-side-first evaluation and others for right-side-first evaluation. Thus, side-effect operands can cause plenty of trouble in those languages.

430 You can, in principle, position two plus signs or two minus signs as suffixes, rather than as prefixes. In either position, the plus signs or minus signs cause a variable's value to change, but, if the incremented or decremented variable is embedded in a larger expression, the value handed over differs. If a variable is prefixed, the value handed over is the new, incremented value; if a variable is suffixed, the value handed over is the old, original value.

Suppose that the value of counter is 3. Then, the value of the expression --counter is 2, and the new value of counter is 2. On the other hand, the value of the expression counter-- is 3, even though the new value of counter is 2.

431 Consider, for example, the following oddball version of powerOf2, in which the decrementing of the counter variable occurs in the Boolean expression, rather than in the normal continuation expression, which is missing. The suffix form, counter--, must be used, rather than the prefix form, --counter, because decrementing is to be done after your program decides whether to go around the loop. Were you to use the prefix form, your program would fail to go around the loop enough times:

```
public class Demonstrate {
 public static void main (String argv[]) {
  System.out.println(powerOf2(4));
 }
 public static int powerOf2 (int n) {
  int result = 1;
  for (int counter = n; counter-- != 0;) {
    result = 2 * result;
  }
  return result;
}}
```

432 There are still other ways to define powerOf2 using a for loop. You can, for example, bring the reassignment of the result variable within the reassignment part of the for loop, joining it to the reassignment of the counter variable. The result is a for loop with an **empty statement**, which consists of a semicolon only, in place of an ordinary statement or block:

```
public class Demonstrate {
 public static void main (String argv[]) {
  System.out.println(powerOf2(4));
 }
 public static int powerOf2 (int n) {
  int result = 1;
  for (int counter = n;              // Initialization
       counter != 0;                 // Test
       --counter, result = result * 2)  // Reassignment
    ;                                // Empty statement
  return result;
}}
```

433 Finally, you can, if you like, terminate a loop immediately by including a break statement at the point where you what termination; in the following contrived example, the break statement eliminates the need for an ordinary testing expression:

```
public class Demonstrate {
 public static void main (String argv[]) {
  System.out.println(powerOf2(4));
 }
 public static int powerOf2 (int n) {
  int result = 1;
  for (int counter = n; ; --counter) {
   if (counter == 0) {break;}
   result = result * 2;
  }
  return result;
}}
```

You can stop `while` loops, as well as `for` loops, with `break` statements.

434 The definition of `powerOf2` that appears in Segment 427 is the best of the lot in many respects: declaration and initialization both are done in the initialization part of the `for` statement, a simple test of a counter variable occurs in the testing part of the `for` statement, the counter variable is reassigned in the reassignment part of the `for` statement, and the computation of the result is separated from the reassignment part. The `for` statement is deployed straightforwardly; there are no parlor tricks.

435
PRACTICE
Write an iterative program that accepts two positive integers, m and n, and computes m sup n.

436
PRACTICE
Write an iterative program that accepts a positive integer, n, and computes the factorial of n, written $n!$, where $n! = n \times n - 1 \times \ldots \times 1$.

437
HIGHLIGHTS

- If you want to repeat a calculation for as long as a Boolean expression's value is `true`, **then** use a `while` loop:

```
while (Boolean expression)
   embedded statement or block
```

- If you want to repeat a calculation involving entry, Boolean, and continuation expressions, **then** use a `for` loop:

```
for (entry expression;
      Boolean expression;
      continuation expression)
   embedded statement or block
```

- If you want to repeat a calculation until a variable is counted down to 0, **then** use a counting loop:

```
for (counter-declaration-and-initialization expression;
      counter-testing expression;
      counter-reassignment expression)
   embedded statement or block
```

- If you want to increment or decrement the value of a variable by 1, **then** instantiate one of the following patterns:

```
++ variable name
-- variable name
```

- **If** you want to change a variable's value by combining it with the value of an expression via addition, subtraction, multiplication, or division, **then** consider instantiating the following pattern:

`variable name` `operator` = `expression`

25 HOW TO WRITE RECURSIVE METHODS

438 In Chapter 24, you learned how to repeat a computation by using Java's iteration statements. In this chapter, you learn how to repeat a computation by using recursive method calls.

439 If you are not yet familiar with recursion, it is best to see how recursion works through an example involving a simple mathematical computation that you already know how to perform using iteration.

440 Suppose, for example, that you want to write a method, recursivePowerOf2, that computes the nth power of 2 recursively. One way to start is to define recursivePowerOf2 in terms of the powerOf2 method already provided in Chapter 24:

```
public static int recursivePowerOf2 (int n) {
 return powerOf2(n);
}
```

Once you see that you can define recursivePowerOf2 in terms of powerOf2, you are ready to learn how gradually to turn recursivePowerOf2 into a recursive method that does not rely on powerOf2.

441 First, note that you can eliminate the need to call powerOf2 in the simple case in which the value of the parameter is 0:

```
public static int recursivePowerOf2 (int n) {
 if (n == 0) {
  return 1;
 }
 else {return powerOf2(n);}
}
```

442 Next, note that you can arrange for recursivePowerOf2 to hand over a little less work to powerOf2 by performing one of the multiplications by 2 in recursivePowerOf2 itself, and subtracting 1 from powerOf2's argument:

```
public static int recursivePowerOf2 (int n) {
 if (n == 0) {return 1;}
 else {
  return 2 * powerOf2(n - 1);
 }
}
```

Clearly, recursivePowerOf2 must work as long as one of the following two situations holds:

- The value of the parameter, n, is 0; in this situation, `recursivePowerOf2` returns 1.

- The value of n is not 0, but `powerOf2` is able to compute the power of 2 that is 1 less than the value of n.

443   Now you are ready to perform the recursion trick: You replace the call to `powerOf2` in `recursivePowerOf2` by a call to `recursivePowerOf2` itself:

```java
public static int recursivePowerOf2 (int n) {
 if (n == 0) {return 1;}
 else {
   return 2 * recursivePowerOf2(n - 1);
 }
}
```

The new version works for two reasons:

- If the value of the parameter, n, is 0, `recursivePowerOf2` returns 1.

- If the value of n is not 0, `recursivePowerOf2` asks itself to compute the power of 2 for a number that is 1 less than the value of n. Then, `recursivePowerOf2` may ask itself to compute the power of 2 for a number that is 2 less than the original value of n, and so on, until the `recursivePowerOf2` needs to deal with only 0.

444   When a method, such as `recursivePowerOf2`, is used in its own definition, the method is said to be **recursive**. When a method calls itself, the method is said to **recurse**.

Given a positive, integer argument, there is no danger that `recursivePowerOf2` will recurse forever—calling itself an infinite number of times—because eventually the argument is counted down to 0, which `recursivePowerOf2` handles directly, without further recursion.

445   There is also no danger that the values taken on by the parameter n will get in one another's way. Each time `recursivePowerOf2` is entered, Java sets aside a storage spot to hold the value of n for that entry.

446   Note that the simple case—the one for which the result is computed directly—is handled by the **base** part of the definition.

The harder case—the one in which the result is computed indirectly, through solution of another problem first—is handled by the **recursive** part of the definition.

447   You can experiment with `recursivePowerOf2` in a program such as this:

```
public class Demonstrate {
 public static void main (String argv[]) {
  System.out.print("2 to the 3rd power is ");
  System.out.println(recursivePowerOf2(3));
  System.out.print("2 to the 10th power is ");
  System.out.println(recursivePowerOf2(10));
 }
 public static int recursivePowerOf2 (int n) {
  if (n == 0) {
   return 1;
  }
  else {
   return 2 * recursivePowerOf2(n - 1);
  }
 }
}
```

──────────────────── Result ────────────────────

```
2 to the 3rd power is 8
2 to the 10th power is 1024
```

---

448 The following diagram shows the four calls involved when the `recursivePowerOf2` method is set to work on 3:

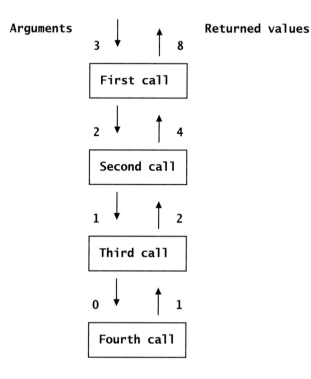

449 The `recursivePowerOf2` method is an instance of the **recursive counting pattern**, in which a specified operand is combined by a specified operand with a recursive call:

```
public static int method name (int n) {
  if (n == 0) {return result for n equal to 0 ;}
  else {
    return combination operand
           combination operator
           method name (n - 1);
  }
}
```

450 Now, suppose that the number of users of your movie-evaluation service is growing like a colony of rabbits. You are asked to predict what the number of users will be after *n* months. Fortunately, Fibonacci figured out long ago how fast his particular breed of rabbits multiply, deriving a formula that gives the number of female Fibonacci rabbits after *n* months, under the following assumptions: Female Fibonacci rabbits mature 1 month after birth. Once they mature, female Fibonacci rabbits have one female child each month. At the beginning of the first month, there is one immature female Fibonacci rabbit. Fibonacci rabbits live forever. And there are always enough Fibonacci males on hand to mate with all the mature females.

451 The following diagram shows the number of female Fibonacci rabbits at the end of every month for 6 months:

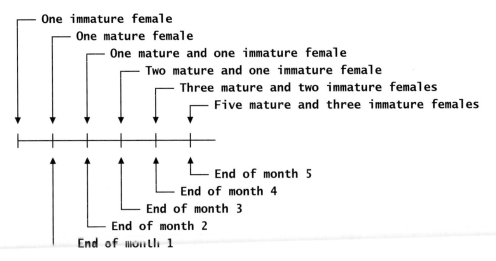

Clearly, the number of female rabbits there are at the end of the *n*th month is the same as the number of females at the end of the previous month plus the number of females that gave birth during the current month. But, of course, the number of females that gave birth during the current month is the number of mature female rabbits at the end of the previous month, which is same as the total number of females at the end of the month before that. Thus, the following formula holds:

$$\text{Rabbits}(n) = \text{Rabbits}(n-1) + \text{Rabbits}(n-2)$$

452 Capturing the Fibonacci rabbit formula in the form of a Java method, you have the following:

```
public class Demonstrate {
 public static void main (String argv[]) {
  System.out.print("At the end of month 3, there are ");
  System.out.println(rabbits(3));
  System.out.print("At the end of month 10, there are ");
  System.out.println(rabbits(10));
 }
 public static int rabbits (int n) {
  if (n == 0 || n == 1) {return 1;}
  else {return rabbits(n - 1) + rabbits(n - 2);}
 }
}
```
——————————————————— Result ———————————————————
```
At the end of month 3, there are 3
At the end of month 10, there are 89
```

453 The following diagram shows the `rabbits` method works, given the task of determining the number of Fibonacci rabbits at the end of 3 months:

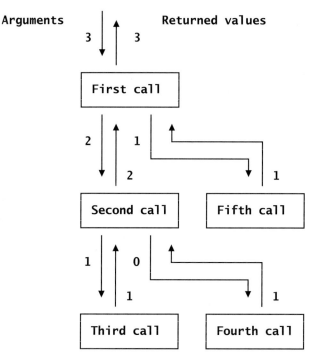

454   Now, suppose that you rewrite the `rabbits` method in terms of two auxiliary methods:

```
public static int rabbits (int n) {
 if (n == 0 || n == 1) {
  return 1;
 }
 else {return previousMonth(n) + penultimateMonth(n);}
}
```

Realizing that `previousMonth` must return the number of rabbits at the end of the previous month, you see that you can define `previousMonth` as follows:

```
public static int previousMonth (int n) {return rabbits(n - 1);}
```

Analogous reasoning leads you to the following definition for `penultimateMonth`:

```
public static int penultimateMonth (int n) {return rabbits(n - 2);}
```

455   No matter how you arrange the three methods inside the `Demonstrate` class, your program refers to at least one method before that method is defined. In the following arrangement, for example, the program refers to both `previousMonth` and `penultimateMonth` before they are defined. Fortunately, because the Java compiler is a **multiple-pass compiler**, such forward references cause no problems.

```
public class Demonstrate {
 public static void main (String argv[]) {
  System.out.print("At the end of month 3, there are ");
  System.out.println(rabbits(3));
  System.out.print("At the end of month 10, there are ");
  System.out.println(rabbits(10));
 }
 public static int rabbits (int n) {
  if (n == 0 || n == 1) {
   return 1;
  }
  else {return previousMonth(n) + penultimateMonth(n);}
 }
 public static int previousMonth (int n) {return rabbits(n - 1);}
 public static int penultimateMonth (int n) {return rabbits(n - 2);}
}
```

—————————————— Result ——————————————
```
At the end of month 3, there are 3
At the end of month 10, there are 89
```

456   The following diagram shows `rabbits` and its two auxiliaries working to determine how many Fibonacci rabbits there are at the end of 3 months:

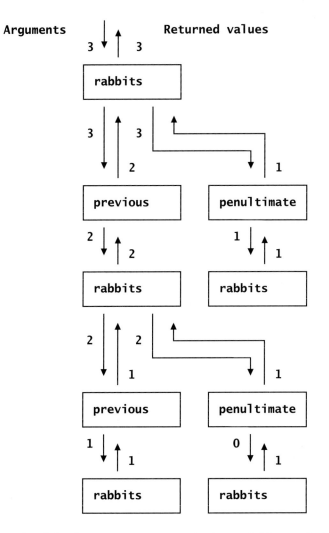

Each of the three cooperating methods can initiate a chain of calls that ends in a call to itself. Thus, the cooperating methods exhibit indirect, rather than direct, recursion.

457 Many mathematically oriented programmers prefer recursive definitions to iterative definitions, when both are possible, believing that there is inherent elegance in defining a method partly in terms of itself.

Other, practically oriented programmers dislike recursive definitions for one or both of two reasons. First, the recursive approach usually produces much slower programs, because each method call takes time. Second, the recursive approach may have problems with large arguments, because the number of method calls in a recursive chain of calls is usually limited to a few hundred.

Recursion aficionados counter by creating compilers that handle certain recursive methods in sophisticated ways that avoid such limits.

458
PRACTICE Write a recursive program that accepts two positive integers, *m* and *n*, and computes *m* sup *n*.

459
PRACTICE Write a recursive program that accepts a positive integer, *n*, and computes the factorial of *n*, written *n*!, where $n! = n \times n - 1 \times \ldots \times 1$.

460
PRACTICE Temporarily suspending disbelief, convert the program that you wrote in Segment 459 into a program consisting of two cooperating methods, `factorial` and `recurse`. The `recurse` method is to call the `factorial` method.

461
HIGHLIGHTS

- Recursive methods work by calling themselves to solve subproblems until the subproblems are simple enough for them to solve directly.

- The portion of a recursive method that handles the simplest cases is called the base part; the portion that transforms more complex cases is called the recursive part.

- If you want to solve a difficult problem, **then** try to break it up into simpler subproblems.

- If you are writing a recursive method, **then** your method must handle the simplest cases, **and** must break down every other case into the simplest cases.

- If your recursive method is to count down a number, **then** you may be able to instantiate the following recursive counting pattern:

```
public static int  method name  (int n) {
  if (n == 0) {
   return  result for n equal 0 ;
  }
  else {
   return  combination operand
           combination operator
           method name (n - 1);
  }
}
```

26 HOW TO WRITE MULTIWAY CONDITIONAL STATEMENTS

462 In this chapter, you learn how to write programs that decide which of many alternatives to execute on the basis of an expression that returns an integer value.

463 The purpose of a switch statement is to execute a particular sequence of statements according to the value of an expression that produces an integer. In most switch statements, each anticipated value of the integer-producing expression and the corresponding sequence of statements is sandwiched between a case keyword on one end and a break or return statement on the other, with a colon separating the anticipated value and the statement sequence:

```
switch ( integer-producing expression ) {
  case integer literal 1 : statements for integer 1 break;
  case integer literal 2 : statements for integer 2 break;
  ...
  default: default statements
}
```

When such a switch statement is encountered, the integer-producing expression is evaluated, producing an integer. That value is compared with the integer literals found following the case keywords. As soon as there is a match, evaluation of the following statements begins; execution continues up to the first break or return statement encountered.

The line beginning with the default: keyword is optional. If the expression produces an integer that fails to match any of the case integer literals, the statements following the default: keyword are executed.

If there is no match and no default: keyword, no statements are executed.

464 The version of the rabbits method shown in the program in Segment 452 contains an if–else statement:

```
public class Demonstrate {
 public static int rabbits (int n) {
  if (n == 0 || n == 1) {
   return 1;
  }
  else {
   return rabbits(n - 1) + rabbits(n - 2);
  }
 }
}
```

If you wish, you can rewrite the program without the || operator, handling separately cases of 0 or 1 rabbit:

```
public class Demonstrate {
 public static int rabbits (int n) {
  if (n == 0) {return 1;}
  else if (n == 1) {return 1;}
  else {return rabbits(n - 1) + rabbits(n - 2);}
 }
}
```

465 If you wish, you can use a switch statement to control recursion. In the following, the first two statement sequences are terminated by return statements, rather than by break statements:

```
public class Demonstrate {
 public static int rabbits (int n) {
  switch (n) {
   case 0: return 1;
   case 1: return 1;
   default: return rabbits(n - 1) + rabbits(n - 2);
  }
 }
}
```

466 When there is no break or return statement to terminate the execution of a sequence of statements, execution is said to **fall through** to the next sequence of statements, where execution continues, once again, in search of a break or return statement.

The reason for the fall-through feature is that you occasionally want to perform the same action in response to any of several conditions.

Note carefully, however, that inadvertently forgetting a break or return statement is a common error.

467 The following switch statement does the work with no duplication of the return statement:

```
public class Demonstrate {
 public static int rabbits (int n) {
  switch (n) {
   case 0: case 1: return 1;
   default: return rabbits(n - 1) + rabbits(n - 2);
  }
 }
}
```

468 The integer literals and the integer-producing expression in switch statements can be any of the integral types. In Chapter 31, you learn about a program in which the integer literals are characters, and the integer-producing expression produces a character.

469

PRACTICE

Write a program that accepts two numbers, representing a year and a month, and displays the number of days in that month. Use a `switch` statement, and be sure to exploit the fall-through feature. Note that leap years occur in years divisible by 4, except for centenary years that are not divisible by 400.

470

HIGHLIGHTS

- If you want a program to decide which of many alternative statements to evaluate, **then** instantiate the following pattern:

```
switch (integer-producing expression) {
  case integer literal 1: statements for integer 1 break;
  case integer literal 2: statements for integer 2 break;
  ...
  default: default statements
}
```

- In `switch` statements, you can omit the keyword `default:` and the default statements.

- In `switch` statements, the integer-producing expression can produce a value belonging to any of the integral data types, including the `char` data type.

- In `switch` statements, once embedded-statement execution begins, execution continues up to the first embedded `break` or `return` statement, or to the end of the `switch` statement, whichever comes first. Bugs emerge when you forget to pair `case` keywords with `break` or `return` statements.

27 HOW TO WORK WITH FILE INPUT STREAMS

471 So far, you have worked exclusively with wired-in information. In this chapter, you learn how to work with information stored in text files. In particular, you learn how to read information from humanly readable text files. Later, in Chapter 33, you learn how to write information into humanly readable text files. In the intervening chapters, you learn how to work with information stored in arrays or vectors and you learn how to work with Java's exception mechanism. Then, in Chapter 34, you learn how to work with information stored efficiently, but not in a humanly readable form, in serialized files.

472 A **stream** is a sequence of values. To read bytes from a file, you create a **file input stream**. Then, to convert those bytes into characters appropriate for your operating system, you create an **input-stream reader**:

```
File input stream

     │
     │  Bytes
     ▼

Input-stream reader

     │
     │  Characters
     ▼

Your program
```

473 To create a file input stream connected to a file, you use an expression that creates an instance of the `FileInputStream` class for a specified file.

The following is an example in which the file specification happens to be `"input.data"`, and the file input stream is assigned to `stream`:

```
                              File specification ─┐
                                                  │
                                                  ▼
                                          _____
FileInputStream stream = new FileInputStream("input.data");
```

474 Of course, the file specification may include an operating-system–specific **path**, as in the following example:

```
FileInputStream stream
 = new FileInputStream("d:/phw/onto/java/input.data");
   _____
                   ▲
                   └── Path
```

475 When you are finished with an file input stream, you should close it, using the `close` method:

`stream.close()`

Java generally closes all streams for you, once they no longer can be accessed, but Java may not close a particular stream for a long time. Accordingly, you should close files, using the `close` method, as a matter of good programming practice.

476 Given a file input stream, you can read 1 byte at a time from that stream.

Generally, however, you want to read 1 character at a time, and characters may occupy more than 1 byte on some operating systems. Accordingly, you insert an input-stream reader between your file input stream and your program.

To create a input-stream reader connected to a file input stream, you use an expression that creates an instance of the `InputStreamReader` class for that file input stream. In the following statement, for example, you declare an `InputStreamReader` variable, and create a `InputStreamReader` instance from a `FileInputStream` instance:

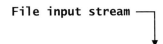

File input stream

`InputStreamReader reader = new InputStreamReader(stream);`

477 To read a line of text, you first need to construct an instance of the `BufferedReader` class from an input-stream reader:

Input stream reader

`BufferedReader buffer = new BufferedReader(reader);`

Then, you can read a line of text, producing a string, using the `readLine` method:

`buffer.readLine()`

If there are no more lines of text in a file, then the `readLine` method returns `null`.

478 Of course, you usually want to get numbers and delimited strings from a data file, rather than to get strings that represent lines of text. To get numbers and delimited strings, you can follow a traditional approach, by which you read lines from a buffered reader and work on those lines with string-manipulation methods. Alternatively, you can follow a more sophisticated approach: You can read tokens from the buffered reader.

You begin to learn about the traditional approach in Segment 482; you begin to learn about the more sophisticated approach in Segment 487; and you learn how the more sophisticated approach is related to the more traditional approach in Segment 500.

479 Before you can do anything with the `FileInputStream` classes, you must inform Java that you wish to use classes defined in a group of classes called the **input–output package**, also known as the **java.io package**.

In general, if you want to use a particular class in a particular package, then you inform Java that you want that class by including an `import` statement, such as the following, in your class definition:

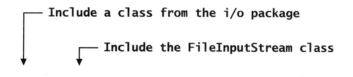

```
import java.io.FileInputStream;
```

Alternatively, if you want to tell Java to be prepared to use any class in a particular package, then you include an asterisk, instead of a class name, in the `import` statement:

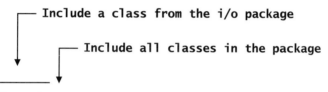

```
import java.io.*;
```

The advantage of using an asterisk is that you can cover all the classes from a single package in one statement; the disadvantage is that your compiler may do its work more slowly.

480 Whenever you create `FileInputStream` instances, you must also tell Java what to do in the event that a lamentable input–output error occurs: for example, your program might try to attach a file input stream to a file that does not exist.

In such lamentable situations, Java is said to **throw an exception**. For example, Java throws an exception that is an instance of the `FileNotFoundException` class whenever you try to connect a file input stream to a file that does not exist.

481 To tell Java what to do when exceptions are thrown, you have two choices.

First, you can embed a group of statements, some of which may throw exceptions, in a `try–catch` statement, in which you specify explicitly what Java is to do when particular exceptions are thrown. You learn about this approach in Chapter 32.

Second, you can indicate that a method contains statements that may throw exceptions with which you do not wish to deal in that method. You so indicate by adding the keyword `throws` and the name of the exception class, or a superclass of the exception class, to the method definition. To handle all sorts of input–output exceptions, including instances of the `FileNotFoundException` class, you use `IOException` as the name of the exception class:

```
public class Demonstrate {                    ────── ──────────
  public static void main(String argv[]) throws IOException {
  ...
  }
}
```

Java insists that you use either a try–catch statement or the throws keyword, to force you to think about what you want to happen in the event that a failure occurs.

Of the two approaches, you see the throws keyword in this chapter, because the focus of this chapter is file input streams, not exception handling. In general, however, using a try–catch statement is better programming practice, because such statements place the solution close to where the problem occurs.

482 At this point, you are ready to start assembling a traditional-approach program, such as the following, which simply displays each line of the input file. The program reads each line from the buffered reader using the readLine method. Reading continues until the readLine method returns null or a string with no characters, detected by way of the equals method with an empty-string ordinary argument:

```
import java.io.*;
public class Demonstrate {
  public static void main(String argv[]) throws IOException {
    FileInputStream stream = new FileInputStream("input.data");
    InputStreamReader reader = new InputStreamReader(stream);
    BufferedReader buffer = new BufferedReader(reader);
    String line;
    int nextSpace, x, y, z;
    while ((line = buffer.readLine()) != null && !line.equals("")) {
      System.out.println("Line read: " + line);
    }
    stream.close();
    return;
  }
}
```

──────────────── Sample Data ────────────────
```
4  7  3
8  8  7
2 10  5
```
──────────────── Result ────────────────
```
Line read:  4  7  3
Line read:  8  8  7
Line read:  2 10  5
```

483 To make use of the strings produced by readLine, you first need to exploit several methods found in the String class:

- The trim method produces a string with no spaces or other whitespace characters on the ends. For example, if line = " 4 7 3 ", then:

  line.trim() ⟶ "4 7 3"

- The indexOf method finds the position of its ordinary argument in its target argument. If line = "4 7 3", then:

  line.indexOf(" ") ⟶ 1

- The substring method, with one indexing argument, extracts a string from its target argument, starting at the index.

  line.substring(2) ⟶ "7 3"

- The substring method, with two indexing arguments, extracts a string from its target argument.

  line".substring(0, 1) ⟶ "4"

484 Using the methods explained in Segment 483, you can readily extract strings representing integers from a line of text. Then, to convert those strings to integers, you use parseInt, a static method of the Integer class, as in the following example, in which the result is an integer.

  Integer.parseInt("4") ⟶ 4

485 Now, you combine trim, indexOf, substring and parseInt to read three successive numbers from each line of text:

```java
import java.io.*;
public class Demonstrate {
 public static void main(String argv[]) throws IOException {
  FileInputStream stream = new FileInputStream("input.data");
  InputStreamReader reader = new InputStreamReader(stream);
  BufferedReader buffer = new BufferedReader(reader);
  String line;
  while ((line = buffer.readLine()) != null && !line.equals("")) {
   line = line.trim();
   int nextSpace = line.indexOf(" ");
   int x = Integer.parseInt(line.substring(0, nextSpace));
   line = line.substring(nextSpace).trim();
   nextSpace = line.indexOf(" ");
   int y = Integer.parseInt(line.substring(0, nextSpace));
   line = line.substring(nextSpace).trim();
   int z = Integer.parseInt(line);
   System.out.println("Numbers read: " + x + ", " + y + ", " + z);
  }
  stream.close();
  return;
 }
}
```

———————————————— Sample Data ————————————————

```
4  7   3
8  8   7
2  10  5
```

———————————————— Result ————————————————

```
Numbers read: 4, 7, 3
Numbers read: 8, 8, 7
Numbers read: 2, 10, 5
```

486 Finally, you can use the three successive numbers read from each line of text to construct a movie. Then, you can report the movie's rating, using, for example, the Movie class definition provided in Segment 316:

```java
import java.io.*;
public class Demonstrate {
 public static void main(String argv[]) throws IOException {
  FileInputStream stream = new FileInputStream("input.data");
  InputStreamReader reader = new InputStreamReader(stream);
  BufferedReader buffer = new BufferedReader(reader);
  String line;
```

```
    while ((line = buffer.readLine()) != null && !line.equals("")) {
     line = line.trim();
     int nextSpace = line.indexOf(" ");
     int x = Integer.parseInt(line.substring(0, nextSpace));
     line = line.substring(nextSpace).trim();
     nextSpace = line.indexOf(" ");
     int y = Integer.parseInt(line.substring(0, nextSpace));
     line = line.substring(nextSpace).trim();
     int z = Integer.parseInt(line);
     Movie m = new Movie(x, y, z);
     System.out.println("Rating: " + m.rating());
    }
    stream.close();
    return;
   }
 }
```

———————————————— Sample Data ————————————————

```
 4  7  3
 8  8  7
 2 10  5
```

———————————————— Result ————————————————

```
Rating: 14
Rating: 23
Rating: 17
```

487 To use the token approach, you insert a **stream tokenizer** between your input-stream reader and your program. You do not need a buffered reader.

To create a stream tokenizer connected to an input-stream reader, you use an expression that creates an instance of the `StreamTokenizer` class for that input-stream reader. In the following statement, for example, you declare a `StreamTokenizer` variable, and create a `StreamTokenizer` instance from a `InputStreamReader` instance:

```
        Input-stream reader instance ─────┐
                                          │
                                          ▼
StreamTokenizer tokens = new StreamTokenizer(reader);
```

`StreamTokenizer` instances are called either **stream tokenizers** or just **tokenizers**.

488 Tokenizers treat whitespace characters as delimiters that divide character sequences into **tokens**. Thus, a file containing the following characters is viewed as a stream of nine tokens divided by spaces and line-terminating characters:

```
 4   7   3
 8   8   7
 2  10   5
```

489 You can think of a tokenizer as though it were a machine that steps through a stream of tokens. The nextToken method moves the machine from one token to the next. Suppose, for example, that you call nextToken with tokens, a StreamTokenizer instance, as the target:

tokens.nextToken()

The first time that Java executes a call to the nextToken method, given that the first token is a number, the value of that token is assigned to the nval instance variable in the tokenizer:

After Java executes the second call to nextToken, the second token is assigned to nval:

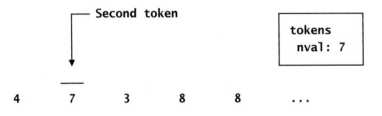

490 Because the value of the current token is stored in the nval instance variable of the tokenizer, you obtain the number using the field-selection operator:

tokens.nval

491 Note that the number stored in the nval instance variable is always a floating-point double value, even if what you see in the file is an integer. The rationale is that you can always cast a double value into any other type. Accordingly, if your file contains integers, and you want to work with int values, you need to cast the number that you obtain from the nval instance variable:

(int) tokens.nval

492 As the token machine moves down a stream of tokens, eventually it reaches the end of the token stream. At that point, the nextToken method returns a special value, which is the same as the value assigned to the TT_EOF instance variable of the tokenizer, where TT is an acronym for token type.

Thus, when nextToken returns a value equal to the value of the TT_EOF instance variable, there are no more tokens to be read. Accordingly, you can read and process all the integer tokens in a token stream with a while loop:

```
while (tokens.nextToken() != tokens.TT_EOF) {
  ...
  ... (int) tokens.nval ...
  ...
}
```

493
SIDE TRIP The value of the TT_EOF variable happens to be an integer, so you could use that integer in your programs instead of TT_EOF. Good programming practice dictates that you should never use an integer in place of an instance variable, because using the instance variable makes it clear, without requiring any inference, that you are testing for the end of the token stream.

494 At this point, at last, you have all the machinery needed to produce a series of int values from the information in a file. When you gather that machinery into a program, you have the following, which simply displays the int values, one to a line.

```
import java.io.*;
public class Demonstrate {
 public static void main(String argv[]) throws IOException {
  FileInputStream stream = new FileInputStream("input.data");
  InputStreamReader reader = new InputStreamReader(stream);
  StreamTokenizer tokens = new StreamTokenizer(reader);
  while (tokens.nextToken() != tokens.TT_EOF) {
   System.out.println("Integer: " + (int) tokens.nval);
  }
  stream.close();
 }
}
```
———————————————— Sample Data ————————————————
4 7 3
———————————————— Result ————————————————
Integer: 4
Integer: 7
Integer: 3

Note that the close method closes the file input stream, when reading is finished, as prescribed in Segment 475.

495 Of course, the program in Segment 494 goes to a lot of trouble to produce int values from the characters in a file, just to display them for you as characters. Accordingly, the next example uses the int values to initialize Movie instances, each of which becomes the target of the rating method.

```
import java.io.*;
public class Demonstrate {
 public static void main(String argv[]) throws IOException {
  FileInputStream stream = new FileInputStream("input.data");
  InputStreamReader reader = new InputStreamReader(stream);
  StreamTokenizer tokens = new StreamTokenizer(reader);
  while (tokens.nextToken() != tokens.TT_EOF) {
   int x = (int) tokens.nval;
   tokens.nextToken(); int y = (int) tokens.nval;
   tokens.nextToken(); int z = (int) tokens.nval;
   Movie m = new Movie(x, y, z);
   System.out.println("Rating: " + m.rating());
  }
  stream.close();
 }
}
```

496 A token stream may produce not only number tokens, but also string tokens. Suppose, for example, that movie names are included in the input file, with delimiting double quotation marks:

"Apocalypse Now"	4 7 3
"The Sting"	8 8 7
"Bedtime for Bonzo"	2 10 5

To process such a file, you must learn how to recognize movie names. In this chapter, you ignore them, once you recognize them; in Chapter 31, you learn how to incorporate them into Movie instances.

497 You know that nextToken returns the value of the TT_EOF instance variable when there are no more tokens.

In the event that there is a token, the value returned by nextToken depends on whether the token is a number or a string. If the token is a number, nextToken returns the value of the TT_NUMBER instance variable; if the token is a string, nextToken returns the value of the TT_WORD instance variable.

498 Whenever the token is a whitespace-delimited string, that token is assigned to the sval instance variable of the tokenizer. For example, if movie names are included in the file, each word in those movie names becomes a value of the sval instance variable:

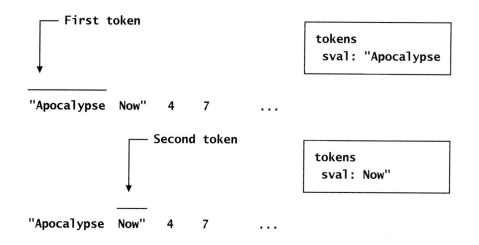

First token

tokens
  sval: "Apocalypse

"Apocalypse   Now"   4   7   ...

Second token

tokens
  sval: Now"

"Apocalypse   Now"   4   7   ...

499 You readily can adapt the program in Segment 495 to deal with both numbers and strings. In the following, the value of the nextToken method is assigned to a local variable, next, which is then compared with the TT_NUMBER and TT_WORD instance variables. In the event that the value returned by the nextToken method is the value of the TT_WORD instance variable, the token is ignored. A switch statement, of the sort you learned about in Chapter 26, responds appropriately to the value:

```
import java.io.*;
public class Demonstrate {
 public static void main(String argv[]) throws IOException {
  FileInputStream stream = new FileInputStream("input.data");
  InputStreamReader reader = new InputStreamReader(stream);
  StreamTokenizer tokens = new StreamTokenizer(reader);
  int next = 0;
  while ((next = tokens.nextToken()) != tokens.TT_EOF) {
   switch (next) {
    case tokens.TT_WORD: break;
    case tokens.TT_NUMBER:
     int x = (int) tokens.nval;
     tokens.nextToken(); int y = (int) tokens.nval;
     tokens.nextToken(); int z = (int) tokens.nval;
     Movie m = new Movie(x, y, z);
     System.out.println("Rating: " + m.rating());
     break;
   }
  }
  stream.close();
 }
}
```

500 You learned about the traditional approach in Segment 482 and you learned about the
SIDE TRIP token approach in Segment 487.

To see how the more sophisticated approach is related to the traditional approach, you can study the following definition of MovieStreamTokenizer, which is derived from the program shown in Segment 486.

```java
import java.io.*;
public class MovieStreamTokenizer {
 FileInputStream stream;
 InputStreamReader reader;
 BufferedReader buffer;
 Movie movie;
 int MORE = 0, EOF = 1;
 public static void main(String argv[]) throws IOException {
  MovieStreamTokenizer tokens = new MovieStreamTokenizer("input.data");
  while(tokens.nextMovie() != tokens.EOF) {
   Movie m = tokens.movie;
   System.out.println("Rating: " + m.rating());
  }
 }
 public MovieStreamTokenizer (String fileName) throws IOException {
  stream = new FileInputStream("input.data");
  reader = new InputStreamReader(stream);
  buffer = new BufferedReader(reader);
 }
 public int nextMovie () throws IOException {
  String line = buffer.readLine();
  if (line != null && !line.equals("")) {
   line = line.trim();
   int nextSpace = line.indexOf(" ");
   int x = Integer.parseInt(line.substring(0, nextSpace));
   line = line.substring(nextSpace).trim();
   nextSpace = line.indexOf(" ");
   int y = Integer.parseInt(line.substring(0, nextSpace));
   line = line.substring(nextSpace).trim();
   int z = Integer.parseInt(line);
   movie = new Movie(x, y, z);
   return MORE;
  }
  stream.close();
  return EOF;
 }
}
```

The MovieStreamTokenizer constructor assigns values to instance variables for the file input stream, the input-stream reader, and the buffered reader. Each call to nextMovie reads a line of text from the buffered reader, processes that line to produce the arguments needed by the Movie constructor, and returns the value of the MORE instance variable. If there are no more lines of text, then nextMovie returns the value of the EOF variable.

Thus, a `MovieStreamTokenizer` instance provides a stream of movie instances, accessible via the `movie` instance variable, just as an ordinary stream tokenizer provides a stream of strings and doubles, accessible via the `nval` and `sval` instance variables.

501
SIDE TRIP The file-reading mechanisms that you have learned about in this chapter work well whenever you run your program on the same computer on which your data reside. In Chapter 45, you learn about more sophisticated mechanisms that work well even when your program is to run via a network browser.

502
PRACTICE Suppose that you are hired as a programmer by a baseball team. Your first job is to write a program that reads a file containing the scores from previous games. All scores are given as the name of the opponent followed by a pair of numbers that represent your team's score and the opponent's score. Here is an example:

```
"Cubs"          4      2
"Yankees"       9      0
"Blue Jays"     4      3
```

Your program is to use the information in the file to display your team's won–lost record.

503
PRACTICE Extend the definition of the `MovieStreamTokenizer` class, which you learned about in Segment 500, such that it can handle files that contain movie names, as well as rating information.

504
HIGHLIGHTS

- If you want to tell Java that you intend to work with file input or file output streams, **then** include the following line in your program:

  ```
  import java.io.*;
  ```

- If you want to read from an input file, one line at a time, **then** instantiate the following pattern:

  ```
  FileInputStream stream variable
    = new FileInputStream( file specification );
  InputStreamReader reader variable
    = new InputStreamReader( stream variable );
  BufferedReader buffered reader variable
    = new BufferedReader( reader variable );
  ```

- If you want to read a line from a buffered reader, **then** instantiate the following pattern:

  ```
  buffered reader variable .readLine()
  ```

- If you need to manipulate strings, **then** deploy methods such as `equals`, `trim`, `indexOf`, and `substring`.

CHAPTER 27 | **161**

- If you need to produce an integer from a string, **then** deploy the `parseInt` static method of the `Integer` class.

- If you want to read from an input file, token by token, **then** instantiate the following pattern:

```
StreamTokenizer token variable
 = new StreamTokenizer( input-stream reader variable );
```

- If you want to move a tokenizer to the next token, **then** instantiate the following pattern:

```
token variable .nextToken()
```

- If you want to read from a tokenizer until it is empty, **then** instantiate the following pattern:

```
while ( nextToken's value != token variable .TT_EOF) {
...
}
```

- If you want to know whether the current token is a number, **then** compare the value produced by `nextToken` to the `TT_NUMBER` instance variable:

```
nextToken's value == token variable .TT_NUMBER
```

- If you want to know whether the current token is a string, **then** compare the value produced by `nextToken` to the `TT_WORD` instance variable:

```
nextToken's value == token variable .TT_WORD
```

- If the current token is a number, **and** you want to use the value of that number, **then** instantiate the following pattern:

```
( desired type ) token variable .nval
```

- If the current token is a string, **and** you want to use the value of that string, **then** instantiate the following pattern:

```
token variable .sval
```

- If you have finished reading from an input file stream, **then** close the file by instantiating the following pattern:

```
stream variable .close();
```

28 HOW TO CREATE AND ACCESS ARRAYS

505 In this chapter, you learn how to store information in arrays, and you learn how to retrieve such information.

506 An **array** contains a collection of **elements**, all of which have the same primitive type or class, that Java stores and retrieves using an integer **index**. In Java, the first element of an array is indexed by zero; hence, Java is said to have **zero-based arrays**.

The following, for example, is a one-dimensional array, of length 4, with integer elements:

```
0   1   2   3      ← Index

65  87  72  75
```

507 The number of bytes allocated for each place in an array is determined by the type of the elements to be stored. If an array is to hold integers of type `short`, for example, Java allocates 2 bytes per integer. On the other hand, if an array is to hold integers of type `int`, Java allocates 4 bytes per integer.

508 To declare a variable with an array as that variable's type, you add brackets to an ordinary variable declaration. For example, to declare `durations` to be a variable to which an integer array will be assigned, you write the following:

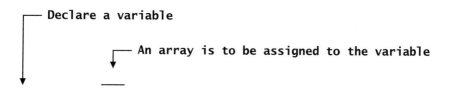

```
Declare a variable

        An array is to be assigned to the variable



_____   ___

int durations [ ];
```

509 Variables typed with arrays are said to be **reference variables**. You learned in Segment 76 that variables typed with classes are also reference variables.

510 To create an array, you need to deploy the `new` operator, just as you need to deploy the `new` operator to create a class instance.

To signal that an array is to be created, you include the type of the elements to be stored and a bracketed number that specifies how many elements the array is to store. For example, to create an array of four integers, you write the following:

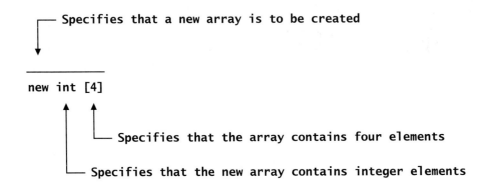

Specifies that a new array is to be created

`new int [4]`

Specifies that the array contains four elements

Specifies that the new array contains integer elements

511 At this point, you can declare an integer-array variable, and can assign an integer array to that variable:

```
int durations [];
durations = new int [4];
```

Alternatively, you can combine variable declaration and array creation:

Declare   Create

`int durations [] = new int [4];`

512 To use an array, once it is created, you need to know how to write into and to read from the various locations in the array, each of which is identified by a numerical index.

Consider durations—the one-dimensional array of integers. To write data into that array, you use assignment statements in which the array name and a bracketed integer index appear on the left side of an assignment operator—the place where you are accustomed to seeing variable names. The following statement, for example, inserts an integer into the place indexed by the value assigned to the counter variable:

```
durations[counter] = 65;
```

513 You can combine array creation and element insertion by using an **array initializer**, in which specific elements appear, separated by commas, and surrounded by brackets:

```
int durations [] = {65, 87, 72, 75};
```

The array initializer shown specifies that an array is to be created, that the array is to store four elements, and that the initial values are to be 65, 87, 72, and 75. Thus, one statement takes the place of five:

```
int durations[] = new int [4];
durations[0] = 65;
durations[1] = 87;
durations[2] = 72;
durations[3] = 75;
```

514 To read data from the `durations` array, once the data have been written, you write an expression containing the array name and a bracketed integer index. The following expression, for example, yields the integer stored in the place indexed by the value assigned to the `counter` variable:

```
durations[counter]
```

515 To obtain the length of an array, you can use the field-selection operator to obtain the value of the `length` instance variable:

```
durations.length
```

516 Whenever you create an array of numbers, all the elements in the array are initialized automatically to 0, the default value for numbers. Whenever you create an array of strings, all the elements in the array are initialized automatically to `null`, the default value for strings.

517 The following program defines an array of four integers, wires in integers via an array initializer, computes the sum of the integers, and displays the average:

```
public class Demonstrate {
 public static void main (String argv[]) {
   int sum = 0;
   int durations [] = {65, 87, 72, 75};
   for (int counter = 0; counter < durations.length; ++counter) {
     sum = sum + durations[counter];
   }
   System.out.print("The average of the " + durations.length);
   System.out.println(" durations is " + sum / durations.length);
  }
}
———————————————— Result ————————————————
The average of the 4 durations is 74
```

518 You can use arrays to store not only numbers, but also class instances. Once you have defined the `Movie` class, for example, you can use the following statement to declare and initialize a `Movie` array variable:

```
┌── Declare        ┌── Initialize
│                  │
▼                  ▼
────────────       ────────────
Movie movies [] = new Movie [4];
```

519 To insert a `Movie` instance into an array, you use an assignment statement, in which the array name and a bracketed integer index are followed by the assignment operator, and by an expression that yields a `Movie` instance:

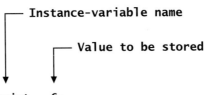

Expression that yields a Movie instance

```
movies[counter] = new Movie();
```

520 Once you have inserted `Movie` instances into an array, you can alter the instance variables in that `Movie` instance. For example, to write into an element of the `movies` array, you use assignment statements in which the array name, a bracketed integer index, and the instance-variable name appear on the left side:

Instance-variable name

Value to be stored

```
movies[counter].script = 6;
```

521 To read data from the `movies` array, once the data have been inserted, you simply write an expression containing the array name, a bracketed integer index, and the instance-variable name. The following expression, for example, yields the value assigned to the `script` instance variable of the `Movie` instance stored in the place indexed by the value assigned to the `counter` variable:

```
movies[counter].script
```

522 Whenever you create an array of class instances, all the elements in the array are initialized to a value that represents the absence of an instance. That value is denoted as `null`. Thus, if you want a program to determine whether it has written into an array of instances at a particular place, you compare the value obtained from that place with `null`. If the value obtained from a place is `null`, you have yet to write an instance into that place:

```
movies[counter] == null
```

523 To use an array element as an instance method target, you write an expression containing the array name, a bracketed integer index, and the instance-method name and arguments. The following expression, for example, yields the value produced by the `rating` method when used on the `Movie` instance stored in the place indexed by the value assigned to the `counter` variable:

```
movies[counter].rating()
```

524 You can combine array creation and element insertion when the elements are of type `Movie`, just as you can combine array creation and element insertion when the elements are of type `int`.

For example, if you wish to create a four-element array of specific movies, you can write the following, in which all `Movie` instances happen to be created with the three-parameter constructor:

```
Movie movies[] = {new Movie(5, 6, 3),
                  new Movie(8, 7, 7),
                  new Movie(7, 2, 2),
                  new Movie(7, 5, 5)};
```

525 The following is a program in which an array of four Movie instances is defined, data are wired in via an array initializer, the sum of the ratings is determined in a for loop, and the average of those ratings is reported via a print statement. The Movie class involved is the one defined in Segment 316:

```
public class Demonstrate {
 public static void main (String argv[]) {
  Movie movies[] = {new Movie(5, 6, 3),
                    new Movie(8, 7, 7),
                    new Movie(7, 2, 2),
                    new Movie(7, 5, 5)};
  int sum = 0;
  for (int counter = 0; counter < movies.length; ++counter) {
    sum = sum + movies[counter].rating();
  }
  System.out.print("The average rating of the " + movies.length);
  System.out.println(" movies is " + sum / movies.length);
 }
}
```
————————————————— Result —————————————————
The average rating of the 4 movies is 16

526 Now, suppose that you have defined the Attraction class, the Movie class, and the Symphony class as in Segment 316. If you then declare an array for instances of the Attraction class, you can place Movie instances and Symphony instances in that array, because the value of an element of an array declared for a particular class can be an instance of any subclass of that class.

For example, you can compute the average rating of a mixed array of Movie and Symphony instances:

```
public class Demonstrate {
 public static void main (String argv[]) {
  int sum = 0;
  Attraction attractions[] = {new Movie(4, 7, 3),
                              new Movie(8, 8, 7),
                              new Symphony(10, 9, 3),
                              new Symphony(9, 5, 8)};
  for (int counter = 0; counter < attractions.length; ++counter) {
    sum = sum + attractions[counter].rating();
  }
  System.out.print("The average rating of the " + attractions.length);
  System.out.println(" attractions is " + sum / attractions.length);
 }
}
```

———————————————— Result ————————————————
The average rating of the 4 attractions is 20

527

SIDE TRIP

Many programmers find it helpful—albeit not absolutely necessary—to understand, in general terms, how arrays are implemented.

In Java, integer arrays contain a `length` instance variable and 4 bytes of memory for every `int` instance in the array. The 4-byte chunks are arranged consecutively in memory. If you want to know the address of the first byte occupied by the nth integer, you add the address of the first byte of the zeroth integer to $4 \times n$.

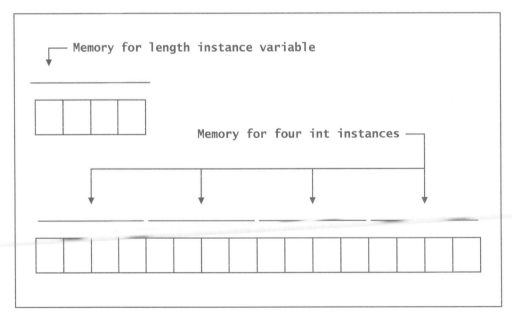

528

SIDE TRIP

All other arrays of primitive types are arranged the same way. The location of the nth element is always the sum of the address of the first byte of the zeroth element and n times the number of bytes occupied by each element.

529
SIDE TRIP Instances of a reference type cannot be stored so straightforwardly, because the number of bytes required for each element may vary.

For example, an instance of the `Attraction` class will need fewer bytes than will instances of the `Movie` and `Symphony` classes, both of which are subclasses of the `Attraction` class. Yet instances of the `Movie` and `Symphony` classes are valid occupants of an `Attraction` array.

Accordingly, you cannot store mixtures of `Attraction`, `Movie`, and `Symphony` instances consecutively, expecting that the *n*th element will be offset from the beginning of the array by *n* times a fixed number of bytes.

530
SIDE TRIP In Java, `Attraction` arrays each contain a `length` instance variable and several bytes of memory for the **address** of every `Attraction` instance in the array.

Even though the instances may occupy different amounts of space, the instance addresses occupy the same amount of space. Hence, the address of the *n*th instance address will be offset from the beginning of the array by *n* times a fixed number of bytes:

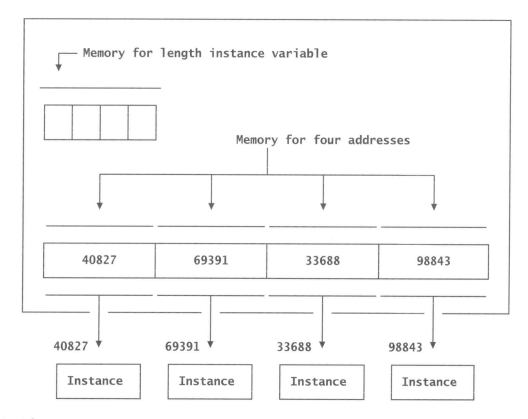

531
SIDE TRIP Whenever you assign a new instance to an array, displacing an existing element, and that displaced instance is not an element of any other array or the value of any variable, then

the memory for that instance is returned to the free-storage list via the garbage-collection process described in Segment 186.

532
SIDE TRIP

The addresses that connect arrays to class instances are called **pointers**. Java moves through the pointers to the instances for you automatically, so you do not need to know even that pointers exist.

C and C++ provide elaborate tools for pointer manipulation. Accordingly, proponents of those languages consider the pointer-manipulation tools to be a strength of those languages.

Explicit pointer manipulation by programmers can be a source of system-endangering bugs, because you can chase an errant pointer into the wrong part of memory, or even, in extreme cases, into some other program. Accordingly, proponents of Java consider the absence of pointer-manipulation tools to be a strength of the language.

Proponents of Java sometimes say that Java has no pointers when what they mean is that Java provides no access to pointers.

533
SIDE TRIP

In C++, you are allowed to create arrays of class instances, as well as arrays of pointers to class instances. If you have an array of class instances, all the elements must be instances of the class, rather than instances of the class's subclasses, because only enough room is reserved for instances of the class itself.

Accordingly, if you want to place subclass instances in an array, you must use a pointer array, which, in C++, requires you to understand pointer dereferencing and virtual functions.

By uniformly implementing reference arrays with automatically handled pointers, Java avoids the need for both pointer dereferencing and virtual functions.

534
SIDE TRIP

When you create an array of class instances, memory is set aside for addresses, but memory for the class instances is not set aside until those class instances are created. Accordingly, if you should overestimate the number of elements that you need, you waste only the memory required by the unnecessary addresses, but do not waste the memory that would be required if memory were set aside for the unnecessary class instances.

In general, setting aside memory for addresses leads to far less memory waste far less than that incurred by the alternative approach of setting aside memory for class instances.

535
PRACTICE

You easily can define arrays with more than one dimension: You simply add more bracketed dimension sizes. For example, to define a double array with 2 rows and 100 columns, you proceed as follows:

```
double 2DArray [] [] = new double[2][100];
```

Amend the program you were asked to write in Segment 502 such that it writes scores into an array with 2 rows and 160 columns. Then, display not only the won–lost record, but also the average difference between your team's score and the opponent's score for games won and for games lost.

- If you want to declare and initialize a one-dimensional array, **then** instantiate the following pattern:

  `data type` `array name` `[]` `=`
    `new` `data type` `[` `number of elements` `];`

- If you have an array, **and** you want to write a value into the array at a specified position, **then** instantiate the following pattern:

  `array name` `[` `index` `]` `=` `expression` `;`

- If you want to know whether an class-instance-containing array has been assigned a value at a specified position, **then** instantiate the following pattern:

  `array name` `[` `index` `]` `==` `null`

- If you have a value stored in an array at a specified position, **and** you want to read that value, **then** instantiate the following pattern:

  `array name` `[` `index` `]`

- If you want to know the length of an array, **then** instantiate the following pattern:

  `array name` `.length`

29 HOW TO MOVE ARRAYS INTO AND OUT OF METHODS

537 In Chapter 27, you learned how to use tokenizers to read integers and strings from a file. In Chapter 28, you learned how to store information in arrays.

Now, you can combine what you learned about files with what you learned about arrays to read movie-rating information from a file, to create movie instances, and to store those instances in an array.

538 The following program creates an array that can hold up to 100 `Movie` instances. Then, it fills part or all of that array with `Movie` instances:

```java
import java.io.*;
public class Demonstrate {
 public static void main(String argv[]) throws IOException {
  FileInputStream stream = new FileInputStream("input.data");
  InputStreamReader reader = new InputStreamReader(stream);
  StreamTokenizer tokens = new StreamTokenizer(reader);
  int movieCounter = 0;
  Movie movies [] = new Movie [100];
  while (tokens.nextToken() != tokens.TT_EOF) {
   int x = (int) tokens.nval;
   tokens.nextToken(); int y = (int) tokens.nval;
   tokens.nextToken(); int z = (int) tokens.nval;
   movies [movieCounter] = new Movie(x, y, z);
   ++movieCounter;
  }
  stream.close();
 }
}
```

539 You probably do not know exactly how many `Movie` instances you need to store. Accordingly, you need to define an array that is sure to be large enough to hold all the elements that you can possibly encounter.

If you cannot determine a maximum size for an array because the number of needed elements is too unpredictable, you probably should store your information in a vector. You learn about vectors in Chapter 30.

540 To make generally useful the file-reading and array-writing program in Segment 538, you must repackage it as a method defined in its own class, rather than retaining it as part of `main` in the `Demonstrate` class. Accordingly, you need to know how to specify that a parameter is an array and that a returned value is an array.

541 To specify that a parameter is an array, you include brackets with the parameter type specification. Similarly, to specify that a method returns an array value, you include brackets with the return-value type specification.

542 Suppose, for example, that you decide to repackage the file-reading and array-storing apparatus into a method named `readData`. You write `readData`, a class method that both accepts and returns an array of `Movie` instances:

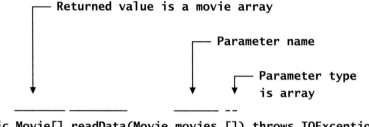

```
public static Movie[] readData(Movie movies []) throws IOException {
  ...
}
```

Equivalently, you can place the brackets in front of the parameter name:

```
public static Movie[] readData(Movie[] movies) throws IOException {
  ...
}
```

543 Now, you can create a movie array in `main`, and can hand that array to the `readData` class method, defined in the `Auxiliaries` class. Evidently, the `readData` method adds elements to the array and returns it, whereupon a `for` loop displays ratings. Note that the `main` program determines that there are no more movies with which to deal by looking for `null`, as explained in Segment 522:

```
import java.io.*;
public class Demonstrate {
 public static void main(String argv[]) throws IOException {
   Movie mainArray [] = new Movie [100];
   mainArray = Auxiliaries.readData(mainArray);
   Movie m;
   for (int counter = 0, (m = mainArray[counter]) != null; ++counter) {
    System.out.println(m.rating());
   }
 }
}
```

544 The required definition for the `readData` method is as follows:

```java
import java.io.*;
public class Auxiliaries {
 public static Movie[] readData(Movie movies []) throws IOException {
  FileInputStream stream = new FileInputStream("input.data");
  InputStreamReader reader = new InputStreamReader(stream);
  StreamTokenizer tokens = new StreamTokenizer(reader);
  int movieCounter = 0;
  while (tokens.nextToken() != tokens.TT_EOF) {
   int x = (int) tokens.nval;
   tokens.nextToken(); int y = (int) tokens.nval;
   tokens.nextToken(); int z = (int) tokens.nval;
   movies [movieCounter] = new Movie(x, y, z);
   ++movieCounter;
  }
  stream.close();
  return movies;
 }
}
```

545 Curiously, the following pair of methods also works, although, at first glance, it might seem that nothing is returned from readData, inasmuch as readData has the void keyword, instead of a return type, and the call to readData does not appear in an assignment statement:

```java
import java.io.*;
public class Demonstrate {
 public static void main(String argv[]) throws IOException {
  Movie mainArray [] = new Movie [100];
  Auxiliaries.readData(mainArray);
  // Remainder as in Segment 543 ...
 }
}
```

```java
import java.io.*;
public class Auxiliaries {
 public static void readData(Movie movies []) throws IOException {
  FileInputStream stream = new FileInputStream("input.data");
  InputStreamReader reader = new InputStreamReader(stream);
  StreamTokenizer tokens = new StreamTokenizer(reader);
  int movieCounter = 0;
  // While loop as in Segment 544 ...
  stream.close();
  // Return statement deleted here
 }
}
```

546 To understand why the program in Segment 545 works, you need to know that, when an

array is assigned to a variable, the value is represented as an address of a chunk of memory representing an array instance:

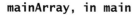

mainArray, in main

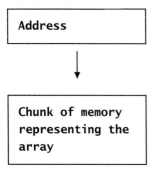

When you hand `mainArray` to `readData`, the value of the parameter, `movies`, becomes a copy of the address of `mainArray`, because Java's parameters are **call-by-value** parameters, as you learned in Segment 131:

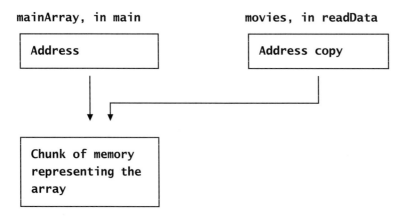

Note, however, that only the address is copied; the contents of the chunk of memory representing the array are not copied. Accordingly, any changes to the elements of the array inside `readData` are retained after `readData` returns. In this respect, the argument–parameter relationship of an array is like the argument–parameter relationship of an instance, as described in Segment 185.

547 So far, you have seen two ways to write the `main–readData` combination:

- You create an array in `main`. The address of the memory representing the array is assigned to a variable in `main`. Then, you hand over the address to `readData`, where it is assigned to a parameter. On return, the address is handed back, and again is assigned to the variable in `main` from whence it came.

- You create an array in `main`. The address of the memory representing the array is assigned to a variable in `main`. Then, you hand over the address to `readData`, where it is assigned to a parameter. Nothing is returned, but the changes to the array stick, because only the address is copied on entering readData, and the array elements are not copied.

There is another alternative:

- You only declare an array variable in main. Thus, there is no array to hand to readData. Instead, you create the array in readData, and hand it back as the value of readData.

548 The following program illustrates the approach that creates the array in the called method. In this version, the file name is passed from main to readData:

```java
import java.io.*;
public class Demonstrate {
 public static void main(String argv[]) throws IOException {
  Movie mainArray [] = Auxiliaries.readData("input.data");
  // Remainder as in Segment 543 ...
 }
}
```

```java
import java.io.*;
public class Auxiliaries {
 public static Movie[] readData(String fileName) throws IOException {
  FileInputStream stream = new FileInputStream(fileName);
  InputStreamReader reader = new InputStreamReader(stream);
  StreamTokenizer tokens = new StreamTokenizer(reader);
  Movie movies [] = new Movie [100];
  int movieCounter = 0;
  // While loop as in Segment 544 ...
  stream.close();
  return movies;
 }
}
```

549 Now that you understand array parameters, you are, at last, ready to understand why the main method has a parameter declared by String arg[].

Evidently, the main method has just one parameter, arg, which is assigned, when the method is called, to an array of String instances. The length of the array is equal to the number of command-line arguments provided; each element corresponds to one command-line argument.

Thus, the following program displays all the command-line arguments provided when the Demonstrate program is called:

```
public class Demonstrate {
 public static void main(String argv []) {
  int max = argv.length;
  for (int counter = 0; counter < max; ++counter) {
   System.out.println(argv[counter]);
  }
 }
}
```

550 Suppose that you run the program shown in Segment 549 by typing the following command line:

```
java Demonstrate This is a test
```

Then, the program displays the arguments, one to a line:

```
This
is
a
test
```

551 You are free, of course, to use the strings provided by the command line in any way you wish.

Frequently, you may wish the strings were numbers, rather than strings. Fortunately, you can convert strings to integers using the parseInt class method of the Integer class.

Thus, if you want to supply rating information as a set of command-line arguments, you can produce integers from those arguments as illustrated in the following program, which computes a movie rating:

```
public class Demonstrate {
 public static void main(String argv[]) {
  Movie m = new Movie(Integer.parseInt(argv[0]),
                      Integer.parseInt(argv[1]),
                      Integer.parseInt(argv[2]));
  System.out.println("The rating is " + m.rating());
 }
}
```

552 Suppose that you run the program shown in Segment 551 by typing the following command line:

```
java Demonstrate 4 7 3
```

Then, the program displays the movie rating:

```
The rating is 14
```

553

Typing in data is tedious; even skilled typists make mistakes. Accordingly, suppose that you decide to have two typists independently create files for your baseball team's season record. Assume that both typists use the format shown in Segment 502.

Next, you write two methods: readScores and verifyScores. The readScores method is to take a filename argument and to return a two-dimensional array of the sort you learned about in Segment 535. The verifyScores method is to take two arguments: a file name and the array produced by readScores. The verifyScores method is to display information about every score for which the two files differ, and to return true only if there are no discrepancies.

554

- If you want to specify that a parameter is an array, **then** include brackets with the parameter type specification.

- If you want to specify that a method produces an array value, **then** include brackets with the return-value type specification.

- When you hand an array argument to a method, the array address is copied, and is assigned to the corresponding method parameter. The array elements are not copied.

- When you return an array value from a method, the array address is returned. The array elements are not copied.

30 HOW TO STORE DATA IN EXPANDABLE VECTORS

555 You learn about vectors in this chapter. You learn that vectors are useful alternatives to arrays, especially when you are unsure about how much information you need to store.

556 An instance of the Vector class, also known as a **vector** by the convention mentioned in Segment 167, contains **elements** that are stored and retrieved in several ways. For example, you can store and retrieve the elements of a vector using an integer **index**, just as you can store and retrieve the elements of an array.

557 Instances of the Vector class differ substantively from array instances:

- You can store any number of elements in any vector. Vectors are not of fixed size.

- You can add elements to the front or back of a vector, or even insert elements into the middle without replacing an existing element.

- You can store only class instances in vectors. Vectors cannot hold elements of primitive type.

558 The Vector class is one of many offerings provided in Java's `java.util` package; `util` is an acronym for **util**ities.

559 You declare Vector variables just as you would any variable to which class instances are assigned. For example, to declare v to be a variable to which a vector will be assigned, you write the following:

```
┌─ Declare a Vector variable
▼

_____

Vector v;
```

To create a vector instance, you deploy the new operator:

```
┌─ Create a Vector instance
▼

_____

new Vector()
```

To declare a vector variable and to create an instance in the same statement, you combine variable declaration and vector creation:

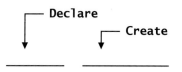

```
Vector v = new Vector();
```

560 To add elements to the back end of a vector, you use the addElement method. For example, if a Movie instance is assigned to a variable m, you add that movie instance to a vector assigned to v as follows:

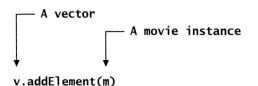

```
v.addElement(m)
```

561 To insert an element at a particular place, you use the insertElementAt method, providing an instance and an integer index as arguments. Thus, if you want to add elements to the front end of a vector, displacing all other elements, you use insertElementAt with an index of 0:

```
v.insertElementAt(m, 0)
```

562 To remove an element from a particular place, you use the removeElementAt method, providing an integer index as the argument. Thus, if you want to remove the first element of a vector, displacing all the other elements to fill in the hole, you use removeElementAt with an index of 0:

```
v.removeElementAt(0)
```

563 To read the element at the front end of a vector, you use the firstElement method:

```
v.firstElement()
```

To access the element at the back end of a vector, you use the lastElement method:

```
v.lastElement()
```

564 Using the addElement, firstElement, and removeElementAt methods, you can represent **first-in, first-out (FIFO) queues** with vectors:

```
  ┌─ firstElement reads elements from the front

  ├─ removeElementAt removes elements from the front
  │
  ▼
┌───┬───┬───┬───┐
│   │   │   │   │
└───┴───┴───┴───┘
          ▲
          └─ addElement adds elements at the back
```

Similarly, you can use vectors to represent **last-in, first-out (LIFO) push-down stacks** by using the insertElementAt, firstElement, and removeElementAt methods:

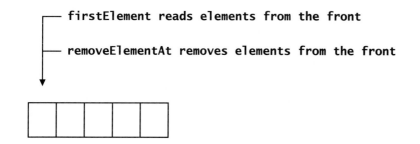

firstElement reads elements from the front

removeElementAt removes elements from the front

insertElementAt adds elements to the front

565 Once an element has been placed in a vector, you can retrieve that element using the `elementAt` method with an integer argument. For example, the following expression retrieves the element identified by an integer variable, `counter`, from the vector, `v`:

`v.elementAt(counter)`

Similarly, you can replace an element using the `setElementAt` method. For example, the following expression replaces the element identified by the value of an integer variable, `counter`, by the instance assigned to the instance variable, `m`:

`v.setElementAt(m, counter)`

Thus, `elementAt` and `setElementAt` allow you to use a vector as though it were an array.

566 The definitions of the `addElement`, `insertElementAt`, and `setElementAt` methods specify that the element added shall be an instance of the `Object` class. Because all classes descend from the `Object` class, you can add any class instance to a vector.

567 To obtain the number of elements in a vector, you use the `size` method:

`v.size()`

Note that `size` is a method; it is not an instance variable.

568 Having stored `Movie` instances in a vector, you might think that you could calculate the rating of one of those instances, using the `rating` method, as follows:

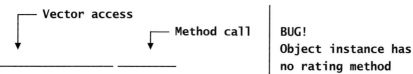

Vector access

Method call

BUG!
Object instance has
no rating method

`v.firstElement().rating()`

The reason such an expression does not work is that the elements of a vector always appear to be instances of the `Object` class, and no `rating` method is defined for the `Object` class.

569 As you learned in Segment 342, you can cast an instance to a class, as long as the instance is, in fact, an instance of the class.

For example, you can work with an element of a vector by casting that element, an `Object` instance, into a `Movie` instance:

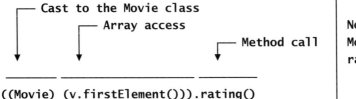

```
((Movie) (v.firstElement())).rating()
```

570 The following combination is based on the combination shown in Segment 548, and reads the same sort of data file, but differs in that the combination stores `Movie` instances in a vector, rather than an array. The highlighted expressions and statements identify the principle differences:

```java
import java.io.*;
import java.util.*;
public class Demonstrate {
 public static void main(String argv[]) throws IOException {
  Vector mainVector = Auxiliaries.readData("input.data");
  int size = mainVector.size();
  for (int counter = 0; counter < size; ++counter) {
   System.out.println(
     ((Movie) mainVector.elementAt(counter)).rating()
   );
  }
 }
}

import java.io.*;
import java.util.*;
public class Auxiliaries {
 public static Vector readData(String fileName) throws IOException {
  FileInputStream stream = new FileInputStream(fileName);
  InputStreamReader reader = new InputStreamReader(stream);
  StreamTokenizer tokens = new StreamTokenizer(reader);
  Vector v = new Vector();
  while (tokens.nextToken() != tokens.TT_EOF) {
   int x = (int) tokens.nval;
   tokens.nextToken(); int y = (int) tokens.nval;
   tokens.nextToken(); int z = (int) tokens.nval;
   v.addElement(new Movie(x, y, z));
  }
  stream.close();
  return v;
 }
}
```

571 If you use a vector, you do not need to worry about how many Movie instances there may be: No matter how many there are, the vector will hold them, unlike an array of fixed size.

572 Instead of using the elementAt method and a counter variable, counter, to access vector elements, as shown in Segment 570, you can create an **iterator**, which offers up vector elements, one element at a time.

573 To produce an iterator from a vector, you define an Iterator variable, then establish a value for that variable using the iterator method with the vector as the target. For example, to produce an iterator named i from the vector assigned to mainVector, you write the following expression:

```
Iterator i = mainVector.iterator()
```

Once you have created an iterator, you can fetch the successive elements from the vector using the next predicate:

```
i.next()
```

Thus, an iterator maintains a pointer to a place in the parent vector. When you call next, the iterator returns the element to the right of the pointer and advances the pointer to the next element.

574 To be sure that there is a next element, you test the iterator using hasNext:

```
i.hasNext()
```

575 Iterators simplify for loops. All you need in a for loop's Boolean expression is a hasNext expression:

```
Iterator i = mainVector.iterator();
for (; i.hasNext();) {
 ··· i.next() ···
 }
```

If you like, you can move variable declaration and initialization inside the for loop, producing a compact expression:

```
for (Iterator i = mainVector.iterator(); i.hasNext();) {
 ··· i.next() ···
 }
```

576 Modifying the Demonstrate definition shown in Segment 570 produces the following:

```
import java.io.*;
import java.util.*;
public class Demonstrate {
 public static void main(String argv[]) throws IOException {
   Vector mainVector = Auxiliaries.readData("input.data");
   for (Iterator i = mainVector.iterator(); i.hasNext();) {
     System.out.println(((Movie) i.next()).rating());
   }
 }
}
```

577 Because iterator-enabled for loops are so compact, relative to counter-enabled for loops, you see iterator-enabled for loops in the rest of this book.

578
SIDE TRIP
Because all vector elements must be instances, you might wonder how you could possibly make a vector of, say, int values, inasmuch as int values are not instances of a class.

The answer is that you use an instance of the Integer class. All such instances have an instance variable to which an integer is assigned. Because instances of the Integer class are instances, in contrast to int values, those instances are valid vector elements.

Because the purpose of Integer instances is to surround int values, in a way that enables those int values to enter into vectors, Integer instances are called **wrappers**.

The Long, Float, and Double classes serve as wrapper classes for other arithmetic types.

579
SIDE TRIP
Another reason for using a wrapper is that a wrapper can be the target of method calls, whereas an arithmetic value cannot be such a target.

580
SIDE TRIP
You get information into and out of wrappers as illustrated for the Integer wrapper:

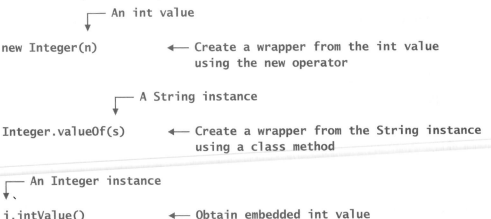

```
                    ┌── An int value
                    ↓
    new Integer(n)          ◄── Create a wrapper from the int value
                                using the new operator


                        ┌── A String instance
                        ↓
    Integer.valueOf(s)      ◄── Create a wrapper from the String instance
                                using a class method


        ┌── An Integer instance
        ↓
    i.intValue()            ◄── Obtain embedded int value
                                using an instance method
```

581
SIDE TRIP
In addition to the highly flexible Vector class, Java also offers other built-in **collection** classes. Of the collection classes, the Vector class is the most useful.

582

PRACTICE

Write a method, readScoreVector, that records baseball-game scores in a vector. You are to obtain the scores from a file, as specified in Segment 502. Each vector element is to be an instance of a class named Game, which you are to define as well. Use instance variables to hold your team's score and the opponent team's score.

583

HIGHLIGHTS

- If you want to store instances, **but** you cannot predict how many there will be, **then** use a vector, rather than an array.

- If you want to implement a queue or a push-down stack, **then** use a vector.

- If you want to declare a vector variable and to create a vector instance, **then** instantiate the following pattern:

  `Vector` `vector name` `= new Vector();`

- If you want to add elements to the front or back of a vector, or to insert an element into a vector, **then** instantiate one of the following patterns:

  `vector name` `.insertElementAt(` `instance` `, 0)`
  `vector name` `.addElement(` `instance` `)`
  `vector name` `.insertElementAt(` `instance` `,` `index` `)`

- If you want to retrieve an element from the front or back of a vector, **then** instantiate one of the following patterns:

  `vector name` `.firstElement()`
  `vector name` `.lastElement()`

- If you want to retrieve an element from a vector, or to replace an element in a vector as though that vector were an array, **then** instantiate one of the following patterns:

  `vector name` `.elementAt(` `index` `)`
  `vector name` `.setElementAt(` `index` `)`

- If you want to know how many elements a vector contains, **then** instantiate the following pattern:

  `vector name` `.size()`

- If you want to use a vector element as a target for a method that belongs to a particular class, **and** that vector element is known to be an instance of the class, **then** cast the vector element to the class by instantiating the following pattern:

  `((` `class name` `)` `vector element` `)`

- If you want to perform a computation using every element of a vector in turn, then instantiate the following pattern:

```
for (Iterator iterator variable = vector .iterator()
    ; iterator variable .hasNext()
    ;) {
 ... iterator variable .next() ...
  }
```

- If you want to store `int` values in a vector, then wrap those values in `Integer` instances.

31 HOW TO WORK WITH CHARACTERS AND STRINGS

584   In this chapter, you learn how to deposit both `Movie` and `Symphony` instances in a vector, by adding a code character to each line of information in a file.

You also learn how to work with strings, so that you can deposit title information in `Movie` and `Symphony` instances.

585   Imagine that your data file has not only information about script, acting, and direction, but also code characters, with M indicating a `Movie` instance and S indicating a `Symphony` instance:

```
┌── Type code
│
▼
M  4   7  3      ←── Script, acting, and direction ratings
M  8   8  7      ←── Script, acting, and direction ratings
S 10   9  3      ←── Music, playing, and conducting ratings
```

586   You learned in Segment 498 that tokenizers read strings, such as the single character string, "M", which become the value of the tokenizer's `sval` instance variable. Accordingly, you can easily extract strings from a file.

587   Once you have a string, you can determine its length using the `length` method. For example, if `codeString` has a string assigned to it, you can obtain the length of the string as follows:

```
┌── Variable with a string assignment
│
│          ┌── length method
│          │
▼          ▼
_____  _____

codeString.length()
```

Note the contrast between arrays and vectors: to obtain the length of an array, you examine the `length` instance variable, rather than calling a method; to obtain the length of a vector, you deploy the `size` method.

588   Strings are constants. Using the + operator, you can concatenate two strings to produce a new, longer string, but you cannot add to, delete from, or change the characters in a string.

589   When you wish to extract a particular character from a string, you use the `charAt` method, with the argument indicating the character that you wish to extract. A 0 argument indicates that you want the first character, because all string indexing is zero based, as is indexing for arrays and vectors:

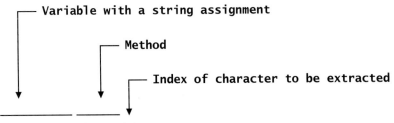

Variable with a string assignment

Method

Index of character to be extracted

```
codeString.charAt(0)
```

590 You denote a particular character by surrounding that character with single quotation marks, thus distinguishing the character from, say, a variable name. For example, you denote the character *M* by writing `'M'`.

If you want to see whether you have extracted a particular character, you compare what you have extracted with that character. Then, if you wish, you can center an `if` statement on that comparison, as in the following example, which executes the block only if the first character in the string is *M*:

```
if (codeString.charAt(0) == 'M') {
  ...
}
```

591 As you learned in Segment 468, you can also use characters in `switch` statements, because characters are considered integral types:

```
switch (codeString.charAt(0)) {
  case 'M': ... break;
  ...
}
```

In this example, the integer-producing expression actually produces a character, and the integer literals actually are characters.

592 You can declare variables to be character variables. You can assign any **literal character**, such as `'X'`, to such variables:

```
char c = 'X';
```

593 The character type is one of the **primitive types**, which you learned about in Segment 180. The **default value** of a character variable is the **null character**, denoted by `'\u000'`.

594 You see strings and characters at work in the following program. This program differs from the one in Segment 570 in two key ways. First, the program reads strings from a file, as well as integers, and interprets the first character of those strings as a code letter. Second, the program uses the code letter to determine whether it should create a `Movie` instance or a `Symphony` instance:

```java
import java.io.*;
import java.util.*;
public class Demonstrate {
 public static void main(String argv[]) throws IOException {
  Vector mainVector;
  mainVector = Auxiliaries.readData("input.data");
  for (Iterator i = mainVector.iterator(); i.hasNext();) {
   System.out.println(((Attraction)i.next()).rating());
  }
 }
}
```

```java
import java.io.*;
import java.util.*;
public class Auxiliaries {
 public static Vector readData(String fileName) throws IOException {
  FileInputStream stream = new FileInputStream(fileName);
  InputStreamReader reader = new InputStreamReader(stream);
  StreamTokenizer tokens = new StreamTokenizer(reader);
  Vector v = new Vector();
  while (tokens.nextToken() != tokens.TT_EOF) {
   String codeString = tokens.sval;
   tokens.nextToken(); int x = (int) tokens.nval;
   tokens.nextToken(); int y = (int) tokens.nval;
   tokens.nextToken(); int z = (int) tokens.nval;
   switch (codeString.charAt(0)) {
     // First character indicates a movie:
     case 'M': v.addElement(new Movie(x, y, z)); break;
     // First character indicates a symphony:
     case 'S': v.addElement(new Symphony(x, y, z)); break;
   }
  }
  stream.close();
  return v;
 }
}
```

595
SIDE TRIP Java's strings differ from the strings of C and C++, because Java's strings are instances of the String class, rather than arrays of characters. In Java, the length of a string is determined by the length instance variable.

In C and C++, you determine length by looking for the first null character in the array. Most programmers believe that Java's approach is simpler from the conceptual perspective, and is easier to work with from the practical perspective.

596 As an illustration of other features of tokenizers, suppose that you have a file that supplies not only movie titles and rating information, but also, optionally, names of poster files, which you learn to use in Chapter 44:

```
"Apocalypse Now"     4  7  3     "apnow.jpg"
"Bedtime for Bonzo"  8  8  7
```

An ordinary tokenizer treats all carriage returns as though they were spaces; it treats double quotation marks as ordinary characters. Accordingly, you need to learn how to alter a tokenizer such that it will recognize carriage returns. You also need to learn how to use double quotation marks to delimit strings that contain embedded spaces.

597 You tell a tokenizer to use a particular character as a delimiter by using the quoteChar method.

For example, to revise the tokens tokenizer to use double quotation marks to delimit strings, you write the following:

```
tokens.quoteChar((int) '"')
```

Note that the double quotation character, ", must be cast to an int before you hand that character over as the argument to quoteChar.

598
The reason that quoteChar requires an integer argument is that the low-level methods that read from files actually read bytes from those files, and those bytes are immediately translated into integer values. Tokenizers translate the integer values into characters only later, after the delimiters have done all their work.

599 You tell a tokenizer to recognize carriage returns using the eolIsSignificant method with true as the argument:

```
tokens.eolIsSignificant(true);
```

Then, you can check the next token to see whether it is equal to the TT_EOL instance variable of the tokenizer.

600 Now, you can write the following movie-reading program, which captures movie names, ratings, and poster files, if any:

```
import java.io.*;
import java.util.*;
public class Demonstrate {
 public static void main(String argv[]) throws IOException {
  Vector mainVector;
  mainVector = Auxiliaries.readMovieFile("input.data");
  for (Iterator i = mainVector.iterator(); i.hasNext();) {
   System.out.println(((Movie) i.next()).rating());
  }
 }
}
```

```
import java.io.*;
import java.util.*;
public class Auxiliaries {
 public static Vector readMovieFile(String fileName) throws IOException
{
  FileInputStream stream = new FileInputStream(fileName);
  InputStreamReader reader = new InputStreamReader(stream);
  StreamTokenizer tokens = new StreamTokenizer(reader);
  tokens.quoteChar((int) '"');
  tokens.eolIsSignificant(true);
  Vector v = new Vector();

  while (tokens.nextToken() != tokens.TT_EOF) {
   String nameString = tokens.sval;
   tokens.nextToken(); int x = (int) tokens.nval;
   tokens.nextToken(); int y = (int) tokens.nval;
   tokens.nextToken(); int z = (int) tokens.nval;
   Movie m = (new Movie(x, y, z));
   m.title = nameString;
   if (tokens.nextToken() == tokens.TT_EOL) {}
   else {m.poster = tokens.sval; tokens.nextToken();}
   v.addElement(m);
  }
  stream.close();
  return v;
 }
}
```

601

SIDE TRIP

Occasionally, you need to denote various special characters. You denote the space character, straightforwardly, as ' '. You denote other characters by using a combination of a **backslash**, \, and a code. In such combinations, the backslash is said to be the **escape character**:

\t	tab
\r	carriage return
\n	line feed
\f	form feed
\b	backspace
\"	double quote
\'	single quote
\\	backslash

The backslash itself appears in the table because you need a way to denote the backslash when you really want a backslash, rather than the escape character.

602

PRACTICE Generalize the program that you were asked to write in Segment 582 such that it records not only game scores, but also opponent names. Assume that the data file includes comments as shown in the following illustration. Have your program record those comments as well.

```
"Cubs"        4    2    "Nearly rained out"
"Yankees"     9    0    "Incredibly exciting"
"Blue Jays"   4    3    "Super boring"
```

603

HIGHLIGHTS

- Strings are constants. You cannot add to, delete from, or change the characters in strings.

- If you want to determine the length of a string, **then** instantiate the following pattern:

  `string .length()`

- If you want to extract a character from a string, **then** instantiate the following pattern:

  `string .charAt( index )`

- If you want to concatenate two strings, to create a new string, **then** instantiate the following pattern:

  `first string + second string`

- If you want to denote a character, **then** surround that character with single quotation marks.

- If you want a tokenizer to return a token for the end of a line, **then** instantiate the following pattern:

  `token variable .eolIsSignificant(true);`

- If you want to know whether the current token represents the end of a line, **then** compare the value produced by nextToken to the TT_EOL instance variable:

  `nextToken's value == token variable .TT_EOL`

- If you want a tokenizer to use the double quotation mark to delimit strings with embedded spaces, **then** instantiate the following pattern:

  `token variable .quoteChar((int) '"');`

32 HOW TO CATCH EXCEPTIONS

604 In Chapter 27, you learned that Java expects you to acknowledge that a method may lead to an error, such as an attempt to open a nonexistent file. Your acknowledgment may appear in the method in the form of the keyword `throws` and the name of the exception class associated with the error. Such an acknowledgment merely passes the problem up to the calling method, which must itself acknowledge the possibility of an error.

In this unit, you learn about a way not only to acknowledge that a method may lead to exceptional behavior, but also to specify the appropriate response to that behavior.

605 If an error occurs, then Java is said to **throw an exception.** Whenever an expression has the potential to cause Java to throw an exception, you can embed that expression in a `try-catch` statement, in which you specify explicitly what Java is to do when an exception actually is thrown.

606 Suppose, for example, that you want to open a file for reading using a `FileInputStream` instance. You can acknowledge that the attempt may throw an exception by embedding the reading expressions in a block following the `try` keyword.

Java stops executing statements in the `try` block as soon as an exception is thrown:

```
try {
  ···    ←─── An attempt to attach a stream to a file occurs here
}
```

607 You specify what to do in the event that the exception is an instance of the `IOException` class by writing the keyword `catch`, followed by a parameter typed by `IOException`, surrounded by parentheses, followed by another block:

```
catch (IOException e) {
  ···
}
```

608 You may want to use the `printStackTrace` method to print a record of the calls leading to the error.

```
catch (IOException e) {
 e.printStackTrace();
}
```

609 Alternatively, you may want to write display statements that include the exception parameter in the `catch` block:

```
catch (IOException e) {
 System.out.println(e);
}
```

Such statements produce informative comments, such as the following:

Name of missing file

java.io.FileNotFoundException: input.data

610 Note that exceptions form a class hierarchy. The exception actually thrown when a file does not exist is an instance of the FileNotFoundException class.

Because the IOException class is a superclass of the FileNotFoundException class, the FileNotFoundException instance is also an instance of the IOException class, enabling the catch block with the IOException parameter to catch FileNotFoundException instances.

A catch block with an Exception parameter will catch instances of any exception.

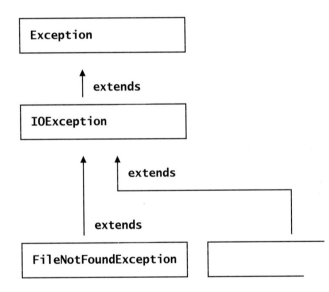

611 If you like, you can write multiple catch blocks so that you can handle different exceptions differently. The catch block actually invoked is the one with a parameter typed by the most specific class of which the exception is an instance.

612 Thus, in the following example, failure to find a file would activate the block associated with the FileNotFoundException class, rather than the one associated with the IOException class:

```
try {
        ◄── An attempt to attach a stream to a file occurs here
}
// More specific exception caught:
catch (FileNotFoundException e) {
 System.out.println("Evidently the input file does not exist.");
}
// More general exception caught:
catch (IOException e) {
 System.out.println("Evidently an input--output error occurred.");
}
```

613 The catch blocks in the following version of the readMovieFile program, which you saw in a previous incarnation in Segment 600, announce where and why an exception is caught:

```
import java.io.*;
import java.util.*;
public class Auxiliaries {
 public static Vector readMovieFile(String fileName) {
  Vector v = new Vector();
  try {
   FileInputStream stream = new FileInputStream(fileName);
   if (stream == null) {return null;}
   InputStreamReader reader = new InputStreamReader(stream);
   StreamTokenizer tokens = new StreamTokenizer(reader);
   tokens.quoteChar((int) '"');
   tokens.eolIsSignificant(true);
   while (tokens.nextToken() != tokens.TT_EOF) {
    String nameString = tokens.sval;
    tokens.nextToken(); int x = (int) tokens.nval;
    tokens.nextToken(); int y = (int) tokens.nval;
    tokens.nextToken(); int z = (int) tokens.nval;
    Movie m = (new Movie(x, y, z));
    m.title = nameString;
    if (tokens.nextToken() == tokens.TT_EOL) {}
    else {m.poster = tokens.sval; tokens.nextToken();}
    v.addElement(m);
   }
   stream.close();
  }
  catch (FileNotFoundException e) {System.out.println(e);}
  catch (IOException e) {System.out.println(e);}
  return v;
 }
}
```

This version of the Auxiliaries definition, which contains a definition of readMovieFile, serves up to Segment 45, where the FileInputStream mechanism is replaced by a more general mechanism that is better suited to handling files accessed via a network browser.

614 If a program fails to find a file, the reason may be that the file has not yet appeared, and the right approach to take is to try again. For example, the following variation on the program shown in Segment 613 loops if the file does not exist, because the catch expression continues to reset the tryAgain variable to true:

```java
import java.io.*;
import java.util.*;
public class Auxiliaries {
 public static Vector readMovieFile(String fileName) {
  boolean tryAgain = true;
  Vector v = new Vector();
  while (tryAgain) {
    try {
     tryAgain = false;
     // Rest of try expression as in Segment 613 ...
    }
    catch (FileNotFoundException e) {
     tryAgain = true;
    }
    catch (IOException e) {
     System.out.println(e);
    }
  }
  return v;
 }
}
```

615 The Java compiler attempts to be smart, anticipating potential exceptions and forcing you to acknowledge those potential exceptions.

Sometimes, however, Java does not detect a potential exception at compile time, but encounters an exception at run time nevertheless. Java compiles the following demonstration program without complaint, but throws an ArrayIndexOutOfBoundsException, because the array has no element indexed by 3:

```java
public class Demonstrate {
 public static void main(String argv[]) {
  int [] threeElements = {1, 2, 3};
  for (int counter = 0; counter < 4; ++counter) {
   System.out.println(threeElements[counter]);
  }
 }
}
```

616 As you work with Java programs, you are likely to encounter other exception instances that you will either have to acknowledge or want to handle. Such exceptions include, for example, instances of the `NegativeArraySizeException` class, thrown by attempts to create arrays with a negative number of elements, and instances of the `ArithmeticException` class, thrown by attempts to divide by zero.

617 If you want a program to stop when an exception is thrown, you use `exit`—a class method of the `System` class, to which you supply an argument of 0:

```
catch (IOException e) {
  System.exit(0);
}
```

When executed, the `exit` statement terminates the program and returns its argument either to the calling program or, if there is no calling program, to the operating system. By general convention, an argument of 0 is taken by the calling program or the operating system to mean that no special action is to be taken.

618 Occasionally, you may want to have a block of statements executed after a `try` statement, whether or not an exception is thrown, activating a `catch` block.

Accordingly, Java provides for `finally` blocks, which are executed after the `try` block is executed, along with any `catch` block that happens to be executed:

```
try {
  ...
}
catch ( exception-class name  e) {
  ...
}
finally {
  clean up statements
}
```

619 You can create and throw your own exceptions. To create an exception, you extend the `Exception` class, as illustrated in the following example:

```
public class StrangeDataException extends Exception {
}
```

Once you have defined an exception class, you can throw instances:

```
throw (new StrangeDataException())
```

Those instances are caught by corresponding catchers:

```
catch (StrangeDataException e) {
  ...
}
```

Amend the program that you were asked to write in Segment 602 such that it creates and throws instances of the StrangeDataException class whenever a baseball score is either negative or greater than 50. Have your program catch such exceptions and then display a brief explanation before terminating itself.

- If you want to catch an exception, **then** instantiate the following pattern:

```
try {
  ...
  Statement with potential to throw exception
  ...
}
catch (exception-class name  parameter) {
  exception-handling statements
}
```

- If you want to catch input–output exceptions, **then** write a try–catch statement focused on the FileNotFoundException or IOException class.

- If you want to shut down a program, **then** write the following statement:

```
System.exit(0);
```

- If you want to add clean-up statements to a try statement, **then** add a finally block by instantiating the following pattern:

```
finally {
  clean-up statements
}
```

33 HOW TO WORK WITH OUTPUT FILE STREAMS

622 In Chapter 27, you learned how to read information from a humanly readable text file. Now, you learn to write information into a humanly readable text file.

623 Much of the required machinery for writing into a file runs parallel to the required machinery for reading from a file.

First, you connect to an output file by creating an instance of the `FileOutputStream` class, also known as a **file output stream,** for a specified file. The following is an example in which the file specification happens to be `"output.data"`, and the file output stream is assigned to `stream`:

File specification

```
FileOutputStream stream = new FileOutputStream("output.data");
```

624 Given a `FileOutputStream` instance, you can write 1 byte at a time to that stream. You are more likely to want to be able to write characters and character strings to the stream, however, so you must declare a `PrintWriter` variable and create a `PrintWriter` instance from a `FileOutputStream` instance:

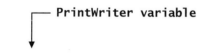

PrintWriter variable

```
PrintWriter writer = new PrintWriter(stream);
```

FileOutputStream instance

625 Once you have a `PrintWriter` instance, you can write strings to that stream, using the `print` and `println` methods.

626 It is good programming practice to **flush** print writers and file output streams when you are finished with them.

You flush a print writer to ensure that any buffered characters are actually written to the stream's destination. You do flushing by using a flush statement:

```
writer.flush();
```

You close file output streams to release system resources. You do closing by using the same sort of `close` statement that you use to close file input streams:

```
stream.close();
```

627 You can use the program in Segment 613 to read movie script, acting, and direction ratings from file. Then, in the following program, you can write overall movie ratings into another file:

```java
import java.io.*;
import java.util.*;
public class Demonstrate {
 public static void main(String argv[]) throws IOException {
  FileOutputStream stream = new FileOutputStream("output.data");
  PrintWriter writer = new PrintWriter(stream);
  Vector mainVector;
  mainVector = Auxiliaries.readMovieFile("input.data");
  for (Iterator i = mainVector.iterator(); i.hasNext();) {
   writer.println(((Movie) i.next()).rating());
  }
  writer.flush();
  stream.close();
  System.out.println("File written");
 }
}
```

—————————————— Sample Data ——————————————
"Apocalypse Now"   4 7 3   "apnow.jpg"
"Bedtime for Bonzo"   8 8 7
—————————————————— Result ——————————————————
File written

Once the main method is executed, the file, output.data, contains the following data:

```
14
23
```

628
PRACTICE Amend the program that you were asked to write in Segment 620 so that it catches all exceptions of the StrangeDataException class and responds by writing a brief explanation into an error file.

Your program is not to stop when it encounters an error, instead, It is to record all legitimate scores in a vector.

629
HIGHLIGHTS

- If you want to tell Java that you intend to work with file input or file output streams, **then** include the following line in your program:

```
import java.io.*;
```

- If you want to write to an output file, **then** instantiate the following pattern:

```
FileOutputStream stream variable
  = new FileOutputStream( file specification );
PrintWriter printer variable
  = new PrintWriter( stream variable );
```

- If you want to write data to a `PrintWriter` instance, **then** instantiate one of the following patterns:

```
print writer .print( information to be printed );
print writer .println( information to be printed );
```

- If you have finished writing to a file stream via a print writer, **then** flush the print writer and close the file by instantiating the following patterns:

```
print writer variable .flush();
file stream variable .close();
```

34 HOW TO WRITE AND READ VALUES USING THE SERIALIZABLE INTERFACE

630 In Chapter 27 and Chapter 33, you learned how to read data from and write data to humanly readable text files. Storing data in text files has serious disadvantages, however. For example, to prepare programs that write values to text files, you must decide how to represent values as character strings, and you must write programs that translate values into such character strings. Then, you must write programs that translate character strings back into values.

Fortunately, Java offers methods that handle details of writing and reading for you. If you use these methods, instead of handling writing and reading details yourself, you simplify your programs, you store data more compactly, and you store and retrieve data faster.

631 Java's `writeObject` method writes into a file information about a class instance. Information about the instance to be stored flows **serially** through the `ObjectOutputStream` and `FileOutputStream` instances as though it is flowing through conduits:

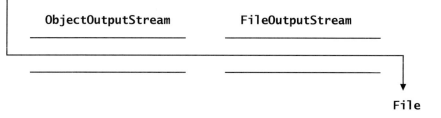

632 After you have stored an instance using Java's `writeObject` method, you can read that instance using `readObject`. Information about the stored instance flows **serially** through the `FileInputStream` instances as though it is flowing through conduits:

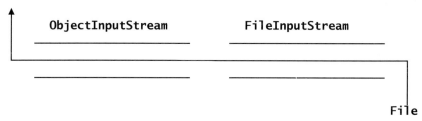

633 Before you can use `writeObject` and `readObject` with the instances of a particular class, you must indicate to the Java compiler that you intend to use instances of that class in **serialized input–output operations**. You use the `Serializable` interface to indicate your intention.

634 Suppose, for example, that you want to use writeObject and readObject with Movie instances. You modify a Movie definition, such as the definition shown in Segment 251, by importing the java.io package and adding the Serializable interface:

```
import java.io.*;
public class Movie extends Attraction implements Serializable {
  // Remainder as in Segment 251 ...
}
```

635 In contrast to the interfaces introduced in Chapter 20, the Serializable interface does not require any method to be defined. Instead, the Serializable interface tells the Java compiler to compile code that enables serialized input–output for the Movie class.

636 Conveniently, Java's Vector class implements the Serializable interface. Thus, inasmuch as the Movie class, defined in Segment 634, also implements the Serializable interface, you can use writeObject and readObject to write entire vectors of movies serially and to read them back serially, as shown in the following demonstration program. The readData method defined in Segment 613 provides the initial vector of Movie instances from a text file:

```
import java.io.*;
import java.util.*;
public class Demonstrate {
 public static void main(String argv[])
   throws IOException, ClassNotFoundException {
   // Read from text file:
   Vector mainVector = Auxiliaries.readMovieFile("input.data");
   // Write out vector of Movie instances:
   FileOutputStream fileOutputStream
    = new FileOutputStream("transit.data");
   ObjectOutputStream objectOutputStream
    = new ObjectOutputStream(fileOutputStream);
   objectOutputStream.writeObject(mainVector);
   objectOutputStream.close();
   // Read in vector of Movie instances:
   FileInputStream fileInputStream
     = new FileInputStream("transit.data");
   ObjectInputStream objectInputStream
     = new ObjectInputStream(fileInputStream);
   mainVector = (Vector) objectInputStream.readObject();
   // Test vector:
   for (Iterator i = mainVector.iterator(); i.hasNext();) {
     System.out.println(((Movie) i.next()).rating());
}}}
```

637 Methods that use writeObject and readObject must either throw IOException and ClassNotFoundException or deal with those exceptions in try–catch statements.

638 Whenever you write a vector of instances using `writeObject`, each element must belong to a class that implements the Serializable interface.

639
SIDE TRIP
You can, in principle, write more than one class instance into a file, but then, to read such a file, your program must know how many class instances have been written, because there is no direct way to test an `ObjectInputStream` instance to determine whether all instances have been read.

Thus, you could use `writeObject` to store a collection of `Movie` instances; however, to read those instances using `readObject`, your program either would have to know how many movies have been written or else make use of the exception throwing done by `readObject` when it tries to read past the end of a file.

Evidently, the designers of Java believe that, if you have a collection of instances to store, you should store it as a collection, rather than store each element of the collection individually.

640
HIGHLIGHTS

- If you want to write and read instances of a particular class, **then** define that class to be an implementer of the `Serializable` interface.

- If you want to write an instance of a particular class, **then** instantiate the following pattern:

```
FileOutputStream output stream
 = new FileOutputStream(" file name ");
ObjectOutputStream object stream
 = new ObjectOutputStream( output stream );
...
object stream .writeObject( instance );
...
output stream .close();
```

- If you want to read an instance of a particular class, **then** instantiate the following pattern:

```
FileInputStream input stream
 = new FileInputStream(" file name ");
ObjectInputStream object stream
 = new ObjectInputStream( input stream );
...
object stream .readObject();
...
input stream .close();
```

35 HOW TO MODULARIZE PROGRAMS USING COMPILATION UNITS AND PACKAGES

641 In Chapter 18, you learned about how to organize, into inheritance hierarchies, classes that share instance variables and instance methods. In this chapter, you learn how to organize, into modular compilation units and packages, classes that work together to solve problems.

642 Consider a demonstration program that consists of five classes. The Attraction class, along with the Movie class and Symphony class, form a class hierarchy that extends the Object class. The Auxiliaries and Demonstrate classes, which stand apart from the Attraction class hierarchy, also extend the Object class:

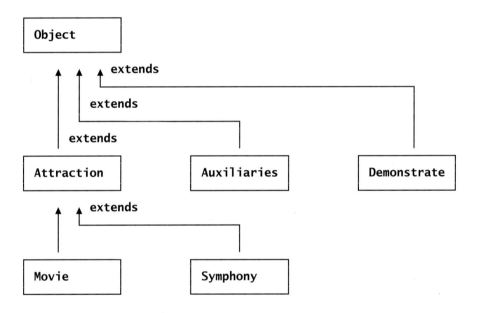

643 Whenever multiple classes can be viewed as functionally related—such as the multiple classes that support entertainment applications—you should use one of Java's mechanisms that enable you to bring together those classes into a **module** that you can develop and maintain independently. Programs divided into modules are said to be **modular**.

644 One way to bring together classes into modules is to define them in the same file. Note, however, that only one such class can be public—the one whose name is the same as the name of the file.

You could, for example, bring the Demonstrate, Auxiliaries, Attraction, Movie, and Symphony classes into one file, named Demonstrate, with only Demonstrate marked as public.

Because all classes in a file are compiled together, with all class names accessible in all other classes, files are said to be **compilation units**.

645 The argument against bringing together many classes into one compilation unit is that only one of the classes can be accessible universally. Accordingly, most Java programmers place each class in its own compilation unit—said another way, they ensure that each file contains just one class definition.

646 Another way to bring together classes into modules is to place them in single-class compilation units, which you then bring together into a common **package**, using a `package` statement at the beginning of each such compilation unit. In general, the package names that appear in package statements consist of components separated by dots:

```
package onto.java.entertainment;
public abstract class Attraction {
 // Remainder of class definition ...
}
```

```
package onto.java.entertainment;
public class Movie extends Attraction {
 // Remainder of class definition ...
}
```

```
package onto.java.entertainment;
public class Symphony extends Attraction {
 // Remainder of class definition ...
}
```

```
package onto.java.entertainment;
import java.io.*;
import java.util.*;
public class Auxiliaries {
 // Remainder of class definition ...
}
```

647 The components of package names always correspond to the final components of the path that specifies the directory in which the corresponding compilation units reside. The initial components of the path are taken from the value of CLASSPATH, an **operating-system environment variable**. Suppose, for example, that you are working in a Windows environment, that the value of the CLASSPATH environment variable includes the d:\phw path, and that the package name for your program is onto.java.entertainment. Then, the compilation units of the package reside in the d:\phw\onto\java\entertainment directory:

```
      ┌── From the CLASSPATH variable
      │
      │        ┌── From the package name
      │        │
      ▼        ▼
   ─────── ────────────────────────
   d:\phw\onto\java\entertainment
```

If you are working in a UNIX environment, the value of the CLASSPATH environment variable includes /usr/phw, and the package name is onto.java.entertainment, then the compilation units of the package are in the /usr/phw/onto/java/entertainment directory.

648 When you set the CLASSPATH environment variable, you must provide for all the directories that contain classes in the value of the CLASSPATH variable, including the directory that is the current directory when you are testing programs. Accordingly, the following is a typical value for the CLASSPATH variable in a Windows environment:

```
┌─ An author has many package names relative to d:\phw
│
│                           ┌─ Include the current directory,
│                           │   whatever it may be
▼                           ▼
─────────                   ───
d:\phw;d:\phw\onto\java;  .
        ─────────────────
                ▲
                └─ Same author uses this directory to test
                   programs that do not use package statements
```

SIDE TRIP 649 On machines that run Windows NT, you set the CLASSPATH variable in the System Properties tab of the System window found in the Control Panel.

On machines that run Windows 95, you set the CLASSPATH variable as follows:

set CLASSPATH=d:\phw;d:\phw\onto\java;.

On machines running the most popular versions of UNIX, you set the CLASSPATH variable as follows:

setenv CLASSPATH d:/usr/phw:/user/phw/onto/java:.

650 The correspondence between package names and path names enables Java to find compilation units specified in import statements. Java simply combines each path specified by the CLASSPATH variable with the path specified by the package name, then searches each combination for the package's compilation units.

SIDE TRIP 651 Dots are used in package names, rather than path-name separators, so as to ensure portability. The translation from package names to path names is done locally in an operating-system–dependent way.

652 As you learned in Segment 479, when you use a package name with an asterisk in an import statement, you tell Java you are interested in all the package's public classes, and in the compilation units in which those classes appear, as follows:

```
                        ┌─ No compilation unit mentioned;
                        │   all compilation units available
                        ▼
import onto.java.entertainment.*
```

Alternatively, you can specify a specific public class, and the compilation unit in which it appears, in place of the asterisk:

```
                            ┌─  A compilation unit mentioned;
                            │   one compilation unit available
                            ▼
                        ──────────

import onto.java.entertainment.Attraction
```

653 Once you have imported an entire package, or just one compilation unit, from a package, you can refer by name to the single public class in each compilation unit. For example, once you have loaded the onto.java.entertainment package, you can refer to the various public classes found in the compilation units:

```
import onto.java.entertainment.*;
import java.io.*;
import java.util.*;
public class Demonstrate {
 public static void main(String argv[]) {
  Vector mainVector;
  mainVector = Auxiliaries.readMovieFile("input.data");
  for (Iterator i = mainVector.iterator(); i.hasNext();) {
   System.out.println(((Movie)(i.next())).rating());
  }
 }
}
```

654 An import statement is not required if you prepend package names to your class names:

```
import java.io.*;
import java.util.*;
public class Demonstrate {
 public static void main(String argv[]) {
  Vector mainVector;
  mainVector =
    onto.java.entertainment.Auxiliaries.readMovieFile("input.data");
  for (Iterator i = mainVector.iterator(); i.hasNext();) {
   System.out.println(
    ((onto.java.entertainment.Movie)(i.next())).rating());
  }
 }
}
```

655 Add to the Entertainment package the Game class that you were asked to write in Seg-
PRACTICE ment 582. Incorporate into the Auxiliaries class defined in the Entertainment package the file-reading method, readScoreVector, that you were asked to write in Segment 582.

- If you want to bring classes together into modules, **then** you can define them in one file, producing a compilation unit. Only one class in a compilation unit can be public, however.

- If you want to bring classes together into modules, **then** you can define them in one directory, declaring them to be part of the same package, with a `package` statement:

  package `package name` **;**

- Package names consist of dot-separated components. Each component corresponds to a component of the path that leads to the directory that contains the package's compilation units; the beginning of that path is specified in the value of the CLASSPATH operating-system variable.

36 HOW TO COMBINE PRIVATE VARIABLES AND METHODS WITH PACKAGES

657 You learned about Java's private, protected, and public machinery in Segment 15, and you learned about Java's package machinery in Chapter 35. In this unit, you learn how these two work together to manage access to variables and methods.

658 Suppose that the `minutes` instance variable lies in the private part of the `Attraction` class's definition. Then, access to that variable is possible only via methods defined in the `Attraction` class:

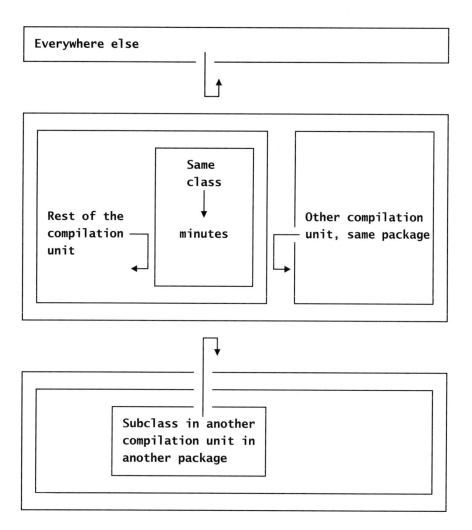

659 You can arrange the access limits shown in Segment 658 by marking the variable with the `private` keyword.

Alternatively, you can mark an instance variable with the `protected` keyword, rather than with the `public` or `private` keywords.

660 Instance variables and instance methods in the protected part of a class definition are accessible from instance methods that are defined in the same class, compilation unit, or package. Protected instance variables and methods are also accessible from any subclass of the class in which they are declared, whether or not that subclass is in the same package. They are not, however, generally accessible from other packages:

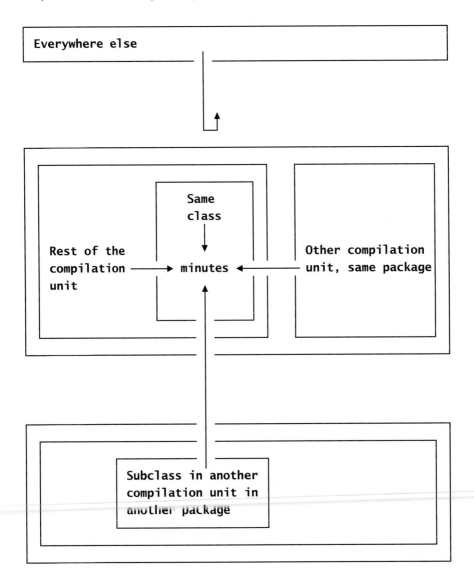

661 The protected `minutes` instance variable is available not only to methods defined in the `Attraction` class definition, but also to methods defined in the `Movie` and `Symphony`

classes, because those classes are subclasses of the `Attraction` class and because both are defined in the same package as the `Attraction` class.

The `minutes` instance variable is also accessible to methods defined in the `Auxiliaries` class, because that class is in the same package as the `Attraction` class.

662   One other possibility remains: If you use none of the protection keywords—`public`, `protected`, or `private`—then you provide access to the rest of the compilation unit and to the rest of the package, but to nothing else:

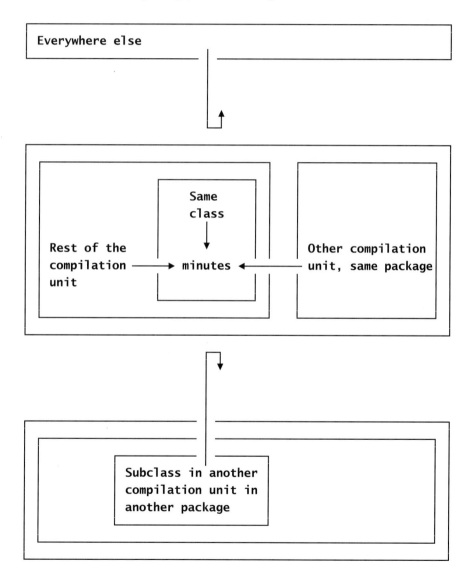

663   Of course, if you mark a variable or method with the `public` keyword, you provide access from all compilation units in all packages:

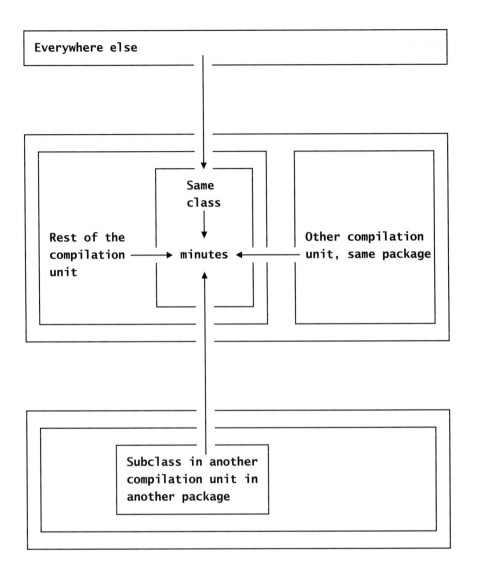

664   Thus, Java allows the public, private, or protected keywords, or nothing, in the place where access is determined:

```
public class Attraction {
 // Define one-parameter constructor:
 public Attraction (int m) {minutes = m;}
 // Define getter:
 public int getMinutes () {return minutes;}
 // Define setter:
 public void setMinutes (int m) {minutes = m;}
 // Declare instance variable:
 keyword  int minutes;
}
```

665 A class itself either is or is not marked public. If it is marked public, then it is accessible from other packages; if it is not marked public, then it is accessible from only the package in which it is defined.

666 Describe and explain what happens when you run the following program:

```
public class Demonstrate {
 public static void main (String argv[]) {
  new Test();
 }
}
class Test {
 Test () {
  System.out.println("Creating a Test instance");
 }
}
```

Then, describe and explain what happens when you mark the zero-parameter constructor with each of the public, protected, and private keywords.

667

- If you want to provide universal access to instance variables and methods, **then** mark them with the public keyword.

- If you want to limit access to instance variables and methods to the package in which they are introduced and to subclasses of the class in which they are introduced, **then** mark them with the protected keyword.

- If you want to limit access to instance variables and methods to the package in which they are introduced, **then** do not mark them with the public, protected, or private keywords.

- If you want to limit access to instance variables and methods to the class in which they are introduced, **then** mark them with the private keyword.

37 HOW TO CREATE WINDOWS AND TO ACTIVATE LISTENERS

668   Programs that have graphical user interfaces are much more powerful than programs that provide services via character-only interfaces, because graphical user interfaces engage the human visual problem-solving faculty. Accordingly, you need to learn how to build graphical user interfaces.

In this chapter, you learn how to create windows; in the next chapter, you learn how to draw lines of the sort needed to produce a meterlike drawing, which eventually becomes part of a movie-rating display. When you have completed this chapter and the next two, you will know the essentials of drawing. That knowledge will enable you to understand how to produce displays such as the following:

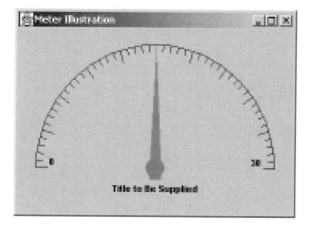

At first, you will be limited to drawing with wired-in data. You learn how to incorporate data from a movie-describing file in Chapter 45.

669   **GUI** is an acronym for **graphical user interface**. Much of the work involved in constructing a GUI centers on the creation of class instances that have a graphical representation, which, in the vernacular of Java, are called **components**. Java's component catalog includes components such as buttons, choice lists, and text fields.

Certain components allow you to nest other containers inside their boundaries; such components are called **containers**.

A **window** is a container's graphical representation. Informally, *window* is used as a synonym for *container*.

670   Component classes are subclasses of the `Component` class; container classes are subclasses of the `Container` class. The following shows the locations of the `Component` and `Container` classes in the Java class hierarchy, as well as the locations of other key classes, `JFrame`, `JApplet`, `JComponent`, and `JPanel`, which are the focus of this chapter, Chapter 43, and Chapter 39.

The class hierarchy shows that all containers are components, but not all components are containers. It so happens that all the components used in this book are containers because they have Container as a superclass.

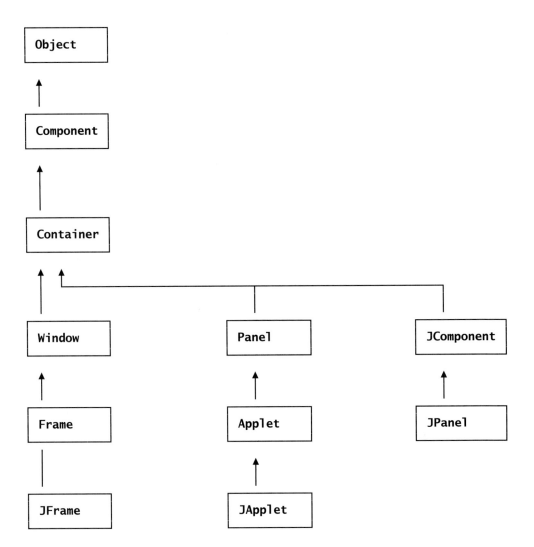

671
SIDE TRIP Note that one of the classes shown in Segment 670 is the Window class. Hence, the word *window* is ambiguous: A window is both the graphical representation of a component and an instance of the Window class. Fortunately, there is no occasion in this book to use the Window class directly, so the word *window* always refers to the graphical representation of a component.

672 As indicated in the class hierarchy shown in Segment 670, JFrame is a subclass of Frame; JApplet is a subclass of Applet; JComponent is a subclass of Component; and JPanel is a subclass of JComponent.

Each of the classes beginning with the letter J is called a **swing** class. Swing classes were developed later than their nonswing superclasses, and because they offer more features and more flexibility, you should use them rather than nonswing analogs.

673 The `Component` and `Container` classes reside in the `java.awt` package; the `java.awt` package is a key part of Java's application programmer's interface (**API**).

The principal swing classes—`JFrame`, `JApplet`, `JComponent`, and `JPanel`—reside in the `javax.swing` package. The `javax.swing` package is another key part of Java's API.

674 The `java.awt` package takes its name from the abstract window toolkit.

SIDE TRIP
The `javax.swing` package takes its name from a demonstration in which a cartoon creature is seen riding on a swing.

675 A component is said to be a **heavyweight component** if it uses programs provided by your SIDE TRIP computer's operating system to display buttons, choice lists, text fields, and the like. Such operating-system programs are said to be the components's **peers**.

A swing component is said to be a **lightweight component** because it does the high-level display work itself, rather than relying on a program provided by your computer's operating system.

Restricting your display work to the swing classes has two major benefits. First, the swing classes offer more features than you find in the common denominator of the popular operating systems. Second, the swing classes offer selectable look and feel. If you use only swing-class components, you can easily have your program look as though it is running on the operating system whose look you prefer.

676 You should never mix heavyweight and lightweight components; a heavyweight compo-SIDE TRIP nent will always hide all lightweight components that occupy the same display area. If your program creates, for example, an instance of the `JPopupMenu` class, you will not see that instance if it lies in an area covered by a heavyweight component, such an instance of the `Canvas` class.

Accordingly, you should do your drawing and text layout on instances of the `JComponent` class, rather than of the `Canvas` class, even though the name might pull you toward the `Canvas` class.

677 You gain access to the classes of the `java.awt` and `javax.swing` packages using the following import statements:

```
import java.awt.*;
import javax.swing.*;
```

By using classes in the `java.awt` and `javax.swing` packages, you gain access to sophisticated graphical machinery.

678 The component and container machinery found in the `java.awt` and `javax.swing` packages is operating-system independent. If you use these packages to construct a GUI for a program, that program will run without change under the UNIX, Windows, or Macintosh operating systems, and you can adapt the program to run as an applet hosted by a web browser, as described in Chapter 44.

679 The following is a simple program that creates a small, titled window and nothing more—the program does not even provide a means to terminate itself:

```
import javax.swing.*;
public class Demonstrate {
 public static void main (String argv []) {
   JFrame frame = new JFrame("Movie Application");
   frame.setSize(350, 150);
   frame.show();
 }
}
```

680 JFrame is an acronym for Java **Frame**. Because the JFrame class is a subclass of the Frame class, the Window class, and the Container class, as indicated in Segment 670, you can refer to an instance of the JFrame class, or instance of subclasses of that class, as a **jframe, frame, window,** or **container.**

You can call a JFrame instance a *jframe* when you want to be precise; you can call the same JFrame instance a *frame* when you are thinking of it as a foundation for an application; you can call the same instance a *window* when you are thinking of it in terms of its graphical representation; and you can call it a *container* when you think of it as a window in which other components appear.

681 The argument of the JFrame constructor, "Movie Application", shown in Segment 679, supplies the title for the window associated with the container. The setSize method fixes the size of the window using width and height arguments. The show method displays the window, which otherwise would exist, but would not be visible. Working together, those methods produce the following window:

682 The program shown in Segment 679 does not terminate. Like the sorcerer's apprentice, it has no way to shut down operations.

To arrange for Java to shut down operations, you need to learn about *events* and *listeners*.

683 In ordinary usage, an **event** is a state change at an instant in time. In the vernacular of programming, there are two type of events. In this chapter, you learn about events associated with a window, such as mouse clicks and key presses. In Chapter 49, you learn about events associated with variable-value changes.

The word *event* also refers to an instance of the EventObject class, or to a subclass of that class. Such an instance describes a state change at an instant in time. That is, an event (a Java class instance) describes a event (a state change at an instant of time).

684 The key to understanding how Java deals with events is to understand **listener classes**. You define listener classes by extending other listener classes or by implementing listener interfaces. Either way, you are sure to include certain prescribed method definitions in those classes.

Suppose, for example, that you define a listener class that extends the WindowListener interface. That interface requires you to define a windowClosing method, among others. You can define your windowClosing method, as shown later, in Segment 685, to shut down your application.

Once you have defined a listener class, you can connect instances of your listener class to your application's window-displaying frame. Then, Java calls your windowClosing method whenever a user of your application's window-displaying frame clicks the window's close button.

685 Once you understand the general explanation in Segment 684, you are ready for the details.

The first step in preparing an application to respond to a click on a window's close button is to define a listener class, such as the following. The WindowListener interface requires you to define various methods, one of which is the windowClosing method. You define that method to shut down the application; you define the others with empty, do-nothing bodies.

Note that you must import the classes in the java.awt.event package whenever you want to define a class that implements the WindowListener interface.

```
import java.awt.event.*;
public class ApplicationClosingWindowListener implements WindowListener
{
 public void windowClosing(WindowEvent e) {System.exit(0);}
 public void windowActivated(WindowEvent e) {}
 public void windowClosed(WindowEvent e) {}
 public void windowDeactivated(WindowEvent e) {}
 public void windowDeiconified(WindowEvent e) {}
 public void windowIconified(WindowEvent e) {}
 public void windowOpened(WindowEvent e) {}
}
```

686 The `windowClosing` method shown in Segment 685 returns no value; and that method has one parameter, an instance of the `WindowEvent` class, which happens to be ignored in the `windowClosing` method, as defined.

In general, however, event parameters are extremely important. In Segment 925, for example, you learn that such parameters allow you to determine exactly which component has generated an event, in situations where multiple components could have generated an event.

687 The second step in preparing an application to respond to a click on a window's close button is to connect a listener instance to your application frame. That is, you connect, using `addWindowListener`, an instance of the listener defined in Segment 685 to a frame such as the one introduced in Segment 679:

```
import javax.swing.*;
public class Demonstrate {
  public static void main (String argv []) {
    JFrame frame = new JFrame("Movie Application");
    frame.setSize(350, 150);
    frame.addWindowListener(new ApplicationClosingWindowListener());
    frame.show();
  }
}
```

688 Once you have defined a window listener, with an appropriate listener method, and have connected a window-listener instance to a particular window, your application's window-displaying frame is ready to handle mouse clicks on the window-closing button. Whenever there is such a click, Java activates machinery, defined by the programmers that implemented the `JFrame` class, that does the following:

- Creates a `WindowEvent` instance

- Calls the `windowClosing` method with the connected listener as the target and the `WindowEvent` instance as an ordinary argument

Then, the `windowClosing` method—defined in the instance's class—does its intended work, shutting down the application by calling the `exit` method.

689 A graphical summary of the window-closing machinery follows:

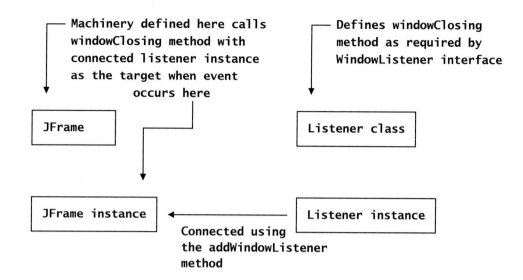

Machinery defined here calls windowClosing method with connected listener instance as the target when event occurs here

Defines windowClosing method as required by WindowListener interface

JFrame

Listener class

JFrame instance ← Listener instance

Connected using the addWindowListener method

690 Remember that you define listener classes, define listener methods, and connect listener instances to components. Built-in machinery calls your connected listener methods when events occur.

691 You have learned about the windowClosing window listener method. More generally, whenever a window is moved, hidden, or exposed, or has a title-bar button clicked, built-in machinery responds by calling **window-listener methods** on **window-listener class instances** connected to the window. The response mechanism also supplies a **window event** as an ordinary argument.

Whenever you click a mouse button with the mouse over a component's graphical representation, built-in machinery responds to that event by calling **mouse listener methods** on **mouse listener class instances** connected to the component. The response mechanism also supplies a **mouse event** as an ordinary argument.

Similarly, whenever you press a key, built-in machinery responds to that event by calling **keyboard listener methods** on **keyboard listener class instances** connected to whatever component is currently responsible for handling key-pressing events. The response mechanism also supplies a **keyboard event** as an ordinary argument.

692 Many interfaces—such as the WindowListener interface—force you to define many methods that do nothing, as shown in Segment 685.

Accordingly, Java frequently provides **adapter classes** that serve as listener-interface companions. Such adapter classes implement all interface-required methods as do-nothing methods: Each such method has an empty body.

Thus, when you want to define a listener that implements only a small subset of the listener-interface methods, you define a subclass of the listener-implementing adapter. Then, you define shadowing methods in your subclass for whatever methods you want to perform real work.

693 For example, you can define the `ApplicationClosingWindowListener` class as a subclass of the Java-provided `WindowAdapter` class, rather than as a class that directly implements the `WindowListener` interface:

```
import java.awt.event.*;
public class ApplicationClosingWindowListener extends WindowAdapter {
 public void windowClosing(WindowEvent e) {System.exit(0);}
}
```

694 Now that you understand how events activate listener methods, you are ready to move most of this work into the constructor of a subclass of the `JFrame` class. This subclass is called the `MovieApplication` class because it will evolve, in easy steps, to become the foundational class of a fully functional movie-rating application.

```
import javax.swing.*;
public class MovieApplication extends JFrame {
 public static void main (String argv []) {
  new MovieApplication("Movie Application");
 }
 public MovieApplication(String title) {
  super(title);
  setSize(350, 150);
  addWindowListener(new ApplicationClosingWindowListener());
  show();
 }
}
```

695 In the definition of the `MovieApplication` class, shown in Segment 694, there is a call to the one-parameter constructor of the superclass, the `JFrame` class. As explained in Segment 300, the first statement in a constructor can be a call to another constructor, which in the `MovieApplication` class is a call to the one-parameter `JFrame` constructor. The title of the window is the argument.

696 The definition in Segment 694 specifies that, when Java creates a `MovieApplication` instance, Java also creates an instance of the `ApplicationClosingWindowListener` class, and connects the two instances, enabling program termination.

697
SIDE TRIP

You may, if you wish, create a subclass of the `ApplicationClosingWindowListener` that alters or supplements the behavior of the superclass. For example, suppose that you want your users to be told when Java is about to exit from an application. Then, you could define the following `PausingWindowListener` subclass. There is no need to define most of the methods required by the `WindowListener` interface, because all but one of those methods is defined adequately in the superclass. You do, however, wish to define `windowClosing` such that it pops up a message window, arranged by the `JOptionPane` class method, `showMessageDialog`. After you click your acknowledgement, `windowClosing` calls the `windowClosing` method in the `ApplicationClosingWindowListener` superclass, which shuts down the application.

```
import javax.swing.*;
import java.awt.event.*;
public class PausingWindowListener
        extends ApplicationClosingWindowListener {
 private MovieApplication application;
 public PausingWindowListener (MovieApplication a) {
  application = a;
 }
 public void windowClosing(WindowEvent e) {
  JOptionPane.showMessageDialog(application, "Shutting down...");
  super.windowClosing(e);
 }
}
```

698
SIDE TRIP
Programming languages that are not object oriented, such as C, support the **callback style** of user-interface programming. When using the callback style, you connect specific procedures to hooks provided for the particular events generated by specific components.

Java offers the much more powerful **delegation style** of user-interface programming. Each component delegates to connected listeners responsibility for responding to events. Use of listeners confers several virtues:

- Listener instances belong to classes that populate a class hierarchy. Thus, the definition of a listener class can refine a portion of the behavior defined in that class's superclasses, while simply reusing other behavior. The example in Segment 697 illustrates.

- Listener instances can be connected and disconnected from components dynamically, at run time.

- Listener instances can maintain state. For example, a listener instance can keep track of the number of times that it responds to an event.

699
PRACTICE
Define a version of the `MovieApplication` class such that deactivating the application window, by clicking in another window, terminates the application.

700
HIGHLIGHTS

- Graphical user interfaces (GUIs) consist of components and containers, both of which have graphical representations.

- An event is a state change at an instant in time. An event is also an instance of the `EventObject` class.

- If you want to respond to an event associated with a component, **then** define a listener class that implements a listener interface, either directly or via a listener adapter, **and then** connect an instance of that listener class to the component. Your listener-class definition will include methods that are actuated in response to events.

38 HOW TO DEFINE INNER CLASSES AND TO STRUCTURE APPLICATIONS

701   Java allows you to embed the definition of one class inside the definition of another. Listener classes, for example, are commonly embedded in application classes, thereby improving program clarity through proximity.

702   Rather than define a listener class, ApplicationClosingWindowListener, as in Segment 685, you can define LocalWindowListener as an **inner class** inside your definition of the MovieApplication class. The two class definitions differ only in that one appears inside the MovieApplication class.

Then, you can alter the constructor of the MovieApplication class defined in Segment 694 to create a LocalWindowListener instance, and you can connect that instance to the movie application frame:

```
import javax.swing.*;
import java.awt.event.*;
public class MovieApplication extends JFrame {
 public static void main (String argv []) {
   new MovieApplication("Movie Application");
 }
 public MovieApplication(String title) {
   super(title);
   setSize(300, 100);
   addWindowListener(new LocalWindowListener());
   show();
 }
 // Define window adapter
 private class LocalWindowListener extends WindowAdapter {
   public void windowClosing(WindowEvent e) {
     System.exit(0);
   }
 }
}
```

703   Because the inner class, LocalWindowListener, defined in Segment 702, is marked with the private keyword, it is not available for use in methods defined for classes other than the MovieApplication class. Thus, you are free to reuse its name in other parts of your program, thus reducing the number of class names that you need to invent.

704   Defining a private subclass of the WindowAdapter class inside the MovieApplication class has two key benefits:

- The definition of the method that responds to a window-closing event appears proximal to the definition of the monitored window.

- You do not need to invent new names for each `WindowListener` subclass. Instead, you can reuse a name you like, such as `LocalWindowListener`.

705
SIDE TRIP
You can reduce still more the number of names that you need to invent by defining inner classes that have no names at all. You use a syntactic convention that replaces the name of the inner class in the new expression with a definition of that inner class. Note that the definition includes the name of the extended class, `WindowAdapter`:

```
import javax.swing.*;
import java.awt.event.*;
public class MovieApplication extends JFrame {
 public static void main (String argv []) {
  new MovieApplication("Movie Application");
 }
 public MovieApplication(String title) {
  super(title);
  setSize(300, 100);
  addWindowListener(new WindowAdapter () {
                      public void windowClosing(WindowEvent e) {
                      System.exit(0);
                     }}
                   );
  show();
 }
}
```

706
SIDE TRIP
Nameless inner classes are not used in the remainder of this book, because many programmers think programs with nameless inner classes are harder to understand than are programs with named inner classes.

707
The program shown in Segment 702 has the following structure:

```
import java.awt.event.*;
public class application name extends JFrame{
 public static void main (String argv []) {
  new application name ();
 }
 public application name () {
  // Call superclass constructor ...
  // Establish window size ...
  // Create and connect class instances ...
  // Show the window ...
 }
 // Define inner classes ...
}
```

In the program shown in Segment 702, there are no class instances other than instances of the MovieApplication and the LocalWindowListener, so there is not much to connect. Nevertheless, both that program and the structure shown in this segment illustrate the following extremely common characteristics:

- The application class is defined to be a subclass of the JFrame class.

- The main method launches the application by creating an instance of the application class.

- The application-class's constructor titles, sizes, and displays a window.

- The application-class's constructor creates class instances as required by the application.

- The application-class's constructor connects appropriately all the required class instances.

708 The main method defined in MovieApplication in Segment 702 generates only one instance of the MovieApplication class. In general, you launch applications by generating a sole instance of an application class.

709

HIGHLIGHTS

- Inner classes are classes defined inside other classes.

- Inner classes are available only in the class in which they are defined, and in that class's subclasses.

- **If** you want to create an application with a window such that the application terminates when the close button is clicked, **then** define a subclass of the JFrame class, **then** define an inner subclass of the WindowListener class, **then** define an appropriate windowClosing method for that inner class, **and then** connect an instance of the inner class to the JFrame subclass instance using addWindowListener:

```
import javax.swing.*;
import java.awt.event.*;
public class application name extends JFrame {
 public static void main (String argv []) {
  new application name (title);
 }
 public application name (String title) {
  super(title);
  setSize(width, height);
  addWindowListener(new LocalWindowListener());
  show();
 }
 // Define window listener
 private class LocalWindowListener extends WindowListener {
  public void windowClosing(WindowEvent e) {
    System.exit(0);
  }
 }
}
```

39 HOW TO DRAW LINES IN WINDOWS

710 In this chapter, you learn how to draw lines that allow you to produce a meterlike drawing, which eventually becomes part of a movie-rating display.

711 You draw on instances of the `JComponent` class, found in the `javax.swing` package. You do not draw on instances of the `Canvas` class, for reasons explained in Segment 676.

712 The `JComponent` class has the following essential properties:

- The definition of the `JComponent` class includes a definition for the `paint` method.

- Whenever you call the `repaint` method, with a component as the target, Java calls the `paint` method on that instance.

- Whenever you iconify, deiconify, or expose a frame's window, Java calls the `paint` method on every component attached to that frame.

713 You create subclasses of the `JComponent` class so that you can shadow the `paint` method of the `JComponent` class. For example, you might define the `Meter` class, anticipating that your new class will evolve into a meter display.

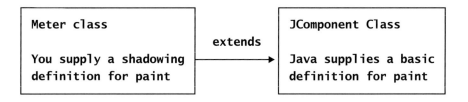

714 Expecting that the `Meter` class will become a real meter, you should follow good programming practice by specifying an interface:

```
public interface MeterInterface {
 // Setters:
 public abstract void setValue (int valueToBeShownByDial) ;
 public abstract void setTitle (String meterLabel) ;
 // Getters:
 public int getValueAtCoordinates (int x, int y) ;
}
```

The `getValueAtCoordinates` method is to return the value that would place the meter's dial nearest the given coordinates; it is put to use in Segment 780.

715 The following definition both extends `JComponent` and implements `MeterInterface`.

Note that the setters required by the MeterInterface include calls to the zero-argument repaint method. You learned in Segment 712 that Java calls paint whenever you call repaint. Thus, calls to the meter setters cause the meter to be redrawn.

```
import java.awt.*;
import javax.swing.*;
public class Meter extends JComponent implements MeterInterface {
 String title = "Title to be Supplied";
 int minValue, maxValue, value;
 // Constructor:
 public Meter (int x, int y) {
  minValue = x;
  maxValue = y;
  value = (y + x) / 2;
 }
 // Setters:
 public void setValue(int v) {value = v; repaint();}
 public void setTitle(String t) {title = t; repaint();}
 // Getter to be defined ...
 // Paint to be defined ...
}
```

716 The argument of a paint method is an instance of the Graphics class:

```
import java.awt.*;
import javax.swing.*;
public class Meter extends JComponent implements MeterInterface {
 String title = "Title to be Supplied";
 int minValue, maxValue, value;
 public Meter (int x, int y) {
  minValue = x;
  maxValue = y;
  value = (y + x) / 2;
 }
 public void setValue(int v) {value = v; repaint();}
 public void setTitle(String t) {title = t; repaint();}
 // Getter to be defined ...
 public void paint(Graphics g) {
  . . .
 }
}
```

717 You never include calls to the paint method in your programs, so you never need to supply the Graphics argument yourself. Whenever you wish to have a window painted, you have repaint called, which calls paint with the necessary argument.

718 A Graphics instance, also known as a **graphics context**, acts as a controller that determines exactly how graphical commands affect the display:

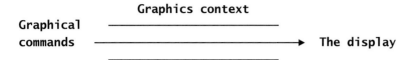

The graphics context determines, for example, color and font properties. You soon learn, in Segment 736, that you can tell a graphics context to have all lines drawn in blue. You then learn, in Segment 745, that you can tell a graphics context to have all text printed in Helvetica.

719 Should you want to draw a simple line, at position (0, 50), with width equal to 100, you use the graphics context as the target of the drawLine method:

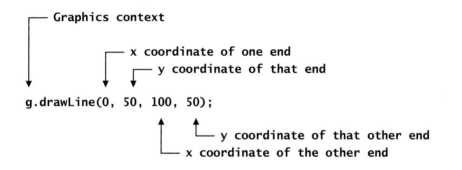

720 The drawLine method appears in the paint method of the Meter class:

```
import java.awt.*;
import javax.swing.*;
public class Meter extends JComponent implements MeterInterface {
 String title = "Title to be Supplied";
 int minValue, maxValue, value;
 public Meter (int x, int y) {
  minValue = x;
  maxValue = y;
  value = (y + x) / 2;
 }
 public void setValue(int v) {value = v; repaint();}
 public void setTitle(String t) {title = t; repaint();}
 // Getter to be defined ...
 public void paint(Graphics g) {
  g.drawLine(0, 50, 100, 50);
  ...
 }
}
```

721 Java draws lines using a coordinate system in which the origin is the upper-left corner. Familiarly, the value of the *x* coordinate increases from 0 as you move right from the left edge of the window. Strangely, the value of the *y* coordinate increases from 0 as you move down from the top edge:

722 You easily can add a short vertical line such that its position along the horizontal line represents the value of the `value` variable. For now, the vertical line lies at midpoint of the horizontal line, with no attention paid to the value of the `value` variable:

```
import java.awt.*;
import javax.swing.*;
public class Meter extends JComponent implements MeterInterface {
 String title = "Title to be Supplied";
 int minValue, maxValue, value;
 public Meter (int x, int y) {
  minValue = x;
  maxValue = y;
  value = (y + x) / 2;
 }
 public void setValue(int v) {value = v; repaint();}
 public void setTitle(String t) {title = t; repaint();}
 // Getter to be defined ...
 public void paint(Graphics g) {
  g.drawLine(0, 50, 100, 50);
  g.drawLine(50, 50, 50, 40);
 }
}
```

723 In Segment 669, you learned that containers contain components and that containers are components.

In particular, a `JFrame` instance is a container that contains a variety of component instances, one of which is the **content pane**, which itself can contain components. The following diagram shows how various components contained by a `JFrame` instance nest together. Note especially that the content pane—generally a `JPanel` instance—can contain components such as `JComponent` instances.

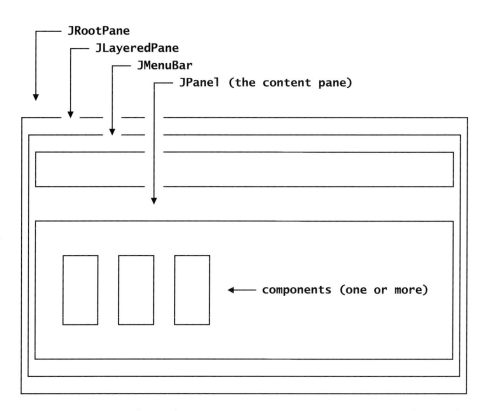

JRootPane

JLayeredPane

JMenuBar

JPanel (the content pane)

← components (one or more)

724
SIDE TRIP A JFrame instance's **layered pane** contains two instances: an optional **menu bar** and a content pane. The **root pane** contains the layered pane and a **glass pane**. You use the glass pane when you need a way to draw above all other panes or to intercept mouse events.

725 To see what the Meter class's paint method draws, you have to attach a Meter class instance to a frame's content pane.

To retrieve the content pane from a frame, you use the getContentPane method with the frame as the target and no arguments. To attach a component to the retrieved content pane, you use the add method with the content pane as the target and two arguments:

getContentPane().add("Center", meter);

The first argument of the add method stipulates where the component is to be placed relative to the content pane, which occupies the entire window, except for space occupied by the menu bar, if any. The second argument supplies the component itself.

726 Thus, to display your nascent meter, you need to augment the MovieApplication class definition provided in Segment 702. You add a declaration that declares an instance variable, meter, you add an initialization statement that creates a Meter instance and assigns that Meter instance to the meter instance variable, and you add an add statement that attaches the meter to the center of the content pane. The meter is created via the two-argument constructor that sets to zero and thirty the minimum and maximum values shown on the meter .

```
import javax.swing.*;
import java.awt.event.*;
public class MovieApplication extends JFrame {
 public static void main (String argv []) {
  new MovieApplication("Movie Application");
 }
 // Declare instance variables:
 private Meter meter;
 // Define constructor
 public MovieApplication(String title) {
  super(title);
  meter = new Meter(0, 30);
  getContentPane().add("Center", meter);
  addWindowListener(new LocalWindowListener());
  setSize(350, 150);
  show();
 }
 // Define window adapter
 private class LocalWindowListener extends WindowAdapter {
  public void windowClosing(WindowEvent e) {
   System.exit(0);
  }
 }
}
```

727 Each frame's content pane is associated with a **layout manager** that specifies how the attached components should be arranged.

The **default layout manager** used with a content pane, the **border layout**, allows five components to be added at positions identified by "Center", "North", "East", "South", and "West". In Segment 726, you learned that "Center" arranges for a component to appear in the center of the window.

728 If you like, you can specify explicitly that you want a content pane to use the border layout. You first create an instance of the BorderLayout class, having imported the java.awt package; then, you add a setLayout statement to the frame's constructor to tie the new border layout to the content pane:

```
import java.awt.*;
import javax.swing.*;
import java.awt.event.*;
public class MovieApplication extends JFrame {
 public static void main (String argv []) {
  new MovieApplication("Movie Application");
 }
 private Meter meter;
```

```
public MovieApplication(String title) {
  super(title);
  meter = new Meter(0, 30);
  getContentPane().setLayout(new BorderLayout());
  getContentPane().add("Center", meter);
  addWindowListener(new LocalWindowListener());
  setSize(350, 150);
  show();
 }
 // Define window adapter
 private class LocalWindowListener extends WindowAdapter {
  public void windowClosing(WindowEvent e) {
    System.exit(0);
}}}}
```

729 Various alternatives to the border-layout manager are described in Appendix E.

SIDE TRIP

730 For a layout manager to place components in a content pane where you want those components, you may have to define getMinimumSize, getMaximumSize, or getPreferredSize methods for the components. Java uses those methods, if they are defined, to determine the ultimate size of each component.

To place a Meter instance in a surrounding MovieApplication's content pane, with other components, you should define getMinimumSize and getPreferredSize methods:

```
import java.awt.*;
import javax.swing.*;
public class Meter extends JComponent implements MeterInterface {
 String title = "Title to be Supplied";
 int minValue, maxValue, value;
 public Meter (int x, int y) {
  minValue = x;
  maxValue = y;
  value = (y + x) / 2;
 }
 public void setValue(int v) {value = v; repaint();}
 public void setTitle(String t) {title = t; repaint();}
 // Getter to be defined ...
 public void paint(Graphics g) {
  g.drawLine(0, 50, 100, 50);
  g.drawLine(50, 50, 50, 40);
 }
 public Dimension getMinimumSize() {return new Dimension(150, 150);}
 public Dimension getPreferredSize() {return new Dimension(150, 150);}
}
```

731 Each getMinimumSize and getPreferredSize method returns a Dimension instance, produced by a call to the Dimension class's constructor with width and height arguments:

Height ———┐
Width ———┐ |
          ↓   ↓

```
public Dimension getMinimumSize() {return new Dimension(150, 150);}
```

732
SIDE TRIP

Many programmers avoid defining `getMinimumSize` and `getPreferredSize` methods on the ground that layout managers should be smart enough to do a good job without advice, and that providing advice, in the form of definitions for `getMinimumSize` and `getPreferredSize` methods, robs the layout manager of potentially useful flexibility.

Other programmers believe that, without a bit of meddling, layout managers act too mysteriously. In this book, we meddle, having found in developing the examples that we need `getMinimumSize` and `getPreferredSize` to ensure that certain components, in certain positions, will appear.

733 Now, it is time for you to learn to produce more sophisticated drawings.

For example, you can obtain an instance of the `Dimension` class using the `getSize` method with a component as the target. The `width` and `height` instance variables of the `Dimension` instance provide the current width and height of the component.

With the width and height in hand, you can draw not just a horizontal line with a simple vertical line at the proper place to represent the value of the `value` instance variable. Instead, you can draw a combination that fills out the window; places the vertical line at the position indicated by the values of the `minValue`, `maxValue`, and `value` variables; scales the vertical line in proportion to the horizontal line; and stays centered, even as you move, or change the size of, the window:

```
import java.awt.*;
import javax.swing.*;
public class Meter extends JComponent implements MeterInterface {
 String title = "Title to be Supplied";
 int minValue, maxValue, value;
 public Meter (int x, int y) {
  minValue = x;
  maxValue = y;
  value = (y + x) / 2;
 }
 public void setValue(int v) {value = v; repaint();}
 public void setTitle(String t) {title = t; repaint();}
 // Getter to be defined ...
```

```
public void paint(Graphics g) {
  // Obtain Dimension instance:
  Dimension d = getSize();
  // Draw:
  int meterWidth = d.width * 3 / 4;
  int meterHeight = meterWidth / 20;
  int dialPosition
    = meterWidth * (value - minValue) / (maxValue - minValue);
  int xOffset = (d.width - meterWidth) / 2;
  int yOffset = d.height / 2;
  g.drawLine(xOffset, yOffset, xOffset + meterWidth, yOffset);
  g.drawLine(xOffset + dialPosition, yOffset,
             xOffset + dialPosition, yOffset - meterHeight);
  }
  public Dimension getMinimumSize() {return new Dimension(150, 150);}
  public Dimension getPreferredSize() {return new Dimension(150, 150);}
}
```

734 You can implement getValueAtCoordinates by reversing the centering and scaling calculations. The method casts the relative x coordinate to a float before division to prevent rounding down to zero, and then uses the round class method in the Math class to round the result returned to the nearest long, which is cast to the required int result:

```
import java.awt.*;
import javax.swing.*;
public class Meter extends JComponent implements MeterInterface {
  String title = "Title to be Supplied";
  int minValue, maxValue, value;
  public Meter (int x, int y) {
    minValue = x;
    maxValue = y;
    value = (y + x) / 2;
  }
  public void setValue(int v) {value = v; repaint();}
  public void setTitle(String t) {title = t; repaint();}
  public int getValueAtCoordinates (int x, int y) {
    Dimension d = getSize();
    int meterWidth = d.width * 3 / 4;
    int xOffset = (d.width - meterWidth) / 2;
    float fraction = (float)(x - xOffset) / meterWidth;
    return (int)Math.round(fraction * (maxValue - minValue) + minValue);
  }
// Define paint as in Segment 733 ...
  public Dimension getMinimumSize() {return new Dimension(150, 150);}
  public Dimension getPreferredSize() {return new Dimension(150, 150);}
}
```

735 Using the definition of the `Meter` class provided in Segment 734, and the definition of the `MovieApplication` class provided in Segment 726, you can produce the following display:

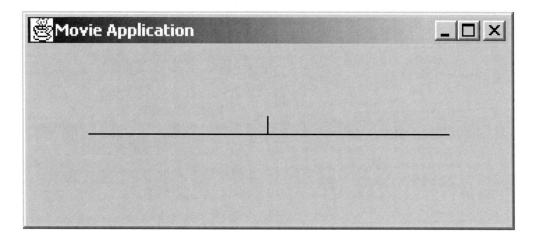

736 You can both get state information from the graphics context and set state information in the graphics context. For example, if you want to draw a blue line, rather than a black one, you easily can modify the example of Segment 734 by adding a statement that provides the graphics context with an instance of the `Color` class.

The definition of the `Color` class includes class variables with values that are instances of the `Color` class itself. One such class variable is the `blue` variable; the value of the `blue` variable is a `Color` instance associated with the color blue:

You use the `setColor` method inside the definition of `paint` to provide the graphics context with a color:

```
public void paint(Graphics g) {
  // Set color:
  g.setColor(Color.blue);
  // Rest of paint definition ...
}
```

737 Whenever you make a change to the value of a graphics-context variable, you should first obtain the current value, and you should restore that value later. For example, you can use the `getColor` method to obtain the current `Color` instance associated with the graphics context. Then, you can change to another `Color` instance temporarily. Finally, you can use the `setColor` method again, this time to restore the graphics context to the original state:

```java
import java.awt.*;
import javax.swing.*;
public class Meter extends JComponent implements MeterInterface {
 String title = "Title to be Supplied";
 int minValue, maxValue, value;
 public Meter (int x, int y) {
  minValue = x;
  maxValue = y;
  value = (y + x) / 2;
 }
 public void setValue(int v) {value = v; repaint();}
 public void setTitle(String t) {title = t; repaint();}
 public int getValueAtCoordinates (int x, int y) {
  Dimension d = getSize();
  int meterWidth = d.width * 3 / 4;
  int xOffset = (d.width - meterWidth) / 2;
  float fraction = (float)(x - xOffset) / meterWidth;
  return (int)Math.round(fraction * (maxValue - minValue) + minValue);
 }
 public void paint(Graphics g) {
  // Obtain current Color instance:
  Color colorHandle = g.getColor();
  // Reset color temporarily:
  g.setColor(Color.blue);
  // Obtain Dimension instance:
  Dimension d = getSize();
  // Draw:
  int meterWidth = d.width * 3 / 4;
  int meterHeight = meterWidth / 20;
  int dialPosition
   = meterWidth * (value - minValue) / (maxValue - minValue);
  int xOffset = (d.width - meterWidth) / 2;
  int yOffset = d.height / 2;
  g.drawLine(xOffset, yOffset, xOffset + meterWidth, yOffset);
  g.drawLine(xOffset + dialPosition, yOffset,
             xOffset + dialPosition, yOffset - meterHeight);
  // Restore color:
  g.setColor(colorHandle);
 }
 public Dimension getMinimumSize() {return new Dimension(150, 150);}
 public Dimension getPreferredSize() {return new Dimension(150, 150);}
}
```

738 The Color class provides class variables for common colors: black, blue, cyan, darkGray, gray, green, lightGray, magenta, orange, pink, red, white, and yellow.

739 You can create your own Color instances via the three-parameter Color constructor. The three arguments specify the intensity of red, green, and blue in the color, on a scale that ranges from 0 to 255. In the following example, the Color constructor produces a Color instance corresponding to dark blue.

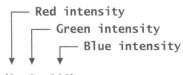

```
new Color(0, 0, 100)
```

To create an instance corresponding to black, you evaluate new Color(0, 0, 0). Similarly, to create an instance corresponding to white, you evaluate new Color(255, 255, 255).

740
PRACTICE Using the Meter class in Segment 737 as a guide, define a class, Thermometer, that produces a drawing that looks like a mercury thermometer with a reading halfway between a given minimum and a given maximum temperature. Use the fillOval method to draw the bulb. Use the drawRect and fillRect methods to draw the rest of the thermometer. All three methods take four arguments: x, y, width, and height.

741
PRACTICE Define a class, TrafficLight, that produces a drawing that looks like a traffic light. Use drawOval, fillOval, and drawRect. All three methods take four arguments: x, y, width, and height. Arrange for each circle to have the proper color.

742
HIGHLIGHTS

- If you want to draw in a window, **then** create a subclass of the JComponent class, by instantiating the following pattern:

```
import java.awt.*;
import javax.swing.*;
public class  subclass name  extends JComponent {
  ...
  public void paint(Graphics g) {
    // Drawing statements go here ...
  }
}
```

and then , attach a new instance of the JComponent subclass to a JFrame instance's content pane by adding the following statement to the frame constructor:

```
getContentPane().add( position ,  subclass instance );
```

The position can be "Center", "North", "East", "South", or "West".

- If you want to draw a line, **then** add a drawLine statement to the paint method defined in a subclass of the JComponent class.

- If you want to determine the size of a component, **then** use the width and height variables of the Dimension instance produced by the getSize method.

- If you want to get the state of the graphics context established by Java for the paint method defined in a subclass of the JComponent class, then use getters such as getColor.

- If you want to set the state of the graphics context established by Java for the paint method defined in a subclass of the JComponent class, then use setters such as setColor.

40 HOW TO WRITE TEXT IN WINDOWS

743 In Chapter 39, you learned how to draw lines on components. In this chapter, you learn how to write text on components.

When you have completed this chapter, you will understand how to create a drawing with both lines and text, using wired-in data. In Segment 45, you learn how to incorporate data into your drawing from a movie-describing file.

744 The following version of `paint` uses the `drawString` method to write the string assigned to the `title` variable, "To be Supplied", with the left side of the T located at x = 100 and the bottom of the T located at y = 50:

```java
import java.awt.*;
import javax.swing.*;
public class Meter extends JComponent implements MeterInterface {
 String title = "Title to Be Supplied";
 int minValue, maxValue, value;
 public Meter (int x, int y) {
  minValue = x;
  maxValue = y;
  value = (y + x) / 2;
 }
 public void setValue(int v) {value = v; repaint();}
 public void setTitle(String t) {title = t; repaint();}
 public int getValueAtCoordinates (int x, int y) {
  Dimension d = getSize();
  int meterWidth = d.width * 3 / 4;
  int xOffset = (d.width - meterWidth) / 2;
  float fraction = (float)(x - xOffset) / meterWidth;
  return (int)Math.round(fraction * (maxValue - minValue) + minValue);
 }
 public void paint(Graphics g) {
  g.drawString(title, 100, 50);
 }
 public Dimension getMinimumSize() {return new Dimension(150, 100);}
 public Dimension getPreferredSize() {return new Dimension(150, 100);}
}
```

745 Naturally, Java allows you to use a variety of **font families**, such as **Roman** and **Helvetica**. Java also allows you to use any of three font **styles**: **plain**, **bold**, and **italic**. And Java allows you to use a variety of font **sizes**, specified in **points**.

To control the font, style, and size, you create instances of the Font class; you then use the `setFont` method to associate those instances with the graphics context.

For example, the following version of the print method writes a string using a 12-point Helvetica bold font:

```
import java.awt.*;
import javax.swing.*;
public class Meter extends JComponent implements MeterInterface {
 String title = "Title to Be Supplied";
 int minValue, maxValue, value;
 public Meter (int x, int y) {
  minValue = x;
  maxValue = y;
  value = (y + x) / 2;
 }
 public void setValue(int v) {value = v; repaint();}
 public void setTitle(String t) {title = t; repaint();}
 public int getValueAtCoordinates (int x, int y) {
  Dimension d = getSize();
  int meterWidth = d.width * 3 / 4;
  int xOffset = (d.width - meterWidth) / 2;
  float fraction = (float)(x - xOffset) / meterWidth;
  return (int)Math.round(fraction * (maxValue - minValue) + minValue);
 }
 public void paint(Graphics g) {
  g.setFont(new Font("Helvetica", Font.BOLD, 12));
  g.drawString(title, 100, 50);
 }
}
```

If you want a plain font, substitute PLAIN for BOLD. If you want an italic font, substitute ITALIC for BOLD.

746 When you write strings, the strings are placed on a **baseline**. Portions of all characters appear above the baseline. Characters such as g and p have **descenders** that appear below the baseline.

The distance by which a font extends above the baseline is that font's **height**, whereas the distance by which the font's characters extends below the baseline is the font's **descent**.

The getFontMetrics method returns an instance of the FontMetrics class. That instance provides height and descent information, via the getHeight and getDescent methods, for the font currently associated with a graphics context. The FontMetrics instance also provides string-width information, via the stringWidth method, for a string argument. The stringWidth method returns the width that the string would occupy if the string were displayed in the font associated with the FontMetrics instance.

You can use information about height and width—using getHeight and stringWidth— to position a string that you draw. In the following example, stringWidth makes it possible to center the string on a baseline located at the middle of the window. The size of the font used varies with the width of the window.

```
import java.awt.*;
import javax.swing.*;
public class Meter extends JComponent implements MeterInterface {
 String title = "Title to Be Supplied";
 int minValue, maxValue, value;
 public Meter (int x, int y) {
  minValue = x; maxValue = y; value = (y + x) / 2;
 }
 public void setValue(int v) {value = v; repaint();}
 public void setTitle(String t) {title = t; repaint();}
// Define getValuesAtCoordinates as in Segment 745 ...
 public void paint(Graphics g) {
  // Determine window size:
  Dimension d = getSize();
  // Prepare font
  int fontSize = d.width / 30;
  g.setFont(new Font("Helvetica", Font.BOLD, fontSize));
  // Write title:
  FontMetrics f = g.getFontMetrics();
  int stringWidth = f.stringWidth(title);
  int xOffset = (d.width - stringWidth) / 2;
  int yOffset = d.height / 2;
  g.drawString(title, xOffset, yOffset);
 }
 public Dimension getMinimumSize() {return new Dimension(150, 100);}
 public Dimension getPreferredSize() {return new Dimension(150, 100);}
}
```

747 The program shown in Segment 746, displayed using the program shown in Segment 726, produces the following result:

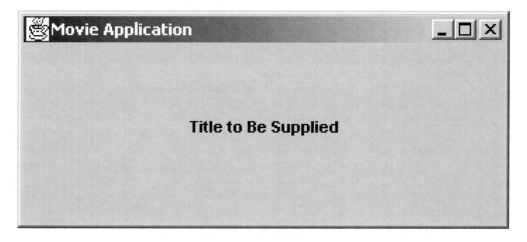

748 Now it is time to combine the definition for the `Meter` class provided in Segment 734 with the definition provided in Segment 746. The text is drawn on a baseline placed far enough under the lines to allow for the text and a reasonable separation from the lines:

```java
import java.awt.*;
import javax.swing.*;
public class Meter extends JComponent implements MeterInterface {
 String title = "Title to Be Supplied";
 int minValue, maxValue, value;
 public Meter (int x, int y) {
  minValue = x; maxValue = y; value = (y + x) / 2;
 }
 public void setValue(int v) {value = v; repaint();}
 public void setTitle(String t) {title = t; repaint();}
 public int getValueAtCoordinates (int x, int y) {
  Dimension d = getSize();
  int meterWidth = d.width * 3 / 4;
  int xOffset = (d.width - meterWidth) / 2;
  float fraction = (float)(x - xOffset) / meterWidth;
  return (int)Math.round(fraction * (maxValue - minValue) + minValue);
 }
 public void paint(Graphics g) {
  // Obtain Dimension instance:
  Dimension d = getSize();
  int meterWidth = d.width * 3 / 4;
  int meterHeight = meterWidth / 20;
  int pointerPosition
   = meterWidth * (value - minValue) / (maxValue - minValue);
  int lineXOffset = (d.width - meterWidth) / 2;
  int lineYOffset = d.height / 2;
  g.drawLine(lineXOffset, lineYOffset,
             lineXOffset + meterWidth, lineYOffset);
  g.drawLine(lineXOffset + pointerPosition, lineYOffset,
             lineXOffset + pointerPosition, lineYOffset - meterHeight);
  // Prepare font
  int fontSize = d.width / 30;
  g.setFont(new Font("Helvetica", Font.BOLD, fontSize));
  // Write title:
  FontMetrics f = g.getFontMetrics();
  int stringWidth = f.stringWidth(title);
  int textXOffset = (d.width - stringWidth) / 2;
  int textYOffset = (d.height / 2) + (2 * f.getHeight());
  g.drawString(title, textXOffset, textYOffset);
 }
 public Dimension getMinimumSize() {return new Dimension(150, 100);}
 public Dimension getPreferredSize() {return new Dimension(150, 100);}
}
```

749 Using the definition in Segment 748 and the definition of `MovieApplication` in Segment 726 produces the following display:

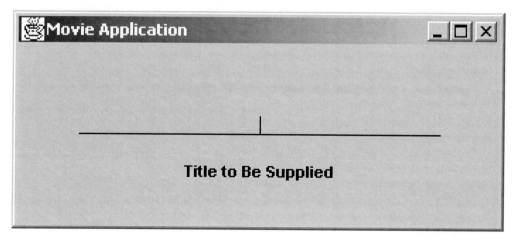

750 Instead of using the definition of `MovieApplication` in Segment 726 to test your meter, you can add a `main` method to the definition of the `Meter` frame itself. That `main` method creates a `JFrame` instance and attaches a meter to that frame. The new `main` method both displays the meter and tests the meter setters:

```java
import java.awt.*;
import javax.swing.*;
public class Meter extends JComponent implements MeterInterface {
 // Rest of definition same as in Segment 748 ...
 public static void main (String argv []) {
  JFrame frame = new JFrame("Meter Test");
  Meter meter = new Meter(0, 100);
  frame.getContentPane().add("Center", meter);
  frame.setSize(350, 150);
  frame.addWindowListener(new ApplicationClosingWindowListener());
  frame.show();
  meter.setValue(25);
  meter.setTitle("Meter Test");
 }
}
```

751 Of course, testing code may become complex. To avoid cluttering your class definitions with complex testing code, and to save space in your compiled code, you should define classes specifically for testing. The following tests the basic `Meter` class shown in Segment 748, without defining a cluttering `main` method inside the `Meter` definition:

In general, you should define your testing class to be a subclass of the tested class, so that you may, if you wish, define shadowing methods for testing purposes.

```
import javax.swing.*;
public class MeterTestor extends Meter {
 public static void main (String argv []) {
  JFrame frame = new JFrame("Meter Test");
  MeterTestor meter = new MeterTestor(0, 100);
  frame.getContentPane().add("Center", meter);
  frame.setSize(350, 150);
  frame.addWindowListener(new ApplicationClosingWindowListener());
  frame.show();
  meter.setValue(25);
  meter.setTitle("Meter Test");
 }
 public MeterTestor (int x, int y) {
  super(x, y);
 }
}
```

752 Now that you know how to produce simple displays, such as the one in Segment 749, you can create more elaborate displays, such as the display shown in Segment 668.

The principal differences between the simple meter defined in Segment 748 and the complex meter defined in Appendix B are:

- The complex meter has a nice look, that you produce by using a little trigonometry to draw a professional-looking dial.

- The complex meter's setters limit the value shown by the pointer to the minimum and maximum values allowed.

On the other hand, the meter defined in Segment 748 and the meter defined in Appendix B both implement the same interface, MeterInterface, defined in Segment 714. Accordingly, you can readily substitute the more elaborate meter for the simple meter in any program that expects the Meter class to implement MeterInterface.

753
PRACTICE Using the Meter class in Segment 748 as a guide, augment the Thermometer definition that you were asked to write in Segment 740 by placing Max and Min labels at the ends of the thermometer. Have the thermometer display the value set.

754
HIGHLIGHTS
- If you want to write a string, **then** add a drawString statement to the paint method, defined in a subclass of the JComponent class, by instantiating the following pattern:

  `graphics context.drawString(a string, x, y);`

- If you want to determine the height of a font or the width of a string, **then** create an instance of the FontMetrics class using the graphics context, **and then** examine that instance's instance variables by instantiating the following patterns:

```
FontMetrics fontMetrics = graphics context .getFontMetrics();
...
fontMetrics.getHeight()                    ⟵ Fetch height
...
fontMetrics.stringWidth( a string );       ⟵ Fetch width
```

- If you want to change to a different font, **then** instantiate the following pattern:

```
graphics context .setFont(new Font( name , Font. style , size ));
```

The *name* is a string, such as "Helvetica". The *style* is the name of a Font class variable, such as BOLD. The *size* is an integer specifying size, such as 12, for a 12-point font.

41 HOW TO USE THE MODEL–VIEW APPROACH TO GUI DESIGN

755 In this chapter, you learn about the model–view approach to building complex systems, and about the classes that Java provides to support the model–view approach. Those classes enables you to construct GUI-oriented systems that would otherwise sink in a mire of complexity.

756 When you adhere to the model–view approach, you separate the classes that embody knowledge about your application's domain, called **model classes**, from classes that embody knowledge about information display, called **view classes**.

757 The `Movie` class, defined later in this chapter, in Segment 768, is a good example of a model class because it embodies knowledge about movies, but embodies no information about information display. Conversely, the `Meter` class, shown in Segment 748 and in Appendix B, is a good example of a view class, because it embodies knowledge about information display, but embodies no information about any particular application domain.

758 The key to the model–view approach is to keep models and views pure. No model is to know anything about information display, and no view is to know anything about any application domain. Thus, no model method is allowed to call a view-defined method or to access a view variable, and no view is allowed to call a model-defined method or to access a model variable.

Accordingly, you define a set of classes, whose only purpose is to enable mediation between model classes and view classes. The **observers** define methods that, for example, fetch information from model instances and relay that information to view instances. The **listeners** symmetrically define methods that, for example, fetch information from view instances and relay that information to model instances.

You learned about listeners in Segment 691. In particular, you learned how to use a window listener to shut down your application. In this chapter, you learn about listeners that have other responsibilities, such as fetching information from view instances and relaying that information to model instances.

759 Model instances are told which observers they should activate at what times. Symmetrically, view instances are told which listeners they should activate at what times.

760 The model–view approach leads to applications defined in terms of four class types:

- **Model** classes, which embody domain knowledge
- **View** classes, which embody information-display knowledge
- **Observer** classes and **listener** classes, which embody knowledge about connections between models and views
- One **application class**, which both serves as a view and performs the following services:

- Creates model, view, observer, and listener instances

- Connects model instances to view instances, via observer instances, and view instances to model instances, via listener instances

- Establishes container–component relations among the views

The application class serves as a view because it provides the master container, such as a frame, that creates a window for the application on a screen.

761   Graphically, the following diagram illustrates how various model–view class instances fit together.

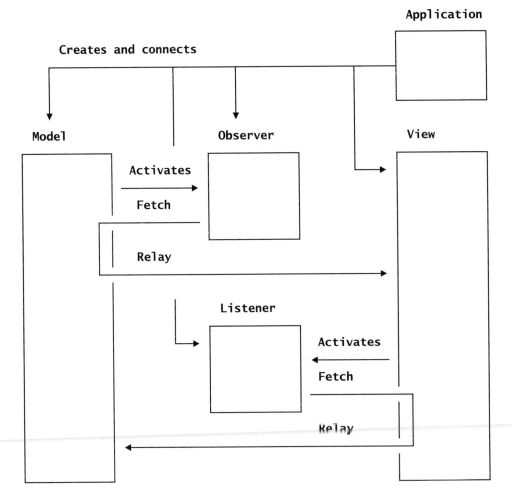

The diagram treats the instances anthropomorphically, using words such as *connect*, *activate*, *fetch*, and *relay*. Later, you learn how to translate those words into calls to particular methods.

Some programmers refer to observers and listeners, collectively, as **adapters**. Regrettably, this language conflicts with the usage of the word *adapter* introduced in Segment 692. In the remainder of this book, we refer to *observers and listeners* rather than to *adapters*.

763 You have already seen three elements of the diagram shown in Segment 761 at work in the example of the `MovieApplication`, defined in Segment 726.

In that definition, you see an application class, a view class, and a listener class:

- `MovieApplication` is the application class, which, like all application classes, is also a view.

- `Meter` is a view class.

- `LocalWindowListener` is a listener class, with a method that you activate by clicking on the window-closing button.

There is no model class. The `LocalWindowListener` listener instance does no fetching from a view or relaying to a model; when activated, the listener's only job is to shut down the application.

764 In the remainder of this chapter, you see how to add a model and an observer to the example of Segment 726 so as to ground the illustration of Segment 761 in a program that exhibits all the elements described in Segment 760:

- The model will be a `Movie` class instance, with the `Movie` class modified so as to extend the `Observable` class.

- The observer will be an instance of a new `MovieObserver` class, which defines a method, that, when activated, fetches a movie's rating from the application's movie instance— the model—and relays that rating to the application's meter instance—the view.

765 Following a principle of good programming practice, the `Movie` class definition implements the `MovieInterface` interface, which insists on the definition of various setters and getters, as well as the `rating` method, which is intended to compute an overall rating from the script, acting, and direction values, and the `changed` method, about which you learn in Segment 767.

```
public interface MovieInterface {
 // Getters
 public abstract int getScript () ;
 public abstract int getActing () ;
 public abstract int getDirection () ;
 public abstract String getTitle () ;
 public abstract String getPoster () ;
 // Setters
 public abstract void setScript (int i) ;
 public abstract void setActing (int i) ;
 public abstract void setDirection (int i) ;
 // Miscellaneous methods
 public abstract int rating () ;
 public abstract void changed () ;
}
```

There are no setters corresponding to getTitle and getPoster, because the title and poster are presumed to be set, once and for all, by a constructor.

766 The following definition implements the interface and declares all the instance variables to be private, ensuring that external access to those variables must go through the setters and getters specified in the interface.

The class definition also extends the Observable class, which is found in the java.util package. Henceforth, Movie instances are also Observable instances, and the Movie class is a model class.

```
import java.util.*;
public class Movie extends Observable implements MovieInterface {
 // Define instance variables:
 private String title, poster;
 private int script = 5, acting = 5, direction = 5;
 // Define three-parameter constructor:
 public Movie (int s, int a, int d) {
   script = s; acting = a; direction = d;
   title = "Title Unknown";
 }
 // Define four-parameter constructor:
 public Movie (int s, int a, int d, String t) {
   this(s, a, d);
   title = t;
 }
 // Define five-parameter constructor:
 public Movie (int s, int a, int d, String t, String p) {
   this(s, a, d, t);
   poster = p;
 }
```

```
// Define setters and getters:
public void setScript(int s) {script = s;}
public void setActing(int a) {acting = a;}
public void setDirection(int d) {direction = d;}
public int getScript() {return script;}
public int getActing() {return acting;}
public int getDirection() {return direction;}
public String getTitle() {return title;}
public String getPoster() {return poster;}
// Define other methods:
public int rating () {
  return script + acting + direction;
}
// changed method defined here ...
}
```

767 Next, you redefine the setters such that they all include calls to the `setChanged` and `notifyObservers` methods, both of which are inherited from the `Observable` class. Calls to `setChanged` establish that a change worthy of note has occurred. If a call to `setChanged` has occurred, establishing that a change worthy of note has occurred, then a call to `notifyObservers` activates all connected observers, and resets the notification apparatus to its initial no-change-worthy-of-note state. You start to learn how to define observers in Segment 773. You learn how to connect observers in Segment 775.

The `Movie` class also defines the `changed` method, which, like the setters, calls `setChanged` and `notifyObservers`.

```
import java.util.*;
public class Movie extends Observable implements MovieInterface {
 // Define instance variables:
 private String title, poster;
 private int script = 5, acting = 5, direction = 5;
 // Constructors as defined in Segment 766 ...
 // Define setters:
 public void setScript(int s) {
  script = s;
  setChanged();
  notifyObservers();
 }
 // Analogous setters defined for acting and direction ...
 // Getters as defined in Segment 766 ...
 // rating method as defined in Segment 766 ...
 public void changed () {
  setChanged();
  notifyObservers();
 }
}
```

768 The fully developed Movie class is as follows. Note that the setters have been brought up to professional standards through two flourishes. First, the setters do nothing unless the value to be set is different from the existing value. This do-nothing behavior prevents the mechanism that activates observers from working with useless information. Second, the setters refuse to set a value outside a prescribed range established by the static variables MIN and MAX.

```java
import java.util.*;
public class Movie extends Observable implements MovieInterface {
 // Define instance and static variables:
 private String title, poster;
 private int script = 5, acting = 5, direction = 5;
 private static int MIN = 0, MAX = 10;
 // Define three-parameter constructor:
 public Movie (int s, int a, int d) {
  script = s; acting = a; direction = d;
  title = "Title Unknown";
 }
 // Define four-parameter constructor:
 public Movie (int s, int a, int d, String t) {
  this(s, a, d);
  title = t;
 }
 // Define five-parameter constructor:
 public Movie (int s, int a, int d, String t, String p) {
  this(s, a, d, t);
  poster = p;
 }
 // Define setters:
 public void setScript(int s) {
  if (script != s) {
   script = Math.max(Math.min(s, MAX), MIN);
   setChanged(); notifyObservers();
  }
 }
 public void setActing(int a) {
  if (acting != a) {
   acting = Math.max(Math.min(a, MAX), MIN);
   setChanged(); notifyObservers();
  }
 }
 public void setDirection(int d) {
  if (direction != d) {
   direction = Math.max(Math.min(d, MAX), MIN);;
   setChanged(); notifyObservers();
  }
 }
```

```
// Define getters:
public int getScript() {return script;}
public int getActing() {return acting;}
public int getDirection() {return direction;}
public String getTitle() {return title;}
public String getPoster() {return poster;}
// Define rating and changed methods:
public int rating () {
  return script + acting + direction;
}
public void changed () {
  setChanged(); notifyObservers();
}
}
```

769   Now, you add a movie instance variable to the definition of the application class, thus installing a model. The definition includes a wired-in Movie instance based on On To Java!,
the forthcoming movie version of this book.

```
import javax.swing.*;
import java.awt.event.*;
public class MovieApplication extends JFrame {
 public static void main (String argv []) {
  new MovieApplication("Movie Application");
 }
 // Declare instance variables:
 private Meter meter;
 private Movie movie;
 // Define constructor
 public MovieApplication(String title) {
  super(title);
  // Construct view instances:
  meter = new Meter(0, 30);
  // Construct model instances:
  movie = new Movie (5, 5, 5, "On to Java");
  // Connect views visually
  getContentPane().add("Center", meter);
  // Connect window listener, size and show
  addWindowListener(new LocalWindowListener());
  setSize(300, 100);
  show();
 }
 // Define window adapter
 private class LocalWindowListener extends WindowAdapter {
  public void windowClosing(WindowEvent e) {
    System.exit(0); return;
}}}
```

770 The movie model that appears in Segment 769 notifies observers whenever there is a call to an instance-variable setter and there are no observers. You begin to learn about observers in Segment 773.

771 From this point forward, the methods of the MovieApplication class access the meter and movie instance variables via getters and setters so as to benefit from data abstraction, as explained in Chapter 13:

```
import javax.swing.*;
import java.awt.event.*;
public class MovieApplication extends JFrame {
 public static void main (String argv []) {
  new MovieApplication("Movie Application");
 }
 // Declare instance variables:
 private Meter meter;
 private Movie movie;
 // Define constructor
 public MovieApplication(String title) {
  super(title);
  // Construct view instances:
  setMeter(new Meter(0, 30));
  // Construct model instances:
  setMovie(new Movie (5, 5, 5, "On to Java"));
  // Connect views visually
  getContentPane().add("Center", getMeter());
  // Connect window listener, size and show
  addWindowListener(new LocalWindowListener());
  setSize(300, 100);
  show();
 }
 // Define getters and setters
 public void setMeter (Meter m) {meter = m;}
 public Meter getMeter() {return meter;}
 public void setMovie (Movie m) {movie = m;}
 public Movie getMovie() {return movie;}
 // Define window adapter
 private class LocalWindowListener extends WindowAdapter {
  public void windowClosing(WindowEvent o) {
   System.exit(0); return;
}}}
```

772 Having arranged to access the meter and movie instance variables via getters, you can move into the getters the meter and movie construction operations, calling the meter or movie constructors only when your program first needs meter or movie values.

The principal benefit of on-demand construction is that you eliminate the danger that your program will ask a variable for a value before that value has been supplied. Liberal use of the idiom involved dramatically reduces the occurrence of bugs that throw instances of a NullPointerException exception.

```java
import javax.swing.*;
import java.awt.event.*;
public class MovieApplication extends JFrame {
 public static void main (String argv []) {
  new MovieApplication("Movie Application");
 }
 // Declare instance variables:
 private Meter meter;
 private Movie movie;
 // Define constructor
 public MovieApplication(String title) {
  super(title);
  // Create model
  getMovie();
  // Create and connect view to application
  getContentPane().add("Center", getMeter());
  // Connect window listener, size and show
  addWindowListener(new LocalWindowListener());
  setSize(300, 100);
  show();
 }
 // Define getters and setters
 public Meter getMeter () {
  if (meter == null) {
   setMeter(new Meter(0, 30));
  }
  return meter;
 }
 public Movie getMovie () {
  if(movie == null) {
   setMovie(new Movie (10, 10, 10, "On to Java"));
  }
  return movie;
 }
 public void setMeter (Meter m) {meter = m;}
 public void setMovie (Movie m) {movie = m;}
 // Define window adapter
 private class LocalWindowListener extends WindowAdapter {
  public void windowClosing(WindowEvent e) {
   System.exit(0); return;
}}}}
```

773 Observers are instances of a class that implements the `Observer` interface defined in the `java.util` package. That interface requires the class to define an `update` method, which is called whenever the observer is activated by a connected model.

In the following preview of an embedded `update` definition, the `update` method fetches a rating and title from a movie and uses that rating and title to set the value and title displayed by a meter. The arguments happen to be ignored:

```java
public void update (Observable observable, Object object) {
  getMeter().setValue(getMovie().rating());
  getMeter().setTitle(getMovie().getTitle());
}
```

774 One way to write the observer class is to define it in the `MovieApplication` class as a local class definition, as shown in the following example.

```java
private class LocalMovieObserver implements Observer {
  public void update (Observable observable, Object object) {
    getMeter().setValue(getMovie().rating());
    getMeter().setTitle(getMovie().getTitle());
}}
```

775 Once you define an observer, you then connect it to a model using the `addObserver` method, which the model inherits from the `Observable` class. You could have your program do the connection in the `MovieApplication` constructor. You should, however, have your program do the connection in the `setMovie` setter to ensure that the observer is connected to the current value of the `movie` variable. You need ensured connection in Chapter 46, where you use a choice list to change the value assigned to the movie variable.

776 The new, more complex, setter does nothing if the new movie is the same as the previous movie. If the previous movie assignment is an instance of the `Movie` class (that is, if it is not `null`), the setter disconnects that previous movie from all previously connected observers using `deleteObservers`, which is a method inherited from the `Observable` class. Then, the setter assigns the new movie to the `movie` variable, adds a new observer if the new movie is an instance of the `Movie` class, and calls `changed` to activate the newly connected, new observer.

```java
public void setMovie (Movie m) {
  if(movie == m) {return;}
  if(movie instanceof Movie) {movie.deleteObservers();}
  if(m instanceof Movie) {
    movie = m;
    movie.addObserver(new LocalMovieObserver());
    movie.changed();
  }
}
```

777 With the new locally defined observer and modified setter installed, you have the following definition of `MovieApplication`.

```
import javax.swing.*;
import java.awt.event.*;
import java.util.*;
public class MovieApplication extends JFrame {
 public static void main (String argv []) {
  new MovieApplication("Movie Application");
 }
 // Declare instance variables:
 private Meter meter;
 private Movie movie;
 // Define constructor
 public MovieApplication(String title) {
  super(title);
  // Create model
  getMovie();
  // Create and connect view to application
  getContentPane().add("Center", getMeter());
  // Connect window listener, size and show
  addWindowListener(new LocalWindowListener());
  setSize(300, 100); show();
 }
 // Define getters and setters
 public Meter getMeter () {
  if (meter == null) {setMeter(new Meter(0, 30));}
  return meter;
 }
 public Movie getMovie () {
  if(movie == null) {setMovie(new Movie (10, 10, 10, "On to Java"));}
  return movie;
 }
 public void setMeter (Meter m) {meter = m;}
 public void setMovie (Movie m) {
  if(movie == m) {return;}
  if(movie instanceof Movie) {movie.deleteObservers();}
  if(m instanceof Movie) {
   movie = m;
   movie.addObserver(new LocalMovieObserver());
   movie.changed();
 }}
 // Define observer:
 private class LocalMovieObserver implements Observer {
  public void update (Observable observable, Object object) {
   getMeter().setValue(getMovie().rating());
   getMeter().setTitle(getMovie().getTitle());
 }}
// Define window adapter as in Segment 772 ...
}
```

778 The definition shown in Segment 777 illustrates all the key elements of the model–view approach: an application instance, a model, a view, an observer, and a listener.

As the constructor creates the movie model, it automatically connects that movie model to a new movie observer and then activates that new observer. The activated observer then looks for a meter view; if it finds that there is none, it creates one. Once the meter view is in hand, the observer fetches information from the movie model and relays that information to the meter view.

Later, in Chapter 46 and Chapter 49, you learn how to use list selection, button pushing, and typing to initiate a chain of calls that leads to calls to model setters. For now, to avoid further complexity, you see how to implement an illustrative listener that sets the movie script, acting, and direction variables to values that direct the meter pointer to any spot on the meter where you click your mouse.

779 You have implemented a window listener by defining a subclass of the WindowAdapter class, which implements the WindowListener interface. Now, you proceed to implement a mouse listener by defining a subclass of the MouseAdapter class, which implements the MouseListener interface.

The MouseListener interface insists on the definition of several methods, one of which is the mouseClicked method, which is defined as a do-nothing method in the MouseAdapter class. In your subclass of the MouseAdapter class, you arrange for the mouseClicked method to reach into the view that produced the mouse event, to fetch a value, and to relay that value to model setters.

780 Specifically, for the sake of illustration, suppose that you want the movie model to have its values set such that the meter pointer moves to the place on the meter where you click your mouse.

First, you must determine the value that the meter would be displaying if the dial were under the mouse at the point of click. Then, because a movie's rating is the sum of the values of the script, acting, and direction instance variables, you divide the value returned from the meter view by 3, and use that result as the argument of the movie model's setters.

The getX and getY methods, called with the mouse event as the target, supply the co-ordinates of the mouse at the point of click, relative to the meter component on which the mouse is clicked. The mouseClicked method uses round, a class method of the Math class, described in Segment 734.

```
public void mouseClicked (MouseEvent e) {
  int x = c.getX();
  int y = e.getY();
  int v = (int) Math.round(getMeter().getValueAtCoordinates (x, y)
              / 3.0);
  getMovie().setScript(v);
  getMovie().setActing(v);
  getMovie().setDirection(v);
}
```

781 One way to write the listener class in which you define the mouseClicked method is to define the listener class as a local class in the MovieApplication class, as shown in the following example, which also features a modification to a setter that calls the addMouseListener method, which the Meter class inherits from the Component class.

The setMeter setter is not as complex as the setMovie setter because setMeter is called just once, whereas setMovie is called many times, once a choice list is added in Chapter 46,

```java
import javax.swing.*;
import java.awt.event.*;
import java.util.*;
public class MovieApplication extends JFrame {
 public static void main (String argv []) {
  new MovieApplication("Movie Application");
 }
 // Declare instance variables:
 private Meter meter;
 private Movie movie;
 // Define constructor
 public MovieApplication(String title) {
  super(title);
  // Create model
  getMovie();
  // Create and connect view to application
  getContentPane().add("Center", getMeter());
  // Connect window listener, size and show
  addWindowListener(new LocalWindowListener());
  setSize(300, 100);
  show();
 }
 // Define getters and setters
 public Meter getMeter () {
  if (meter == null) {setMeter(new Meter(0, 30));}
  return meter;
 }
 public Movie getMovie () {
  if(movie == null) {setMovie(new Movie (10, 10, 10, "On to Java"));}
  return movie;
 }
 public void setMovie (Movie m) {
  if(movie == m) {return;}
  if(movie instanceof Movie) {movie.deleteObservers();}
  if(m instanceof Movie) {
   movie = m;
   movie.addObserver(new LocalMovieObserver());
   movie.changed();
 }}
```

```
public void setMeter (Meter m) {
 meter = m;
 meter.addMouseListener(new LocalMeterListener());
}
// Define observer:
private class LocalMovieObserver implements Observer {
 public void update (Observable observable, Object object) {
  getMeter().setValue(getMovie().rating());
  getMeter().setTitle(getMovie().getTitle());
 }
}
// Define mouse adapter:
private class LocalMeterListener extends MouseAdapter {
 public void mouseClicked (MouseEvent e) {
  int x = e.getX();
  int y = e.getY();
  int v = (int) Math.round(getMeter().getValueAtCoordinates (x, y)
               / 3.0);
  getMovie().setScript(v);
  getMovie().setActing(v);
  getMovie().setDirection(v);
 }
}
// Define window adapter
private class LocalWindowListener extends WindowAdapter {
 public void windowClosing(WindowEvent e) {
  System.exit(0); return;
 }
}
}
```

782 Now it is time to consolidate what you have learned. One way to consolidate is to follow what happens when you click on the meter:

- Your click activates a mechanism that calls mouseClicked with the listener connected to the meter instance as the target.

- The mouseClicked method fetches a value based on mouse coordinates from the meter instance.

- Then, the mouseClicked method relays a result to the movie instance using the setters, setScript, setActing, and setDirection, each of which calls setChanged and notifyObservers.

- Each call to the notifyObservers method activates a mechanism that calls the update method in the observer connected to the movie instance.

- The update method fetches information from the movie model and relays that information to the meter view.

The following diagram traces the call sequence:

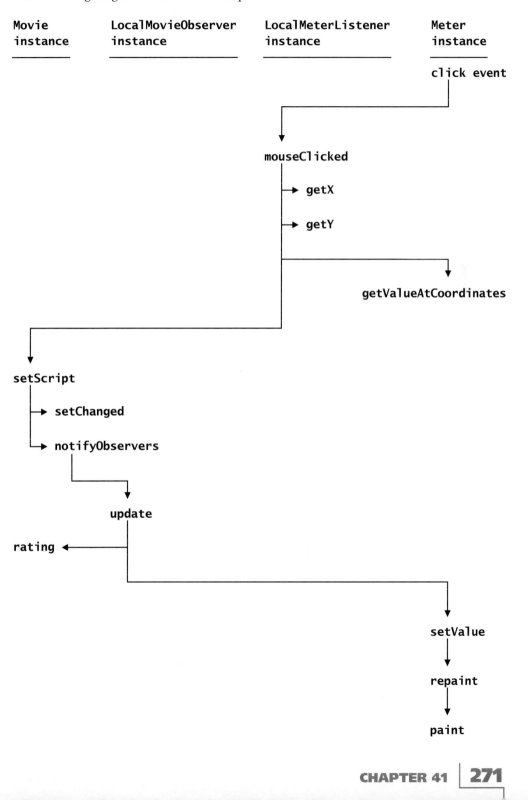

783 Another way to consolidate what you have learned is to reflect on how the methods defined for models, observers, components, and listeners implement the *connecting*, *activating*, *fetching*, and *relaying* depicted in the diagram shown in Segment 761:

The Observable class provides model classes with three essential methods:

- The addObserver method *connects* observer instances to model instances.

- The setChanged and notifyObservers methods jointly *activate* connected observers by calling their update methods.

The Observer interface insists that you define one essential method:

- The update method is called by inherited machinery whenever setChanged is called, followed by a call to notifyObservers.

The update method does whatever you tell it to do; typically it *fetches* values from models and *relays* those values to views.

784 Similarly, the Component class provides view classes with the following:

- Methods, such as addMouseListener, that *connect* listeners to view instances

- An event-noting mechanism that calls methods, such as mouseClicked to *activate* listeners

Listener interfaces insist that you define various essential methods:

- Methods, such as mouseClicked, are called by inherited machinery whenever an event occurs.

Listener methods do whatever you tell them to do. Typically, listener methods *fetch* values from views and *relay* those values to models.

785 Note that you can understand models by understanding only the Observable class and the Observer interface.

On the view side, however, there are several kinds of events, such as mouse events and window events. Each of the corresponding interfaces insists on the definition of its own particular set of methods.

786
PRACTICE
Replace the meter used in the application defined in Segment 781 with an instance of the Thermometer class that you were asked to define in Segment 753.

787
HIGHLIGHTS

- If you want to build a GUI, **then** adopt the model–view approach.

- If you want your program to react to model changes, **then**

  - Arrange for the model class to extend the Observable class.

  - Insert calls to setChanged and notifyObservers in the setters of the model.

- Define an observer class that implements the `Observer` interface.

- Define an `update` method in the observer class such that `update` fetches information from the model and relays that information to a view.

- Connect an observer to the model using `addObserver`.

- If you want your program to react to view events, **then**

  - Define a listener class that implements an appropriate listener interface.

  - Define listener methods as dictated by the listener interface such that those methods fetch information from the view and relay that information to a model.

  - Connect the listener to the appropriate component.

42 HOW TO DEFINE STANDALONE OBSERVERS AND LISTENERS

788 The MovieApplication definition shown in Segment 781 contains a locally defined observer and two locally defined listeners. One benefit of local definition is that the observer and listener code is readily located. Another benefit is that the methods of the locally defined classes can employ MovieApplication instance methods. For example, the observer employs the getMovie and getMeter methods.

When you design practical applications, however, the benefit of having everything in one place can become the burden of having too much in one place, and you find yourself more inclined to define your observers and listeners separately.

In this chapter, you learn how standalone observers and listeners can access the required application instance methods.

789 Consider, for example, the movie observer, defined separately from the application class, as follows. As written, you cannot even compile the definition, because the getMeter and getMovie getters are defined in the MovieApplication class, not the MovieObserver class.

```
import java.util.*;
public class MovieObserver implements Observer {
 public void update (Observable observable, Object object) {
   getMeter().setValue(getMovie().rating());          // BUG!
   getMeter().setTitle(getMovie().getTitle());        // BUG!
 }
}
```

790 You solve the undefined-variable problem by making your application instance available to methods defined in the MovieObserver class. You make that application instance available in a three-step idiom:

- Establish an application instance variable in the observer class.

- Include the application instance as an argument to the observer's constructor.

- Assign the application instance variable in the observer's constructor.

The following illustrates. Both the meter and the movie become accessible via the value of the applet variable.

```
import java.util.*;
public class MovieObserver implements Observer {
 private MovieApplication applet;
 public MovieObserver (MovieApplication a) {
  applet = a;
 }
 public void update (Observable observable, Object object) {
  applet.getMeter().setValue(applet.getMovie().rating());
  applet.getMeter().setTitle(applet.getMovie().getTitle());
 }
}
```

791 Of course, you can make analogous changes to the locally defined mouse listener, producing a standalone mouse listener.

- Establish an application instance variable in the listener class.

- Include the application itself as an argument to the listener's constructor.

- Assign the application instance variable in the listener's constructor.

The following illustrates. Again, both the meter and the movie become accessible via the value of the applet variable.

```
import java.awt.event.*;
public class MeterListener extends MouseAdapter {
 MovieApplication applet;
 public MeterListener (MovieApplication a) {
  applet = a;
 }
 public void mouseClicked (MouseEvent e) {
  int x = e.getX();
  int y = e.getY();
  int v =
    (int) Math.round(applet.getMeter().getValueAtCoordinates (x, y)
                    / 3.0
                    );
  applet.getMovie().setScript(v);
  applet.getMovie().setActing(v);
  applet.getMovie().setDirection(v);
 }
}
```

792 Having defined a new observer and a new listener, you can adjust the definition of the MovieApplication class accordingly, making it simpler.

Note that both the observer constructor and the listener constructor now require the application instance to be handed over as an argument:

```java
import javax.swing.*;
import java.awt.event.*;
import java.util.*;
public class MovieApplication extends JFrame {
 public static void main (String argv []) {
  new MovieApplication("Movie Application");
 }
 // Declare instance variables:
 private Meter meter;
 private Movie movie;
 // Define constructor
 public MovieApplication(String title) {
  super(title);
  // Create model
  getMovie();
  // Create and connect view to application
  getContentPane().add("Center", getMeter());
  // Connect window listener, size and show
  addWindowListener(new LocalWindowListener());
  setSize(300, 100);
  show();
 }
 // Define getters and setters
 public Meter getMeter () {
  if (meter == null) {setMeter(new Meter(0, 30));}
  return meter;
 }
 public Movie getMovie () {
  if(movie == null) {setMovie(new Movie (10, 10, 10, "On to Java"));}
  return movie;
 }
 public void setMeter (Meter m) {
  meter = m;
  meter.addMouseListener(new MeterListener(this));
 }
 public void setMovie (Movie m) {
  if(movie == m) {return;}
  if(movie instanceof Movie) {movie.deleteObservers();}
  if(m instanceof Movie) {
   movie = m;
   movie.addObserver(new MovieObserver(this));
   movie.changed();
 }}
 // Define window adapter
 private class LocalWindowListener extends WindowAdapter {
  public void windowClosing(WindowEvent e) {
   System.exit(0); return;
}}}
```

- If your application class definition grows too large, **then** consider converting your inner class listener and observer definitions into standalone class definitions.

- If you define a listener or observer as a standalone class, **then** provide access to the application's variables as follows:

  - Establish an application instance variable in the standalone class.

  - Assign the application instance variable in the standalone class's constructor.

43 HOW TO DEFINE APPLETS

794 The raison d'être of Java is that Java allows you to access programs via a web browser. In this chapter, you learn how to convert frame classes, of the sort you learned about in Chapter 39 and Chapter 40, into applet classes for such web browsers.

The word *applet* is derived from *application* + *let*; thus, an applet is a little application. Certain applets, however, are quite large.

795 You refer to instances of the `JApplet` class, or subclasses of that class, as **applets**. An applet differs from an ordinary, standalone program in several respects:

- Java creates an applet in response to requests issued by a web browser, by calling the zero-argument applet-class constructor. There is no role for a `main` method.

- An applet has its size determined by the web browser in cooperation with the HTML file that references the applet, as explained in Chapter 44. There are no calls to `setSize` or `show`.

- An applet has no close button; hence, there are no `WindowAdapter` subclass and no `windowClosing` method in `JApplet` classes.

796 Suppose that you want to transform into an applet the `MovieApplication` class defined in Segment 792. You need to make several changes:

First, define the class to extend the `JApplet` class, rather than the `JFrame` class.

```
public class MovieApplication extends JApplet {
...
}
```

Second, remove the definition of the `main` method.

Third, because applets have no close button, remove the `LocalWindowAdapter` subclass definition and remove the call to `addWindowListener`. Because you remove the listener, you no longer need to import the `java.awt.event` package.

Fourth, transform the one-parameter constructor, which passes along a title to the constructor in the direct superclass, into a zero-parameter constructor. Eliminate the calls to the superclass constructor and to the `setSize` and `show` methods.

797 With all the changes in place, you have the following definition of the `MovieApplication` class:

```
import javax.swing.*;
import java.awt.event.*;
import java.util.*;
public class MovieApplication extends JApplet {
 // Declare instance variables:
 private Meter meter;
 private Movie movie;
 // Define constructor
 public MovieApplication () {
  // Create model
  getMovie();
  // Create and connect view to application
  getContentPane().add("Center", getMeter());
 }
 // Define getters and setters
 public Meter getMeter () {
  if (meter == null) {setMeter(new Meter(0, 30));}
  return meter;
 }
 public Movie getMovie () {
  if(movie == null) {setMovie(new Movie (10, 10, 10, "On to Java"));}
  return movie;
 }
 public void setMeter (Meter m) {
  meter = m;
  meter.addMouseListener(new MeterListener(this));
 }
 public void setMovie (Movie m) {
  if(movie == m) {return;}
  if(movie instanceof Movie) {movie.deleteObservers();}
  if(m instanceof Movie) {
   movie = m;
   movie.addObserver(new MovieObserver(this));
   movie.changed();
  }
 }
}
```

798 The nesting of components inside a JApplet instance is the same as the nesting inside a JFrame instance. Thus, the diagram shown in Segment 723 serves for both instances.

799
SIDE TRIP When a browser loads an applet, it calls not only the constructor, but also the init method, which contains computations to be performed once the applet is loaded. The inherited init does nothing.

A browser also calls the start method each time that the page containing an applet is visited or revisited. The start method is meant to contain computations to be performed to start the applet. For example, if an applet involves animation, the `start` method would start the animation.

On the other end, a browser calls the `stop` method each time that the page containing an applet is replaced by another page. A browser also calls the `stop` method just before calling the `destroy` method. For example, if an applet involves animation, the `stop` method would stop the animation.

Finally, a browser calls the `destroy` method each time that the page containing an applet is abandoned completely. The `destroy` method contains computations to be performed to exit from the applet application. The `destroy` method is called, for example, when the browser shuts down, or, in some browsers, when the page containing an applet is replaced by another page.

800 Ordinarily, applet classes define no `main` method, inasmuch as no use is made of a `main` method by a web browser. Nevertheless, you may wish to define a `main` method for testing an applet, either in the applet itself, or as explained in Segment 751, in a testing class. In the testing class, the `main` method embeds a `MovieApplicationTestor` instance in a `JFrame` instance, which is perfectly legitimate, because `JApplet` instances are components.

```
import javax.swing.*;
public class MovieApplicationTestor extends MovieApplication {
 public static void main (String argv []) {
   JFrame frame = new JFrame("Applet Testor");
   MovieApplicationTestor applet = new MovieApplicationTestor();
   frame.getContentPane().add("Center", applet);
   frame.setSize(350, 150);
   frame.addWindowListener(new ApplicationClosingWindowListener());
   frame.show();
 }
}
```

801
SIDE TRIP
If your applet happens to define `init` and `start` methods, your testing class must call those methods explicitly, as in the following example, to provide a faithful simulation of browser behavior:

```
import javax.swing.*;
public class MovieApplicationTestor extends MovieApplication {
 public static void main (String argv []) {
   JFrame frame = new JFrame("Applet Testor");
   MovieApplicationTestor applet = new MovieApplicationTestor();
   frame.getContentPane().add("Center", applet);
   frame.setSize(350, 150);
   frame.addWindowListener(new ApplicationClosingWindowListener());
   frame.show();
   applet.init();
   applet.start();
 }
}
```

802 When you use the testing program defined in Segment 800, you see the following. Note that, from this point forward, the fancy meter, defined in Appendix B, appears instead of the simple meter, defined in Segment 748. The substitution is easy, because both definitions implement the same interface.

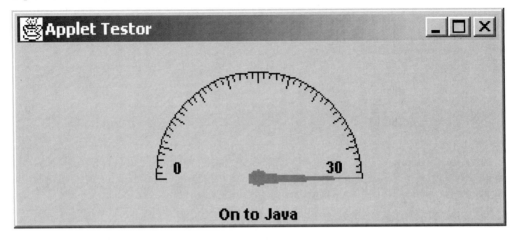

803

HIGHLIGHTS

- Applets are window-producing containers used by web browsers

- Applets have no close button, no window listeners, no sizing method, and no show method.

- Applets have `init`, `start`, `stop`, and `destroy` methods, as well as a zero-argument constructor.

- If you want to test an applet, **then** you may want to define a testing class with a `main` method that creates an instance of the applet and attaches that applet to a frame's content pane.

44 HOW TO ACCESS APPLETS FROM WEB BROWSERS

804 In Chapter 43, you learned how to define applets for web browsers. In this chapter, you learn how to place references to applets in the files with which web browsers work. Thus, you learn how to prepare files for testing applets and for deploying those applets over the Internet.

805 **Web browsers** look at text files that are **marked up** according to the conventions the hypertext markup language (**HTML**). HTML is derived from the standard generalized markup language (**SGML**).

806 When you mark up a text file, you insert **formatting tags** that dictate appearance and provide special effects. Text files with HTML formatting tags are often called **HTML files**. HTML files typically have filename extensions.

807 HTML tags consist of **directives** surrounded by angle brackets. The <p> tag, for example, terminates paragraphs. The <hr> tag draws a horizontal line.

808 HTML is not case sensitive. Thus, <p> does the same work as <P>, and <hr> does the same work as <HR>.

809 Many HTML tags are one-half of a pair that surrounds a block of text. The second tag is like the first, except that it carries a forward slash just inside the first angle bracket. For example, the <title>–</title> pair surrounds that portion of the file intended to serve as the file's title. Similarly, the <head>–</head> pair surrounds the title and other, optional, marked material, such as indexing words. The <body>–</body> pair surrounds the file's body; and the <html>–</html> pair surrounds the entire contents.

Thus, the following is a simple HTML file that contains nothing but a title, two horizontal rules, and a few lines of text:

```
<html>
<head>
<title>Welcome to a simple HTML file</title>
</head>
<body>
<hr>
This text can be viewed by a web browser.<p>
It consists of only text, arranged in two
paragraphs, between horizontal rules.
<hr>
</body>
</html>
```

810 When displayed, the text-containing HTML file produces the following:

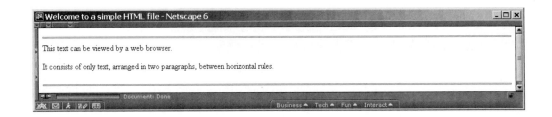

811 HTML files can refer to applets using <applet>–</applet> pairs. The <applet> tag includes width and height specifications, as well as the name of the applet file; the file is presumed to be in the same directory as the HTML file:

```
<html>
<head>
<title>Welcome to the Meter Applet Demonstration</title>
</head>
<body>
<hr>
<applet code="MovieApplication.class" width=350 height=150></applet>
<hr>
</body>
</html>
```

812 Unfortunately, browser development tends to lag behind Java development, and at any

SIDE TRIP   given moment, the latest browsers, without help, tend to be unable to run programs written in the latest version of Java. Nevertheless, you can tell the popular browsers to use the latest **plug-in** Java, rather than their built-in versions.

Note, however, that you should not try to supply a plug-in prescription yourself. Instead, you use a translation tool to modify your <applet>-containing HTML file. See the **Software** page, at the end of this book, for instructions on how to obtain such a translation tool.

813 If your computer is running a **web server**, you can access your HTML file, and its applet, from your own computer, or from any other computer on the Internet, by providing a web browser with an appropriate network address in that browser's location field:

Location: `appropriate network address`

814 An appropriate address is given in the form of a **u**niform **r**esource **l**ocator (**URL**). The general form for a URL for an HTML file accessed via a network includes several parts:

- The first part, http:, specifies that the URL adheres to a scheme known as the **h**ypertext **t**ransfer **p**rotocol.

- The second part, separated from the `http:` specifier by two slashes, specifies an Internet address, such as `www.ascent.com`. Such specifications consist of the name of the web-accessible computer, such as `www`, and the name of the **domain** with which that computer is associated, such as `ascent.com`, separated by a period. Domain names usually consist of organization names, such as `ascent`, and types, such as `com` (or `edu`, `mil`, `gov`, or `org`) separated by a period.

- The third part, separated from the Internet address by a slash, specifies a path to your HTML file, relative to a **root path** established by the web server. If the web server specifies a root path of `d:/InetPub/wwwroot/`, and you supply `books/java/test.html`, then `d:/InetPub/wwwroot/books/java/test.html` is the location of your file on the computer.

The following—with all necessary syntax—illustrates what a URL typically contains:

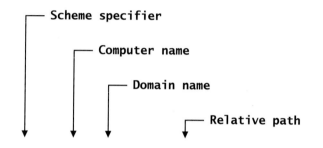

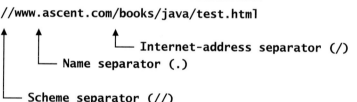

Note that the computer name used by many organizations for their web server is, appropriately enough, www—but it can be any name.

815   If the web server happens to be running on the same computer as your web browser, then you can leave out the Internet address, producing a URL with three slashes in a row:

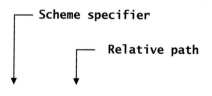

816   URLs may or may not be case sensitive, depending on the server. Thus, the following URLs may or may not be equivalent:

```
http://www.ascent.com/books/java/test.html
HTTP://WWW.ASCENT.COM/BOOKS/JAVA/TEST.HTML
```

817 If a URL ends in a slash, then the web server provides a default file name and extension. Typical web servers use `index.html` for the default file name and extension, but some web servers use other default names and extensions, such as `homepage.html` and `home.html`.

818 If you do not happen to be running a web server on your computer, you can still access an HTML file using a URL that follows the **file scheme**. The following illustrates what such a URL typically contains for a file located on a Windows system. The key change is that the `http:` specifier is replaced by the `file:` specifier:

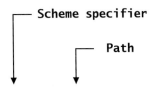

```
file:///d:/phw/onto/java/test.html
```

819 Using the file scheme, you can view via a web browser the HTML file described in Segment 811. Because that HTML file references the applet defined in Segment 797, you see the following result:

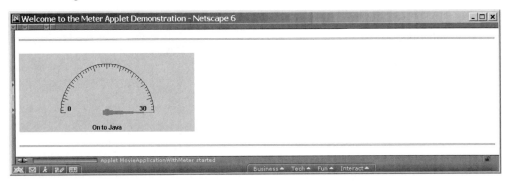

820 You specify the desired width and height of an applet in only the HTML file. Basically, you provide a hole into which the applet adjusts itself.

821 For debugging, you can use Java's command line applet viewer to view the applets embedded in an HTML file. You type, for example, the following:

```
appletviewer file:///d:/phw/onto/java/test.html
```

When you use the applet viewer on the HTML file shown in Segment 811, you see the following. Note that, when you use the applet viewer on an HTML file that contains an applet, you see only the embedded applet; you do not see the other entries in the HTML file.

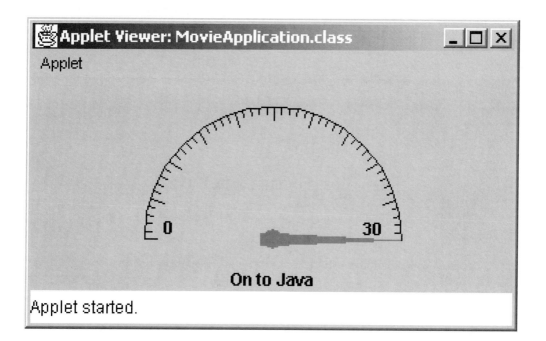

822 In Chapter 54, you begin to learn about servlets, which, in turn, requires you to understand HTML links.

Within your HTML file, you can place a **link** that refers to another HTML file. Links consist of URLs embedded in the first tag of an **address–tag pair**. For example, the following text contains a link:

```
<html>
<head>
<title>Welcome to the Link Demonstration</title>
</head>
<body>
<hr>
This file contains only a link to the
<a href="file:///d:/phw/onto/java/test.html">
meter demonstration.
</a>
<hr>
</body>
</html>
```

Network browsers generally highlight the text between the two tags in some way that marks that text as a link. If you click on that text, your web browser will switch to the referenced HTML file.

823 You learn in Appendix C how to write HTML files that pass parameter values to applets.

SIDE TRIP

The `http:` and `file:` specifiers are but two of the specifiers recognized by web browsers and by other network-oriented applications; another example is the `ftp:` specifier, which specifies a file-transfer protocol.

The HTML language offers a great deal of flexibility, yet the essentials are easy to learn. Many HTML users do not even bother to look at any of the many tutorials on the subject. Instead, they see a display they like in their web browsers, and then they examine the related HTML file, typically by clicking through the web browser's View menu.

- Formatting tags are provided by the hypertext markup language (HTML).

- If you want to embed an applet in an HTML file, **then** instantiate the following pattern:

  `<applet code="`applet name`.class" width=`width` height=`height`>`
  `</applet>`

- If you want to view an applet using a web browser, **then** provide the web browser with the URL address of the HTML file that contains the applet:

  `http://`machine and domain name`/`path relative to root path
  `file:///`full path to file

- If you want to view, for debugging, an applet that is embedded in an HTML file, **then** you may want to use the command-line applet viewer by instantiating the following pattern:

  `appletviewer file:///`full path to file

45 HOW TO USE RESOURCE LOCATORS

827 In Chapter 27 through Chapter 32, you learned how to read movie descriptions from files identified by an operating-system–specific path. Such identifiers work well for standalone applications.

In this chapter, you learn how to use general-purpose resource locators that allow you to specify files in a manner that works both for standalone applications and for browser applications.

828 **Resource locators** help you in two conspicuous ways:

- Resource locators find files even after you have moved your program from one directory to another. You need this feature when you develop a Java program on your personal machine in the expectation of moving it later to some other machine.

- Resource locators find files properly not only for standalone applications, but also for browser applications. You need this feature when you develop a program for a browser, which must honor the security constraints described in Segment 836.

829 In Segment 613, you saw how to establish a reader stream for reading movie vectors as follows:

```
import java.io.*;
import java.util.*;
public class Auxiliaries {
 public static Vector readMovieFile(String fileName) {
  Vector v = new Vector();
  try {
   FileInputStream stream = new FileInputStream(fileName);
   InputStreamReader reader = new InputStreamReader(stream);
   ...
  }
  ...
 }
}
```

The more general way to establish a reader stream for reading movie vectors, using a resource locator, is as follows:

```
public class MovieAuxiliaries {
 public static Vector readMovieFile(String fileName) {
  Vector v = new Vector();
  try {
   URL url = MovieAuxiliaries.class.getResource(fileName);
   InputStream stream = (InputStream) (url.getContent());
   InputStreamReader reader = new InputStreamReader(stream);
   ...
  }
  ...
 }
}
```

830   You can use the two marked statements of the general-purpose mechanism, shown in
       Segment 829, in place of the one marked statement of the file-specific mechanism, without
       attempting to understand how those statements work in detail. Alternatively, you can dive
       into the details, learning about a special class used in connection with resource locators.

       If you wish to avoid the details, you should skip ahead to Segment 836 to learn about the
       general-purpose mechanism's characteristics.

831   Whenever the Java virtual machine loads a class or interface, it creates for that class
       or interface a companion instance of a special class called, confusingly enough, Class.
       Instances of the Class class generally provide access to useful information about their
       companion class, such as, for example, the companion class's name and the names of its
       instance variables.

       The companion Class instance also provides access to methods that are capable of locating
       resources, such as text and image files.

832   Consider, for example, the MovieAuxiliaries class. When the class is loaded by the Java
       virtual machine, an instance of the Class class also is created:

       ┌───┐
       │ MovieAuxiliaries class loaded   │
       └───┘
            │
            ▼
       ┌───┐
       │ Instance of Class class created   │
       └───┘

833   You can get the Class instance for the MovieAuxiliaries class by way of the class
       instance variable attached to the MovieAuxiliaries class:

```
             ┌── MovieAuxiliaries class
           ┌─┘
           ▼
MovieAuxiliaries.class
────────────────────────
           ┌─┐
           │ │
           ▲
           └── Instance of Class class, the companion class
```

Once you retrieve a class's companion Class instance, you can use the getResource method on that instance, together with a file name, to produce a location description:

```
              ┌── Instance of Class class,
            ┌─┘      the companion of the MovieAuxiliaries class
            │
            ▼
            ─────────────
URL url = MovieAuxiliaries.class.getResource(fileName)
          ────────────────────────────────────────────
              ┌─┐
              ▲
              └── A location description
```

834   Next, you can use the location description, an instance of the URL class, as the target of the getContent method. The getContent method returns an object instance that can be cast into an instance of the InputStream class:

```
InputStream stream= (InputStream) (url.getContent())
                    ─────────────────────────────────
                       ┌─┐
                       ▲
                       └── An input stream
```

835   There are two reasons why accessing movie-describing files uses a process that starts with the instance of the Class class that serves as the companion to the MovieAuxiliaries class.

Recall that a companion instance of the Class class is created by the Java virtual machine when that virtual machine loads the MovieAuxiliaries class.

Thus, the virtual machine must know where the MovieAuxiliaries class is located. The resource locator starts looking for the movie-describing file in the same location as that MovieAuxiliaries class, assuming that the movie-describing files are close to—in a sense described in Segment 836—the method for reading those files.

Also, the virtual machine knows whether it is part of a browser; if it is, it deploys security rules different from those for standalone applications.

836   The Java security rules dictate that, when a browser runs a Java program, the resource locator allows files to be loaded from only a location identified with the place that produced the class.

Suppose, for example, that the file name is general.movies. Then, the resource locator will look for general.movies in the directory that holds the MovieAuxiliaries class.

Alternatively, if the file name includes a relative path, such as data/general.movies, then, the resource locator will look for general.movies in the data subdirectory of the directory that holds the MovieAuxiliaries class.

837 Thus, if an applet reads a file in the course of doing its work, that file must come from the same computer and from the same directory as the applet, or possibly from a subdirectory of that directory. Java prevents an applet, obtained via a network, from opening, reading, or writing local files, but allows that applet to open, read, and write files that reside in the directory tree associated with the place from which the applet came.

838 Suppose, for example, that you run a browser that loads an applet stored in the following file:

`d:/phw/onto/java/MeterApplication.class`

Then, that applet can access only files stored in that same directory, and, if relative paths are provided, in the two subdirectories of the java directory, entertainment and data:

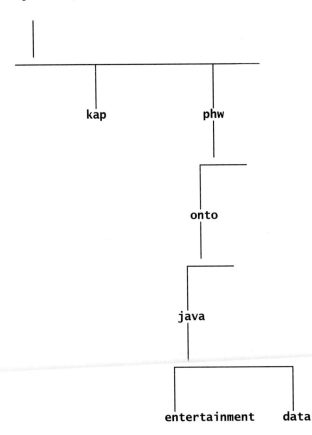

839 Insisting on the same-place restriction helps you to prevent applet providers from poking around in your files to gather information.

840 In ordinary standalone applications, a resource locator can access information in any directory specified by the CLASSPATH operating-system environment variable, or, if a relative path is supplied, in subdirectories of those directories specified by CLASSPATH.

Suppose, for example, that you run a standalone application on a computer that has the directory structure shown in Segment 838. Further suppose that the value of the CLASSPATH variable is as follows:

`\kap;phw\onto\java;.`

Then, your application can access files in the current directory (specified by the `.` in the value of the CLASSPATH variable), in the `\kap` directory, and in the `\phw\onto\java` directory—and, if relative paths are provided, in the subdirectories of those directories.

841 You can access image files in much the same way as you access text files. The only difference is that you cast the value returned by `getContent` into an `ImageProducer` instance, rather than into an input stream:

```
URL url = MovieAuxiliaries.class.getResource(fileName);
ImageProducer producer = (ImageProducer) (url.getContent());
```

The `getContent` method has the intelligence required to deal with both text and image files, as well as with audio files, using both file extensions and file content as a guide.

842 To create an `Image` instance from an `ImageProducer` instance, you must use methods associated with the `Toolkit` class, which specializes in providing connections between your Java program and operating-system mechanisms, such as those that actually spray images on your display.

You obtain a required `Toolkit` instance by way of a class method, `getDefaultToolkit`, which returns the appropriate, operating-system–specific toolkit:

```
Toolkit tk = Toolkit.getDefaultToolkit()
```

843 Next, you use the `createImage` method, provided by the default toolkit, to create an image from the `ImageProducer` instance:

```
Image image = tk.createImage(producer)
```

844 Finally, you are ready to look at the definition of the `MovieAuxiliaries` class, which defines two methods: one for reading movie descriptions from text files, and one for reading images from image files.

Note that several packages are loaded, including `java.net` and `java.awt.image`.

Note also that the method that reads movie descriptions is much like the method defined in Segment 613, except that it uses a resource locator to create a file stream. The method that reads images is used in Chapter 47:

```java
import java.io.*;    import java.awt.*;
import java.net.*;   import java.util.*;
import java.awt.image.*; // Provides ImageProducer
public class MovieAuxiliaries {
 public static Vector readMovieFile(String fileName) {
  Vector v = new Vector();
  try {
   URL url = MovieAuxiliaries.class.getResource(fileName);
   if (url == null) {return null;}
   InputStream stream = (InputStream) (url.getContent());
   if (stream == null) {return null;}
   InputStreamReader reader = new InputStreamReader(stream);
   StreamTokenizer tokens = new StreamTokenizer(reader);
   tokens.quoteChar((int) '"'); tokens.eolIsSignificant(true);
   while (tokens.nextToken() != tokens.TT_EOF) {
    Movie m;
    String nameString = tokens.sval;
    tokens.nextToken(); int x = (int) tokens.nval;
    tokens.nextToken(); int y = (int) tokens.nval;
    tokens.nextToken(); int z = (int) tokens.nval;
    if (tokens.nextToken() == tokens.TT_EOL) {
     m = new Movie(x, y, z, nameString);
    }
    else {
     String posterString = tokens.sval;
     m = new Movie(x, y, z, nameString, posterString);
     tokens.nextToken();
    }
    v.addElement(m);
   }
   return v;
  }
  catch (IOException e) {System.out.println(e);}
  return null;
 }
 public static Image readMovieImage(String fileName) {
  try {
   URL url = MovieAuxiliaries.class.getResource(fileName);
   if (url == null) {return null;}
   ImageProducer producer = (ImageProducer) (url.getContent());
   if (producer == null) {return null;}
   Toolkit tk = Toolkit.getDefaultToolkit();
   Image image = tk.createImage(producer);
   return image;
  }
  catch (IOException e) {System.out.println(e);};
  return null;
}}
```

845 There is no equivalent to closing a file when you are reading a file via a URL. The reason is that the entire file is read all at once into a buffer.

846

HIGHLIGHTS

- Java's resource locators provide a flexible means for accessing text, image, and audio files.

- Resource locators used with standalone applications can obtain files in the directories specified by the value of the CLASSPATH variable, and in subdirectories of those directories.

- Java's security mechanism restricts all files read via a browser to the directory where the applet is stored, and to the subdirectories of that location.

- **If** you want to open an input stream on a text file, **then** instantiate the following pattern:

```
URL url
  = name of colocated class .class.getResource( file name );
InputStream stream = (InputStream) url .getContent();
InputStreamReader reader = new InputStreamReader( stream );
```

- If you want to load an image file, **then** instantiate the following pattern:

```
URL url =
  name of colocated class .class.getResource( file name );
ImageProducer producer = (ImageProducer) url .getContent();
Toolkit toolkit = Toolkit.getDefaultToolkit();
Image image = toolkit .createImage(producer);
```

46 HOW TO USE CHOICE LISTS TO SELECT INSTANCES

847 The illustration program shown in Segment 797 works with but a single, wired-in movie. To witness more interesting behavior, you need to learn to work with a vector of movies, produced by the movie-reading program introduced in Chapter 45.

When you have completed this chapter, you will have learned about a complete application, with a rating meter connected to a displayed list of movies.

848 The following shows an applet with a choice list added. The display was produced by a web browser using the applet defined in this chapter, in Segment 856 and Segment 857, viewed through an HTML file:

849 The applet shown in Segment 848 involves not only a choice list but also a new model class, MovieData. As usual, before you define that class, you begin with an interface definition. That definition establishes a setter and getter for a vector of movies. It also establishes a getter for the movie at a particular place in the vector, and a method that activates observers.

```
import java.util.*;
public interface MovieDataInterface  {
 // Put movies into data source:
 public abstract void setMovieVector (Vector v) ;
 // Extract movies from data source:
 public abstract Vector getMovieVector () ;
 // Find a particular movie at given index:
 public abstract Movie getMovie(int index) ;
 // Miscellaneous method:
 public abstract void changed () ;
}
```

850   Having defined the interface, you proceed to define the class. The new class, like the `Movie` class, is an observable, with a setter that activates observers when the movie vector is set, and a miscellaneous method, `changed` that activates observers when called.

```
import java.util.*;
public class MovieData extends Observable implements MovieDataInterface
{
 private Vector vector;
 public MovieData () {
  setMovieVector(MovieAuxiliaries.readMovieFile("general.movies"));
 }
 public void setMovieVector (Vector v) {
  vector = v;
  setChanged();
  notifyObservers();
 }
 public Vector getMovieVector () {
  return vector;
 }
 public Movie getMovie (int i) {
  if (i >= 0 && i <= vector.size()) {
   return (Movie)(vector.elementAt(i));
  }
  else {return null;}
 }
 public void changed () {
  setChanged();
  notifyObservers();
 }
}
```

851   Testing the index in the `getMovie` method, defined in Segment 850, is an example of **defensive programming**. Although it might seem unlikely that an out-of-bounds argument could be supplied, you should be sure that nothing horrible happens if the argument is, in fact, out of bounds.

852   Adding an instance of the new `MovieData` model class produces the following modification of the applet defined in Segment 797.

```
import javax.swing.*;
import java.awt.event.*;
import java.util.*;
public class MovieApplication extends JApplet {
 // Declare instance variables:
 private Meter meter;
 private Movie movie;
 private MovieData movieData;
```

```java
  // Define constructor
  public MovieApplication() {
   // Create models
   getMovie();
   getMovieData();
   // Create and connect view to application
   getContentPane().add("Center", getMeter());
  }
  // Define getters and setters
  public Meter getMeter () {
   if (meter == null) {setMeter(new Meter(0, 30));}
   return meter;
  }
  public Movie getMovie () {
   if(movie == null) {setMovie(new Movie (10, 10, 10, "On to Java"));}
   return movie;
  }
  public MovieData getMovieData () {
   if(movieData == null) {setMovieData(new MovieData ());}
   return movieData;
  }
  public void setMeter (Meter m) {
   meter = m;
   meter.addMouseListener(new MeterListener(this));
  }
  public void setMovie (Movie m) {
   if(movie == m) {return;}
   if(movie instanceof Movie) {movie.deleteObservers();}
   if(m instanceof Movie) {
    movie = m;
    movie.addObserver(new MovieObserver(this));
    movie.changed();
   }
  }
  public void setMovieData (MovieData m) {
   movieData = m;
  }
 }
```

853 On the view side, a **choice list** is an instance of the JList class, or a subclass of that class. Such instances produce graphical displays of choices on which you can click to make a selection.

There is no need to modify the behavior of the basic JList class; the built-in methods suffice. Accordingly, you do not need to define a subclass; you can install a JList directly into the evolving applet.

```java
import javax.swing.*;
import java.awt.event.*;
import java.util.*;
public class MovieApplication extends JApplet {
 // Declare instance variables:
 private Meter meter;
 private JList jList;
 private Movie movie;
 private MovieData movieData;
 // Define constructor
 public MovieApplication() {
  // Create models
  getMovie();
  getMovieData();
  // Create and connect views to application
  getContentPane().add("Center", getMeter());
  getContentPane().add("East", getJList());
 }
 // Define getters and setters
 public Meter getMeter () {
  if (meter == null) {setMeter(new Meter(0, 30));}
  return meter;
 }
 public JList getJList () {
  if (jList == null) {setJList(new JList());}
  return jList;
 }
 public Movie getMovie () {
  if(movie == null) {setMovie(new Movie (10, 10, 10, "On to Java"));}
  return movie;
 }
 public MovieData getMovieData () {
  if(movieData == null) {setMovieData(new MovieData ());}
  return movieData;
 }
 public void setMeter (Meter m) {
  meter = m;
  meter.addMouseListener(new MeterListener(this));
 }
 public void setMovie (Movie m) {
  if(movie == m) {return;}
  if(movie instanceof Movie) {movie.deleteObservers();}
  if(m instanceof Movie) {
   movie = m;
   movie.addObserver(new MovieObserver(this));
   movie.changed();
 }}
```

```
 public void setMovieData (MovieData m) {
  movieData = m;
 }
 public void setJList (JList j) {
  jList = j;
 }
}
```

854 Next, you must wire together your new model, an instance of `MovieData`, and your new view, an instance of `JList`.

To begin, you define an observer. When activated, the observer fetches the vector of movies from the model, generates a vector of strings from the titles in the vector of movies, and relays the vector of strings to the choice list. The choice list setter, `setListData`, conveniently takes as its argument a vector of strings.

```
import java.util.*;
import javax.swing.*;
public class MovieDataObserver implements Observer {
 private MovieApplication applet;
 public MovieDataObserver (MovieApplication a) {
  applet = a;
 }
 public void update (Observable observable, Object object) {
  Vector titles = new Vector();
  for (Iterator i = applet.getMovieData().getMovieVector().iterator();
       i.hasNext();) {
   Movie movie = (Movie) (i.next());
   titles.add(movie.getTitle());
  }
  applet.getJList().setListData(titles);
 }
}
```

855 Now, you define a listener class for your choice list. The choice list will activate your listener by calling an interface-imposed method, `valueChanged`, whenever you select with a mouse click an item in the choice list.

Because the storage of strings in the choice list parallels the storage of movies in the `MovieData` instance, the index used by `getMovieData` will fetch the movie from the `MovieData` instance that corresponds to the selection from the choice list, determined by `getSelectedIndex`:

```
import javax.swing.*;
import javax.swing.event.*;
public class MovieListListener implements ListSelectionListener {
 private MovieApplication applet;
 public MovieListListener (MovieApplication a) {
  applet = a;
 }
 public void valueChanged(ListSelectionEvent e) {
  int index = applet.getJList().getSelectedIndex();
  applet.setMovie(applet.getMovieData().getMovie(index));
 }
}
```

856 Now, you are ready to complete your applet revision by installing your new movie-data observer and list listener.

```
import javax.swing.*;
import java.awt.event.*;
import java.util.*;
public class MovieApplication extends JApplet {
 // Declare instance variables:
 private Meter meter;
 private JList jList;
 private Movie movie;
 private MovieData movieData;
 // Define constructor
 public MovieApplication() {
  // Create models
  getMovie();
  getMovieData();
  // Create and connect views to application
  getContentPane().add("Center", getMeter());
  getContentPane().add("East", getJList());
 }
 // Define getters and setters
 public Meter getMeter () {
  if (meter == null) {setMeter(new Meter(0, 30));}
  return meter;
 }
 public JList getJList () {
  if (jList == null) {setJList(new JList());}
  return jList;
 }
 public Movie getMovie () {
  if(movie == null) {setMovie(new Movie (10, 10, 10, "On to Java"));}
  return movie;
 }
```

```
public MovieData getMovieData () {
 if(movieData == null) {setMovieData(new MovieData ());}
 return movieData;
}
public void setMeter (Meter m) {meter = m;}
public void setMovie (Movie m) {
 if(movie == m) {return;}
 if(movie instanceof Movie) {movie.deleteObservers();}
 if(m instanceof Movie) {
  movie = m;
  movie.addObserver(new MovieObserver(this));
  movie.changed();
}}
public void setMovieData (MovieData m) {
 movieData = m;
 movieData.addObserver(new MovieDataObserver(this));
 movieData.changed();
}
public void setJList (JList j) {
 jList = j;
 jList.addListSelectionListener(new MovieListListener(this));
}
}
```

The mouse listener, previously attached to the meter for use in demonstration, is removed, as the choice list now illustrates viewer-initiated action.

857 If you have more than a few movies, you will want to view those movies in a choice list with a scroll bar. Using Java, you add a scroll bar to a choice list by viewing the choice list through a **scroll pane**, which automatically adds vertical or horizontal scroll bars, as needed. This addition requires just a small flourish: You create a scroll pane, an instance of the JScrollPane class, with the choice list as its argument. Then, instead of adding the choice list to the applet's content pane, you add the scroll pane.

```
getContentPane().add("East", getJList());
```

                              │ Replaced by
                              ▼

```
getContentPane().add("East", new JScrollPane(getJList()));
```

Testing the applet with the scroll pane installed produces the display shown in Segment 848.

858 Add a print statement to the MovieData observer and the JList listener so that you can
PRACTICE determine when they are called. Experiment with your redefined observer and listener using the tester defined in Segment 800

859 Modify the definition of the MovieApplication class in Segment 856 such that two lists
PRACTICE of movies are shown. One list is to be taken from the general.movies file; the other list is to be taken from the horror.movies file.

- If you want display a choice list, **then** create a new `JList`. Use the `setListData` method, with a vector-of-strings argument, to establish the contents of the choice list.

- If you want to determine which element is selected from a choice list, **then** implement a listener class that defines a `valueChanged` method, **then** obtain the selected element's index inside `valueChanged` using `getSelectedIndex`, **and then** use `addListSelectionListener` to attach a listener instance to the choice list.

- If you want to display a choice list with scroll bars, **then** embed your choice list in an instance of the `JScrollPane` class by instantiating the following pattern:

  new JScrollPane(`choice list`)

  and then add the scroll pane, rather than the choice list itself, to the surrounding applet or frame.

47 HOW TO BRING IMAGES INTO APPLETS

861 This chapter, in concert with Chapter 48, Chapter 51, and Chapter 50, enriches the application about which you learned in Chapter 46 by adding an image, a marqueelike display, a form, a custom-tailored layout manager, and a pull-down menu.

In this chapter, in particular, you learn how to move information from image files into your applets. You also learn that the movement of image files is handled by a separate thread—an arrangement that enables your application to present a snappy look and feel, even though the movement of image files may be slow.

When you have completed this chapter, the movie application about which you are learning will have not only a rating meter and a displayed list of movies, but also an image display for those movies for which image files are available.

862 The following shows an applet with an image added. The display was produced by a web browser using the applet defined in this chapter, in Segment 872, viewed through an HTML file.

863 To display images, you need to define a subclass of the `JComponent` class that, like the `Meter` class, produces instances that are viewers. The new class will be the `Poster` class.

864 Following the conventions of good-programming practice, you precede the definition of the `Poster` class with the definition of an interface:

```
public interface PosterInterface {
 // Setter
 public abstract void setImageFile (String fileName) ;
}
```

Evidently, all you can do to a poster is to call a setter that takes a `String` instance naming a file containing an image.

865 With the interface defined, you proceed to define the required class. If the file name supplied is different from the current value of the `file` variable, and is not null, then `setImage` creates an image using that argument and the `readMovieImage` auxiliary defined in Segment 844. Then, the setter calls `repaint`, which in turn calls `paint`.

```
import java.awt.*;
import javax.swing.*;
import java.util.*;
public class Poster extends JComponent implements PosterInterface {
 private String file;
 private Image image;
 public void setImageFile (String s) {
  if (s != file) {
   file = s;
   if (file == null) {image = null;}
   else {
    image = MovieAuxiliaries.readMovieImage(file);
   }
   repaint();
  }
 }
 // Definition of paint ...
 }
 public Dimension getMinimumSize() {return new Dimension(200, 300);}
 public Dimension getPreferredSize() {return new Dimension(200, 300);}
}
```

866 You display images within a `paint` method using `drawImage`, an instance method of the `Graphics` class.

First, however, you have to determine the appropriate size for the image. You first determine the size of the `Poster` instance by using the `getSize` method to obtain a `Dimension` instance, d, which then provides `width` and `height` instance-variable values for the image component:

```
Dimension d = getSize();
...   d.width ...
...   d.height ...
```

867 Then, with dimensions in hand, you have `paint` call the `drawImage` method, which takes arguments specifying the image, the origin, and the dimensions. Also, because the `drawImage` method needs to know about the image-displaying properties of the component on which the image is to be drawn, that component, the value of `this`, is supplied as the final argument:

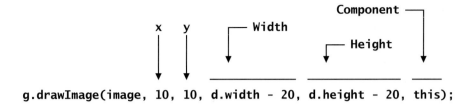

```
g.drawImage(image, 10, 10, d.width - 20, d.height - 20, this);
```

As illustrated, the image is drawn with a 10-unit border.

868 Thus, you can define paint as follows:

```
public void paint(Graphics g) {
 if (image != null) {
  Dimension d = getSize();
   g.drawImage(image, 10, 10, d.width - 20, d.height - 20 , this);
 }
}
```

869 The definition of paint shown in Segment 868 works, but it is likely to distort the image, because the height-to-width ratio of the image will differ from the height-to-width ratio of the component in which the image is to be displayed.

Accordingly, you might choose to use the getWidth and getHeight methods to obtain the width and height of the image, so that you can adjust the arguments provided to drawImage. The getWidth and getHeight methods each use an image as the target, and because the getWidth and getHeight methods need to know about the image-displaying properties of the component on which the image is to be drawn, that component, the value of this, is supplied as well, as an ordinary argument.

```
image.getWidth(this)
```

870 The scaling computations required to adjust the arguments of drawImage are straightforward, albeit tedious:

```java
import java.awt.*;
import javax.swing.*;
import java.util.*;
public class Poster extends JComponent implements PosterInterface {
 private String file;
 private Image image;
 public void setImageFile (String s) {
  if (s != file) {
   file = s;
   if (file == null) {image = null;}
   else {
    image = MovieAuxiliaries.readMovieImage (file);
   }
   repaint();
  }
 }
 public void paint(Graphics g) {
  if (image != null) {
   Dimension d = getSize();
   int x, y, width, height, border = 20;
   // Tedium begins
   double imageRatio = (float) image.getHeight(this)
                           / image.getWidth(this);
   double windowRatio = (float) d.height / d.width;
   if (imageRatio > windowRatio) {
    height = d.height - border;
    width = image.getWidth(this) * (d.height - border)
            / image.getHeight(this);
   }
   else {
    width = d.width - border;
    height = image.getHeight(this) * (d.width - border)
             / image.getWidth(this);
   }
   x = (d.width - width) / 2;
   y = (d.height - height) / 2;
   // Tedium ends
   g.drawImage(image, x, y, width, height, this);
  }
 }
 public Dimension getMinimumSize() {return new Dimension(200, 300);}
 public Dimension getPreferredSize() {return new Dimension(200, 300);}
}
```

871 Now, you need to arrange for the movie observer to fetch information from the movie model that is then relayed to a new poster view. Accordingly, you need to modify the definition of `MovieObserver` previously supplied in Segment 789.

```java
import java.util.*;
public class MovieObserver implements Observer {
 private MovieApplication applet;
 public MovieObserver (MovieApplication a) {
  applet = a;
 }
 public void update (Observable observable, Object object) {
  applet.getMeter().setValue(applet.getMovie().rating());
  applet.getMeter().setTitle(applet.getMovie().getTitle());
  applet.getPoster().setImageFile(applet.getMovie().getPoster());
 }
}
```

872 An instance of the new `Poster` class, defined in Segment 870 is put to use in the following revision of the applet defined previously in Segment 856:

```java
import javax.swing.*;
import java.awt.event.*;
import java.util.*;
public class MovieApplication extends JApplet {
 // Declare instance variables:
 private Meter meter;
 private JList jList;
 private Poster poster;
 private Movie movie;
 private MovieData movieData;
 // Define constructor
 public MovieApplication() {
  // Create models
  getMovie();
  getMovieData();
  // Create and connect views to application
  getContentPane().add("West", getMeter());
  getContentPane().add("East", new JScrollPane(getJList()));
  getContentPane().add("Center", getPoster());
 }
 // Define getters and setters
 public Meter getMeter () {
  if (meter == null) {setMeter(new Meter(0, 30));}
  return meter;
 }
```

```
public JList getJList () {
 if (jList == null) {setJList(new JList());}
 return jList;
}
public Movie getMovie () {
 if(movie == null) {setMovie(new Movie (10, 10, 10, "On to Java"));}
 return movie;
}
public MovieData getMovieData () {
 if(movieData == null) {setMovieData(new MovieData ());}
 return movieData;
}
public Poster getPoster () {
 if (poster == null) {setPoster(new Poster());}
 return poster;
}
public void setMeter (Meter m) {
 meter = m;
}
public void setMovie (Movie m) {
 if(movie == m) {return;}
 if(movie instanceof Movie) {movie.deleteObservers();}
 if(m instanceof Movie) {
  movie = m;
  movie.addObserver(new MovieObserver(this));
  movie.changed();
 }
}
public void setMovieData (MovieData m) {
 movieData = m;
 movieData.addObserver(new MovieDataObserver(this));
 movieData.changed();
}
public void setJList (JList j) {
 jList = j;
 jList.addListSelectionListener(new MovieListListener(this));
}
public void setPoster (Poster p) {
 poster = p;
}
}
```

873 The drawImage method displays the image incrementally, as the image's chunks are loaded. Meanwhile, the rest of your display shows the properties of the current movie quickly.

Separation of image loading and display from the operation of the rest of your program ensures a responsive look and feel. The separation is possible because Java is **multithreaded**.

You learn about multithreading in Chapter 48.

874
PRACTICE
Modify the definition of the `MovieObserver` class, shown in Segment 871, such that an image is displayed only if the rating of the current movie is 25 or greater.

875
PRACTICE
Modify the definition of the `Poster` class defined in Segment 870 such that, if no image is available for the current movie, the message "No image" is displayed instead.

876
HIGHLIGHTS

- Because each image is displayed by its own thread, image display does not stop other processing.

- If you want to display an **Image** instance, **then** instantiate the following pattern inside the `paint` method of the component in which the image is to appear:

  `graphics-context` `.drawImage`
  `(` `image` `,` `x` `,` `y` `,` `width` `,` `height` `,` `drawing component` `);`

- If you wish to determine the width and height of an image, **then** instantiate the following patterns:

  `image` `.getWidth(` `drawing component` `);`
  `image` `.getHeight(` `drawing component` `);`

48 HOW TO USE THREADS TO IMPLEMENT DYNAMIC APPLETS

877   In Segment 873, you learned that you can write a program that appears to be loading an image at the same time that the program is doing other computations. Such apparently simultaneous computations are possible because Java is **multithreaded**. In this chapter, you learn about multithreading in the context of a program that moves a message across the bottom of a display as though the message were presented on a theater marquee.

878   The following shows an applet with a moving message added. The display was produced by a web browser using the applet defined in this chapter, in Segment 898, viewed through an HTML file.

The display was captured at a moment when the message is mostly—but not completely— exposed:

879   A **process** is a running computer program. In a **multiprocessing system**, the operating system maintains a collection of values, called an **execution context**, for each process that keeps track of the process's state. Execution contexts allow the operating system to interrupt one process, to run another process for a time, and then to resume the first process.

880   Each process in a multiprocessing system runs in **time slices** that are interdigitated with the time slices of other processes, thus sharing the computer's time. If the time slices are short enough, all processes appear to be running simultaneously, although each process appears to run more slowly than it would were it to have all the computer's time to itself.

881   In an ordinary multiprocessing system, because each process operates in its own private chunk of memory, each program is said to have its own **address space**.

882   A running Java program is like a multiprocessing system, because it runs multiple processes that share time. However, a running Java program also is unlike a multiprocessing system, because all the processes share a single address space.

A **thread** is a process that shares a single address space with other processes. Each thread works independently, sharing time and a single address space with other threads.

Because Java supports threads, Java is said to be **multithreaded**.

883　Creating and running your own thread is a three-step process:

- You define a subclass of the Thread class. In that definition, you include a definition for a run method.

- You create an instance of your subclass of the Thread class.

- You call the start method with the instance as the target, whereupon the run method begins to run independently.

884　Suppose, by way of illustration, that you define the following thread. When run, by calling the start method in main, the thread prints Looping..., as fast as it can, ad nauseam.

```
import java.lang.*;
public class DemoThread extends Thread {
 public static void main (String argv []) {
  DemoThread thread = new DemoThread();
  thread.start();
 }
 public void run () {
  while (true) {
   System.out.println("Looping...");
  }
 }
}
```

Note that the Thread class is provided by the java.lang package.

885　You can slow down a looping thread by adding sleep expressions. They must be in try–catch expressions to handle interruptions.

The following version of DemoThread prints Looping..., every 200 milliseconds, ad nauseam.

```
import java.lang.*;
public class DemoThread extends Thread {
 public static void main (String argv []) {
  DemoThread thread = new DemoThread();
  thread.start();
 }
 public void run () {
  while (true) {
   System.out.println("Looping...");
   try{sleep(200);}
   catch (InterruptedException e) {}
  }
 }
}
```

886 Of course, you can substitute any statement you like for the print statement in Segment 885. For example, you can arrange for a thread to increment the position of the text displayed on a component.

Suppose that you decide to define a Marquee class such that instances can display a message, provided via a constructor, at a position dictated by the values of the position and drop instance variables.

The paint method uses the graphics context to display the message in a large bold font. If the value of the ready variable is false, then paint first uses the graphics context to initialize all instance variables, other than message:

```
import java.awt.*;
import javax.swing.*;
public class Marquee extends JComponent {
 private String message;
 private int position, drop, initialPosition, delta, messageWidth;
 private Font messageFont = new Font("TimesRoman", Font.BOLD, 24);
 private boolean ready = false;
 public Marquee (String s) {
  message = s;
 }
 public void decrementPosition() {
  if (position + messageWidth < 0) {
   position = initialPosition;
  }
  else {
   position = position - delta;
  }
  repaint();
 }
```

```
public void paint(Graphics g) {
 // Determine size:
 Dimension d = getSize();
 // Set font
 g.setFont(messageFont);
 if (initialPosition != d.width) {ready = false;}
 if (!ready) {
  // Set initial position to be the width:
  position = initialPosition = d.width;
  // Set the font and determine the message width:
  FontMetrics f = g.getFontMetrics();
  messageWidth = f.stringWidth(message);
  // Set delta to be equal to the width of the letter e:
  delta = f.stringWidth("e");
  // Set drop so as to center the text vertically:
  drop = (d.height + f.getHeight() + f.getDescent()) / 2;
  ready = true;
 }
 System.out.println("Painting");
 g.drawString(message, position, drop);
}
public Dimension getMinimumSize() {return new Dimension(300, 50);}
public Dimension getPreferredSize() {return new Dimension(300, 50);}
}
```

887 At first, the message's position is off the display, on the right side. Then, each time that decrementPosition is called, the position shifts left by the value of delta.

Eventually, with sufficient calls, the message shifts entirely to the left of the component, at which point decrementPosition resets the position variable.

888 By arranging to call decrementPosition at regular intervals, you can ensure that the message will scroll from right to left.

Accordingly, you need to define a subclass of the Thread class—say MarqueeThread—that runs independently, and that calls decrementPosition, with the component as the target, at regular intervals.

889 So that the run method in the MarqueeThread class has access to the appropriate instance of the Marquee class, that instance of the Marquee class is provided to the thread via the thread's constructor, and is held by the marquee instance variable.

Then, with the Marquee instance available as the value of the marquee instance variable, the run method is readily defined to call decrementPosition periodically.

```
import java.lang.*;
public class MarqueeThread extends Thread {
  private Marquee marquee;
  public MarqueeThread (Marquee c) {
    marquee = c;
  }
  public void run () {
   while (true) {
    // Call to decrementPosition ...
    try{sleep(200);}
    catch (InterruptedException e) {}
   }
  }
}
```

890 You could write the call to decrementPosition straightforwardly, as in the following illustration. Such a call is exceedingly dangerous, and likely to fail in a large application, because decrementPosition may be called while your program's main thread is in the process of executing display operations. Thus, the display operations initiated by your program's main thread and the display operations initiated by the MarqueeThread may step on each other. In such situations, your display goes haywire.

```
import java.lang.*;
public class MarqueeThread extends Thread {
  private Marquee marquee;
  public MarqueeThread (Marquee c) {
    marquee = c;
  }
  public void run () {
   while (true) {
    // Bad programming practice, do not do this!
    marquee.decrementPosition();
    try{sleep(200);}
    catch (InterruptedException e) {}
   }
  }
}
```

891 The main thread in your program maintains a work queue of display operations. Fortunately, a not-well-known Java mechanism enables you to add your own work-describing class instances to that work queue. That way, your work occurs in between other work on the queue, rather than simultaneously with that other work.

892 To put work on the display-operations queue, you define a class that implements the Runnable interface, with a run method that calls the decrementPosition method of the Marquee class. If you call that class ChangeHandler, then you call decrementPosition by adding a ChangeHandler instance to the display work queue, as described in Segment 893

```
import java.util.*;
import java.awt.event.*;
import javax.swing.*;
public class ChangeHandler implements Runnable {
 private Marquee marquee;
 public ChangeHandler (Marquee c) {
  marquee = c;
 }
 public void run() {
  marquee.decrementPosition();
 }
}
```

893 To add to the display work queue a Runnable instance, or an instance of a subclass of Runnable, you call the invokeLater class method of the SwingUtilities class found in the javax.swing package:

```
SwingUtilities.invokeLater( runnable );
```

894 Once you understand how to place Runnable instances on the display work queue, you are ready to define MarqueeThread properly.

```
import java.lang.*;
import javax.swing.*;
public class MarqueeThread extends Thread {
 private Marquee marquee;
 public MarqueeThread (Marquee c) {
   marquee = c;
 }
 public void run () {
  while (true) {
    // Good programming practice; do it this way!
    ChangeHandler changeHandler = new ChangeHandler(marquee);
    SwingUtilities.invokeLater(changeHandler);
    try{sleep(200);}
    catch (InterruptedException e) {}
  }
 }
}
```

895 You can test the MarqueThread class with the following program:

```
import javax.swing.*;
public class ThreadTestor {
 public static void main (String argv []) {
  JFrame frame = new JFrame("Thread Test");
  Marquee marquee = new Marquee("Buy On To Java Today!");
  MarqueeThread thread = new MarqueeThread(marquee);
  thread.start();
  frame.getContentPane().add("Center", marquee);
  frame.setSize(550, 200);
  frame.addWindowListener(new ApplicationClosingWindowListener());
  frame.show();
 }
}
```

896 At this point, you readily can install a marquee in the evolving movie-rating application. Because none of the other application instances send information to the marquee, you can add the marquee by subclassing the MovieApplication class provided in Segment 872, placing the marquee in the south slot:

```
import javax.swing.*;
import java.awt.event.*;
import java.util.*;
public class MovieApplicationWithThread extends MovieApplication {
 // Declare variables
 private Marquee marquee;
 private MarqueeThread thread;
 // Define constructor
 public MovieApplicationWithThread () {
  super();
  marquee = new Marquee("Buy On To Java Today!");
  thread = new MarqueeThread(marquee);
  thread.start();
  getContentPane().add("South", marquee);
 }
}
```

897 Once you understand how the Marquee, MarqueeThread, and ChangeHandler classes work together, you can bring all three into one class using locally defined classes. The thread is created, and started, in the constructor.

```
import java.awt.*;
import javax.swing.*;
public class Marquee extends JComponent {
 private MarqueeThread thread;
 private String message;
 private int position, drop, initialPosition, delta, messageWidth;
 private Font messageFont = new Font("TimesRoman", Font.BOLD, 24);
 private boolean ready = false;
 public Marquee (String s) {
  message = s;
  thread = new MarqueeThread(this);
  thread.start();
 }
 // Definition of decrementPosition as in Segment 886 ...
 // Definition of paint as in Segment 886 ...
 class MarqueeThread extends Thread {
  private Marquee marquee;
  public MarqueeThread (Marquee c) {
   marquee = c;
  }
  public void run () {
   while (true) {
    ChangeHandler changeHandler = new ChangeHandler(marquee);
    SwingUtilities.invokeLater(changeHandler);
    try{sleep(200);}
    catch (InterruptedException e) {}
   }
  }
 }
 class ChangeHandler implements Runnable {
  private Marquee marquee;
  public ChangeHandler (Marquee c) {
   marquee = c;
  }
  public void run() {
   marquee.decrementPosition();
  }
 }
 public Dimension getMinimumSize() {return new Dimension(300, 50);}
 public Dimension getPreferredSize() {return new Dimension(300, 50);}
}
```

898 Using the definition of the Marquee class shown in Segment 897, you can write the following variation on the program defined in Segment 896:

```
import javax.swing.*;
import java.awt.event.*;
import java.util.*;
public class MovieApplicationWithThread extends MovieApplication {
 // Declare variables
 private Marquee marquee;
 // Define constructor
 public MovieApplicationWithThread () {
  super();
  marquee = new Marquee("Buy On To Java Today!");
  getContentPane().add("South", marquee);
 }
}
```

899   To stop a thread, you assign a signaling value to a variable tested inside the run method. In the following, for example, a mouse listener assigns true to the stopper variable, which is tested each time that run loops inside the marquee thread. As soon as stopper is true, run returns. Thus, you can stop the marquee by clicking on it.

```
import java.awt.*;
import java.awt.event.*;
import javax.swing.*;
public class Marquee extends JComponent {
 MarqueeThread thread;
 String message;
 int position, drop, initialPosition, delta, messageWidth;
 Font messageFont = new Font("TimesRoman", Font.BOLD, 24);
 boolean ready = false;
 boolean stopper = false;
 public Marquee (String s) {
  message = s;
  addMouseListener(new MarqueeListener());
  thread = new MarqueeThread(this);
  thread.start();
 }
 // Definition of decrementPosition as in Segment 886 ...
 // Definition of paint as in Segment 886 ...
 class MarqueeListener extends MouseAdapter {
  public void mouseClicked(MouseEvent e) {
   stopper = true;
  }
 }
}
```

```
class MarqueeThread extends Thread {
 private Marquee marquee;
 public MarqueeThread (Marquee c) {
  marquee = c;
 }
 public void run () {
  while (true) {
   if (stopper) {return;}
   ChangeHandler changeHandler = new ChangeHandler(marquee);
   SwingUtilities.invokeLater(changeHandler);
   try{sleep(200);}
   catch (InterruptedException e) {}
  }
 }
}
class ChangeHandler implements Runnable {
 private Marquee marquee;
 public ChangeHandler (Marquee c) {
  marquee = c;
 }
 public void run() {
  marquee.decrementPosition();
 }
}
public Dimension getMinimumSize() {return new Dimension(300, 50);}
public Dimension getPreferredSize() {return new Dimension(300, 50);}
}
```

900
SIDE TRIP
You can direct a program to wait for a thread to finish its work—that is, for the run method to return—using the join method, as shown in the following example, in which the thread is the value of the thread variable:

```
thread.join(0);
```

The argument specifies a time interval in milliseconds that your program is to wait. A time interval of zero indicates that you want your program to wait until the thread finishes its work, no matter how long the wait.

901
SIDE TRIP
You can use the setPriority method to tell Java about the importance of a particular thread in your application. If the thread assigned to thread is not at all important, you evaluate the following statement:

```
thread.setPriority(Thread.MIN_PRIORITY);
```

On the other hand, if the thread is extremely important, you evaluate the following statement:

```
thread.setPriority(Thread.MAX_PRIORITY);
```

902

SIDE TRIP

Multithreaded programs may require **synchronization**, which is a way of ensuring that two methods will not run at the same time with the same class instance as their target.

One classic example is that of bank-account deposits and withdrawals. If you have different threads call `deposit` and `withdraw` methods on the same bank-account instance, there is a chance that both methods will fetch the current balance from an instance variable before either method performs the appropriate addition or subtraction. Thus, one method may work on an out-of-date balance, as illustrated by the following event sequence, producible by two threads running `deposit` and `withdraw` methods on the same bank-account instance at the same time:

```
Deposit thread                          Withdraw thread
_____                         _____

Fetch current balance, 100

                                        Fetch current balance, 100


Add 10 to 100,
Write balance, 110

                                        Subtract 10 from 100
                                        Write balance, 90
```

903

SIDE TRIP

To solve the interference problem illustrated in Segment 902, you need to ensure that the `deposit` method does not allow the `withdraw` method to run on the same bank-account instance before the `deposit` method has finished its work, even though both methods are under the control of independent threads.

To ensure that the two methods do not work on the same bank-account instance at the same time, you need only to mark both method definitions with the `synchronized` keyword:

```
public synchronized void deposit(int amount) { ··· }
public synchronized void withdraw(int amount) { ··· }
```

Such synchronized methods cannot run on the same bank-account instance at the same time, because Java has what is called a **locking mechanism**. Conceptually, each class instance has exactly one **lock**, and any synchronized method must have that lock to start. Once a synchronized method starts, it holds onto the lock until it has completed its work. Thus, no other synchronized method can run on that class instance during that time.

904

PRACTICE

Develop a dynamic logo consisting of your initials, which are to change color from red to blue and back again once every 10 seconds. Modify the `MovieApplet` definition shown in Segment 896 to include your dynamic logo.

- If you want to create a thread that calls a method defined in another class, the controlled class, **then** instantiate the following pattern:

```
public class class name extends Thread {
  controlled-class name  instance variable ;
  public class name (controlled-class name  parameter) {
    instance variable = parameter ;
  }
  public void run () {
    // Method calls with { instance variable} as the target ...
  }
}
```

- If one thread is to call a method in another thread that involves display, **then** the calling thread should call the called thread indirectly via a change handler and the SwingUtilities class method, invokeLater.

- If you want a thread to pause, **then** instantiate the following pattern:

```
try{sleep( time, in milliseconds );}
catch (InterruptedException e) {return;}
```

- If you want to stop a thread, **then** assign a new value to a variable that is tested by the thread's run method **and then** arrange for the new value to cause the run method to return.

49 HOW TO CREATE FORMS AND TO FIRE YOUR OWN EVENTS

906   In this chapter, you learn how to deploy components that allow data to be typed into text fields, so that you can display and edit a movie's instance variables. You also learn about labels and buttons.

Next, you learn about what property-change listeners are and how you can fire events that activate property-change listeners.

When you have completed this chapter, the movie application about which you are learning will have not only a rating meter and a displayed list of movies, but also mechanisms that allow you to change ratings easily.

907   The following shows an applet with text fields, labels, and buttons added. The display was produced by a web browser using the applet defined in this chapter, in Segment 930, viewed through an HTML file.

908   The key elements in a form are instances of the `JLabel` class, the `JTextField` class, and the `JButton` class. All are components, so you can connect instances of each to an applet's content pane.

In practice, however, you are unlikely to connect labels, text fields, or buttons directly to an applet. Instead, you connect them to an instance of a subclass of the `JPanel` class, which you connect to an applet's content pane. Thus, you implement a form by creating a subclass of the `JPanel` class.

909   The `JPanel` class is Java's generic component container. Each `JFrame` instance and `JApplet` instance has a content pane, and that content pane is, by default, an instance of the `JPanel` class.

You refer to instances of the `JPanel` class, or subclasses of that class, as **panels**.

910 Following good programming practice, in preparation for defining your new panel, you define an interface:

```
public interface RatingPanelInterface {
 // Setters
 public abstract void setValue1 (int value) ;
 public abstract void setValue2 (int value) ;
 public abstract void setValue3 (int value) ;
 // Getters
 public abstract int getValue1 () ;
 public abstract int getValue2 () ;
 public abstract int getValue3 () ;
}
```

The interface shows good taste in that none of the setters and getters have names that hint of movies, thus adhering to the principle that views should exhibit no knowledge of a particular domain. Any view that implements the interface will serve well whenever three values are to be displayed and manipulated.

911 Having defined the interface in Segment 910, you can begin to implement the RatingPanel class, by declaring the instance variables whose assignments will be instances of the int, JTextField, and JButton classes:

```
import java.awt.*;
import java.util.*;
import java.awt.event.*;
import javax.swing.*;
import javax.swing.event.*;
public class RatingPanel extends JPanel implements RatingPanelInterface
{
 private int value1, value2, value3;
 private JTextField field1, field2, field3;
 private JButton button1Plus, button2Plus, button3Plus;
 private JButton button1Minus, button2Minus, button3Minus;
 // Constructor defined here ...
 // Setters and getters defined here ...
 // Local listener defined here ...
 }
 public Dimension getMinimumSize() {return new Dimension(300, 75);}
 public Dimension getPreferredSize() {return new Dimension(300, 75);}
}
```

912 Before you can define the RatingPanel constructor, you need to know a little about the embedded components and the grid layout.

For example, you need to know that instances of the JLabel class, when added to a panel, display the string provided to the JLabel constructor. Thus, when the following add statement appears inside a panel's constructor, the string assigned to `label` appears at a place dictated by the panel's layout manager:

add(new JLabel(label));

913 The constructor for instances of the `JTextField` class specifies an initial string and the number of columns associated with the text field. For example, the following statement creates a 20-column text field, initialized to display a one character string, "0", and assigned to a `JTextField` variable, `field1`:

field1 = new JTextField("0", 20);

Then, when the following add statement appears inside the constructor for a panel, the initial string, "0", is displayed in a text field at a place dictated by the panel's layout manager:

add(field1);

914 Of course, you may wish to construct a text field using an integer, rather than a string. Such a wish requires you to convert the integer into a string first, using the `valueOf` class method found in the `String` class. In the following, the value of the `int` variable, `value1`, is converted:

field1 = new JTextField(String.valueOf(value1), 20);

915 To fetch the current string that appears in a text field, possibly after you edit that field and press the Enter key, you use the `getText` method:

field1.getText()

916 Often, you want the value of an integer that a string represents, so you have to convert the string into an integer using the `parseInt` class method found in the `Integer` class. Thus, the following produces an integer from a text-field's string:

Integer.parseInt(field1.getText());

917 Later on, if you want a program to change what appears in a text field, the `setText` method does the work. To deal with integers, you must first convert the number into a string using the `valueOf` class method found in the `String` class. Thus, the following sets the text from a string obtained from the integer, `value1`:

field1.setText(String.valueOf(value1))

918 The constructor for the `JButton` class produces a button labeled by the constructor's argument, a string. Thus, the following produces a button labeled with a plus sign, and assigns that button to the `button1Plus` instance variable:

button1Plus = new JButton("+");

919 You arrange all the labels, text fields, and buttons in a panel using an instance of the GridLayout layout manager. The GridLayout constructor takes four arguments: the number of rows, the number of columns, the spacing between rows, and the spacing between columns.

To specify that you want three rows and four columns, with reasonable spacing, you specify the following layout manager:

```
setLayout(new GridLayout (3, 4, 3, 3));
```

920 Having learned a little about labels, text fields, buttons, and the grid layout manager, you can define the RatingPanel class's constructor. That constructor takes three arguments, which become row labels via instances of the JLabel class. The constructor arranges three labels, three text fields, and six buttons in a grid layout:

```
import java.awt.*;
import java.util.*;
import java.awt.event.*;
import javax.swing.*;
import javax.swing.event.*;
public class RatingPanel extends JPanel implements RatingPanelInterface
{
 private int value1, value2, value3;
 private JTextField field1, field2, field3;
 private JButton button1Plus, button2Plus, button3Plus;
 private JButton button1Minus, button2Minus, button3Minus;
 RatingPanel (String x, String y, String z) {
  setLayout(new GridLayout (3, 4, 3, 3));
  value1 = 0; value2 = 0; value3 = 0;
  field1 = new JTextField(String.valueOf(value1), 20);
  button1Plus = new JButton("+");
  button1Minus = new JButton("-");
  // Ditto for other text fields and buttons ...
  add(new JLabel (x));
  add(field1); add(button1Minus); add(button1Plus);
  // Ditto for other labels, text fields, and buttons ...
  // Listeners connected here ...
 }
 // Setters and getters defined here ...
 // Local listener defined here ...
 }
 public Dimension getMinimumSize() {return new Dimension(300, 75);}
 public Dimension getPreferredSize() {return new Dimension(300, 75);}
}
```

921 Having defined the RatingPanel constructor, you now proceed to the setters and getters required by the RatingPanelInterface interface.

The getters are straightforward; each returns a value:

```
public int getValue1() {return value1;}
```

Elementary setters also are straightforward; each assigns an instance variable and updates a text field:

```
public void setValue1(int v) {
 value1 = v;
 field1.setText(String.valueOf(value1));
}
```

922 At this point, you have seen the following:

- A `RatingPanel` constructor that creates and arranges labels, text fields, and buttons

- Definitions of `RatingPanel` setters and getters; the setters both assign values and update text fields

923 Now, you must augment your definition so that your form becomes a view capable of supplying information to a model. Your augmentation involves two steps:

- You connect a listener to the text fields and buttons. That listener calls the form's setters, thus maintaining the form's instance variables.

- You arrange for the entire form to produce events and to activate listeners that are connected to the form.

Thus, there are two listener levels:

- A lower-level listener, connected directly to text fields and buttons, operates inside the form, maintaining the form's instance variables.

- A higher-level listener, connected to the form itself, is in charge of fetching information from the form, using the form's getters, and relaying that information to a model.

924 First, you learn how to connect the event-producing text fields and buttons to listeners that maintain the form's instance variables.

In particular, you need to know that both text fields and buttons activate connected action-event listeners, to which they supply action events, which are instances of the `ActionEvent` class.

Action-event listeners implement the `ActionListener` interface, which requires the definition of the `actionPerformed` method; that `actionPerformed` method is called when the connected view activates an action-event listener.

Text fields activate connected action-event listeners when you press Enter or click on another component; buttons produce action events when you click on them.

925 You could define a different action listener for each text field and each button. If there are many components to which to listen, however, you should follow the less cumbersome practice of defining just one listener, which you connect to all the text fields and buttons you wish to have monitored. Then, you define the actionPerformed method such that it determines, when called, which component has produced the action event.

In the following definition, for example, there is just one listener, which is connected to all action-event-producing components. The actionPerformed method calls getSource with the action event as the target. This call produces the action-event-producing component, which actionPerformed matches against each text field and button. Then, having identified the action-event-producing component, actionPerformed calls an appropriate setter:

```java
import java.awt.*;
import java.util.*;
import java.awt.event.*;
import javax.swing.*;
import javax.swing.event.*;
public class RatingPanel extends JPanel implements RatingPanelInterface
{
 private int value1, value2, value3;
 private JTextField field1, field2, field3;
 private JButton button1Plus, button2Plus, button3Plus;
 private JButton button1Minus, button2Minus, button3Minus;
 RatingPanel (String x, String y, String z) {
  setLayout(new GridLayout (3, 4, 3, 3));
  value1 = 0; value2 = 0; value3 = 0;
  field1 = new JTextField(String.valueOf(value1), 20);
  button1Plus = new JButton("+");
  button1Minus = new JButton("-");
  field2 = new JTextField(String.valueOf(value2), 20);
  button2Plus = new JButton("+");
  button2Minus = new JButton("-");
  field3 = new JTextField(String.valueOf(value3), 20);
  button3Plus = new JButton("+");
  button3Minus = new JButton("-");
  add(new JLabel (x));
  add(field1); add(button1Minus); add(button1Plus);
  add(new JLabel (y));
  add(field2); add(button2Minus); add(button2Plus);
  add(new JLabel (z));
  add(field3); add(button3Minus); add(button3Plus);
  LocalActionListener listener = new LocalActionListener();
  field1.addActionListener(listener);
  button1Plus.addActionListener(listener);
  button1Minus.addActionListener(listener);
  // Ditto for other text fields and buttons ...
 }
 // Setters and getters defined here ...
```

```
class LocalActionListener implements ActionListener {
 public void actionPerformed(ActionEvent e) {
  if          (e.getSource() == field1) {
   setValue1(Integer.parseInt(field1.getText()));
  } else if (e.getSource() == button1Plus) {
   setValue1(value1 + 1);
  } else if (e.getSource() == button1Minus) {
   setValue1(value1 - 1);
  }
  // Ditto for other text fields and buttons ...
 }
}
public Dimension getMinimumSize() {return new Dimension(300, 75);}
public Dimension getPreferredSize() {return new Dimension(300, 75);}
}
```

926 The definition in Segment 925 includes the definition of a listener that connects text fields and buttons to setters inside the form, maintaining the form's instance variables.

For example, if you type a new value into the first text field, and press the Enter key, you initiate the following sequence of calls:

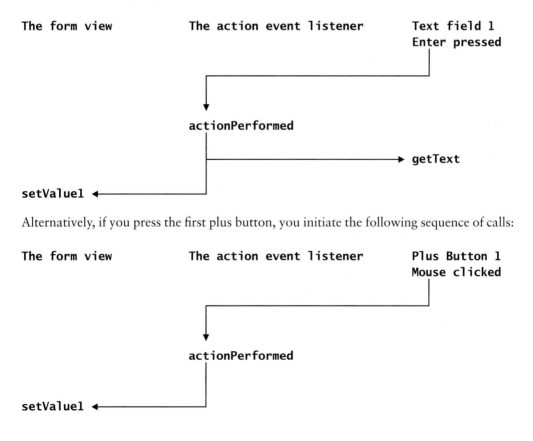

Alternatively, if you press the first plus button, you initiate the following sequence of calls:

927 Now, you must learn how to have the form activate external listeners that are in charge of fetching information from the form, using the form's getters, and of relaying that information to a model.

928 Components, such as `JPanel` instances and instances of `JPanel` subclasses, support a marvelous mechanism for activating connected **property-change listeners**.

The mechanism, in overview, works as follows:

- The `firePropertyChange` method, called on a component, activates each connected property-change listener by calling the listener's `propertyChange` method.

- The `propertyChange` method does whatever you like; typically, the `propertyChange` method fetches values from views and relays those values to models.

- The `addPropertyChangeListener` method connects property-change listeners to the components in which calls to the `firePropertyChange` method occur.

929 To incorporate the property-change mechanism into the form, you need only to modify the setters. In particular, you modify the definition of the setters shown previously in Segment 921 such that they include calls to the `firePropertyChange` method with three arguments: a property-naming string, the previous value, and the new value.

In the following example, the property-naming string is `"value1"`. Conveniently, if the old value is the same as the new value, `firePropertyChange` does nothing.

```
public void setValue1(int v) {
  int oldValue = value1;
  value1 = v;
  field1.setText(String.valueOf(value1));
  firePropertyChange("value1", oldValue, value1);
}
```

930 The modification of the setters finishes the evolution of the form class, producing the following complete definition:

```java
import java.awt.*;              import java.util.*;
import java.awt.event.*;        import javax.swing.*;
import javax.swing.event.*;
public class RatingPanel extends JPanel implements RatingPanelInterface
{
 private int value1, value2, value3;
 private JTextField field1, field2, field3;
 private JButton button1Plus, button2Plus, button3Plus;
 private JButton button1Minus, button2Minus, button3Minus;
 RatingPanel (String x, String y, String z) {
  setLayout(new GridLayout (3, 4, 3, 3));
  value1 = 0; value2 = 0; value3 = 0;
  field1 = new JTextField("0", 20);
  button1Plus = new JButton("+"); button1Minus = new JButton("-");
  // Ditto for other text fields and buttons ...
  add(new JLabel (x));
  add(field1); add(button1Minus); add(button1Plus);
  // Ditto for other labels, text fields, and buttons ...
  LocalActionListener listener = new LocalActionListener();
  field1.addActionListener(listener);
  button1Plus.addActionListener(listener);
  button1Minus.addActionListener(listener);
  // Ditto for other text fields and buttons ...
 }
 public void setValue1(int v) {
  int oldValue = value1;
  value1 = v;
  field1.setText(String.valueOf(value1));
  firePropertyChange("value1", oldValue, value1);
 }
 // Ditto for other setters ...
 public int getValue1() {return value1;}
 // Ditto for other getters ...
 class LocalActionListener implements ActionListener {
  public void actionPerformed(ActionEvent e) {
   if       (e.getSource() == field1) {
    setValue1(Integer.parseInt(field1.getText()));
   } else if (e.getSource() == button1Plus) {
    setValue1(value1 + 1);
   } else if (e.getSource() == button1Minus) {
    setValue1(value1 - 1);
   }
   // Ditto for other text fields and buttons ...
  }
 }
 public Dimension getMinimumSize() {return new Dimension(300, 75);}
 public Dimension getPreferredSize() {return new Dimension(300, 75);}
}
```

931 With the property-change mechanism incorporated into the form, you can define a form listener to be activated by property-change events.

That listener implements the PropertyChangeListener interface, which requires the definition of the propertyChange method and the importation of the java.beans package.

The propertyChange method determines the property name from an instance of the PropertyChangeEvent class using the getPropertyName method. Then, acting typically, the propertyChange method fetches information from the form and relays that information to a model. The constructor ensures that the required movie application is in hand, ready to produce the currently selected movie model:

```java
import java.beans.*;
public class RatingPanelListener implements PropertyChangeListener {
 private MovieApplication applet;
 public RatingPanelListener(MovieApplication a) {
  applet = a;
 }
 public void propertyChange (PropertyChangeEvent e) {
  String property = e.getPropertyName();
  if (applet.getMovie() instanceof Movie) {
   if      (property.equals("value1")) {
    applet.getMovie().setScript(applet.getForm().getValue1());
   }
   else if (property.equals("value2")) {
    applet.getMovie().setActing(applet.getForm().getValue2());
   }
   else if (property.equals("value3")) {
    applet.getMovie().setDirection(applet.getForm().getValue3());
   }
  }
 }
}
```

932 Now, with the listener defined, you can modify the applet defined in Segment 872, inserting a form and form-listening augmentations:

```java
import javax.swing.*;
import java.awt.event.*;
import java.util.*;
public class MovieApplication extends JApplet {
 // Declare instance variables:
 private Meter meter;
 private JList jList;
 private Poster poster;
 private RatingPanel form;
 private Movie movie;
 private MovieData movieData;
```

```java
// Define constructor
public MovieApplication() {
 // Create models
 getMovie();
 getMovieData();
 // Create and connect views to application
 getContentPane().add("West", getMeter());
 getContentPane().add("East", new JScrollPane(getJList()));
 getContentPane().add("Center", getPoster());
 getContentPane().add("South", getForm());
}
// Define getters and setters
public Meter getMeter () {
 if (meter == null) {setMeter(new Meter(0, 30));}
 return meter;
}
public JList getJList () {
 if (jList == null) {setJList(new JList());}
 return jList;
}
public Movie getMovie () {
 if(movie == null) {setMovie(new Movie (10, 10, 10, "On to Java"));}
 return movie;
}
public MovieData getMovieData () {
 if(movieData == null) {setMovieData(new MovieData ());}
 return movieData;
}
public Poster getPoster () {
 if (poster == null) {setPoster(new Poster());}
 return poster;
}
public RatingPanel getForm () {
 if (form == null) {
   setForm(new RatingPanel("Script", "Acting", "Direction"));
 }
 return form;
}
public void setMeter (Meter m) {
 meter = m;
}
public void setMovieData (MovieData m) {
 movieData = m;
 movieData.addObserver(new MovieDataObserver(this));
 movieData.changed();
}
```

```
public void setMovie (Movie m) {
 if(movie == m) {return;}
 if(movie instanceof Movie) {movie.deleteObservers();}
 if(m instanceof Movie) {
  movie = m;
  movie.addObserver(new MovieObserver(this));
  movie.changed();
 }
}
public void setJList (JList j) {
 jList = j;
 jList.addListSelectionListener(new MovieListListener(this));
}
public void setPoster (Poster p) {
 poster = p;
}
public void setForm (RatingPanel f) {
 form = f;
 form.addPropertyChangeListener(new RatingPanelListener(this));
 }
}
```

933 Now, if you should press enter in a text field or click on a button, apparatus in the form view calls a form setter, such as setValue1, as described in Segment 926.

Then, the setter initiates the call sequence that includes property-change firing and listening, as illustrated by a call to the setValue1 setter:

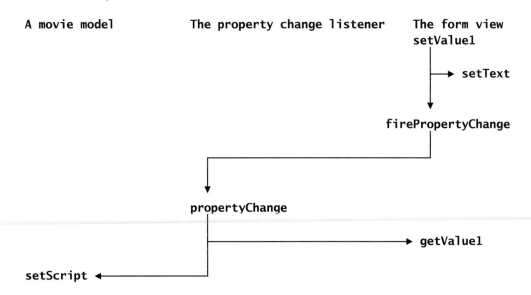

934 The definition shown in Segment 932 enables information to flow from the form view to the currently selected movie model, but you still must do a little more work to get information

to flow from the currently selected movie model to the form view. In particular, you need to modify the movie observer, previously defined in Segment 871, such that the update method calls the form's setters:

```java
import java.util.*;
public class MovieObserver implements Observer {
 private MovieApplication applet;
 public MovieObserver (MovieApplication a) {
  applet = a;
 }
 public void update (Observable observable, Object object) {
  applet.getMeter().setValue(applet.getMovie().rating());
  applet.getMeter().setTitle(applet.getMovie().getTitle());
  applet.getPoster().setImageFile(applet.getMovie().getPoster());
  applet.getForm().setValue1(applet.getMovie().getScript());
  applet.getForm().setValue2(applet.getMovie().getActing());
  applet.getForm().setValue3(applet.getMovie().getDirection());
 }
}
```

935 Now, if activity in the form view causes a value change in the movie model, the movie setter initiates the call sequence illustrated in the following diagram:

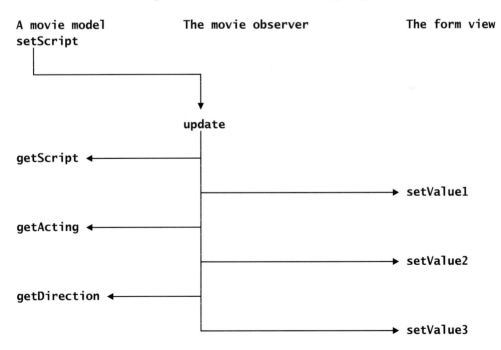

936 A review of the diagrams in Segment 926, Segment 933, and Segment 935 suggests that the form view could initiate an endless loop. It does not, for two reasons:

- The `firePropertyChange` method does not activate listeners if the old value and new value are the same.

- The setters defined in the movie model, in Segment 768, do not activate observers if the old value and the new value are the same.

937

PRACTICE The form definition provided in Segment 930 has one conspicuous defect from the defensive programming point of view: A user can type in the text fields something other than an integer and thus can wreak havoc.

To protect against such disasters, replace the direct calls to the setters in the local listener with calls to private setters that take string arguments. In those new private setters, check to see whether the strings are integers by trying to interpret them as integers, and catching a `NumberFormatException` if you fail. Then, if you succeed, call the regular integer-argument setter on the resulting interpretation; otherwise, if you fail, call the regular integer-argument setter with the current value.

938

PRACTICE Create a panel with one label and one text field. The purpose of the text field is to allow you to type in the name of a movie file.

Then, modify the definition of the `MovieApplication` class in Segment 932 such that your new panel is displayed and such that, each time the name of a new movie file is typed, you replace the list of movies shown in the choice list with the movies in that new file.

939

HIGHLIGHTS

- If you want labels, text fields, and buttons in your application, **then**

  - Use `JLabel` instances to create labels.

  - Use `JTextField` instances to create text fields.

  - Use `JButton` instances to create new buttons.

  - Use `getText` to retrieve strings from text fields.

  - Use `setText` to insert strings into text fields.

- If you need to convert strings to integers, then use `parseInt`, from the `Integer` class.

- If you need to convert integers to strings, **then** use `valueOf` from the `String` class.

- If you want text fields and labels to initiate action, **then** define a listener:

```
class LocalActionListener implements ActionListener {
 public void actionPerformed(ActionEvent e) {
  if (e.getSource() == text field or button ) {
    ··· appropriate response ···;
  } else if (e.getSource() == another text field or button ) {
    ··· appropriate response ···;
  ...
  }
 }
}
```

and then add the listener to the text or button field:

```
text field or button .addActionListener(
  new LocalActionListener()
);
```

- If you want to lay out a group of text and button fields in a rectangular array, then instantiate the following pattern:

```
setLayout(new GridLayout( rows , columns ,
                          row spacing , column spacing )
       );
...
add( text field or button )
...
```

- If you want to deploy your own event creation and listening apparatus, **then** use the firePropertyChange method to create PropertyChangeEvent instances and call property-change listeners.

- If you want to define a property-change listener, **then** define a class that implements the PropertyChangeListener interface, **then** define the propertyChange method, **and then** connect an instance of your listener to a property-change-firing component using the addPropertyChangeListener method.

50 HOW TO DISPLAY MENUS AND DIALOG WINDOWS

940 In this chapter, you learn to incorporate menu bars and popup menus in an applet. Thus, the fully developed movie applet will have menus as well as a rating meter, a displayed list of movies, an image display, and a rating change mechanism. Such features enable your application to present a polished look and feel.

941 **Menu bars** exhibit labels, each of which, when clicked, exhibits a **menu**. Each menu, in turn, exhibits **menu items**, some of which may, themselves, be menus.

942 The following shows an applet with a menu bar, a menu, and two menu items added. The display was produced by an applet viewer using the applet defined in this chapter, in Segment 857, viewed through an HTML file.

943 As shown, the applet has a menu bar with one menu, the `File` menu. When clicked, the `File` menu presents two menu items: `General` and `Horror`. Clicking on one of the two menu items launches a method that reads movies from one of two movie files.

944 You create `JMenu` and `JMenuItem` instances as illustrated in the following examples:

```
new JMenu("File");
new JMenuItem("General");
```

The strings provide labels for menus and menu items.

945 To create a menu bar for the evolving movie application, you create a subclass of the `JMenuBar` class.

```
import java.awt.*;
import java.util.*;
import java.awt.event.*;
import javax.swing.*;
import javax.swing.event.*;
public class MovieMenuBar extends JMenuBar {
 MovieApplication applet;
 private JMenu menu = new JMenu("File");
 private JMenuItem fileMenuGeneral = new JMenuItem("General");
 private JMenuItem fileMenuHorror = new JMenuItem("Horror");
 public MovieMenuBar (MovieApplication a) {
  applet = a;
  // Remainder of constructor ...
 }
 // Remainder of class ...
}
```

946 You connect menus to menu bars, and menu items to menus, using add.

```
import java.awt.*;
import java.util.*;
import java.awt.event.*;
import javax.swing.*;
import javax.swing.event.*;
public class MovieMenuBar extends JMenuBar {
 MovieApplication applet;
 private JMenu menu = new JMenu("File");
 private JMenuItem fileMenuGeneral = new JMenuItem("General");
 private JMenuItem fileMenuHorror = new JMenuItem("Horror");
 public MovieMenuBar (MovieApplication a) {
  applet = a;
  add(menu);
  menu.add(fileMenuGeneral);
  menu.add(fileMenuHorror);
  // Remainder of constructor ...
 }
 // Remainder of class ...
}
```

947 If you wish, you can divide menu items into groups by adding **separators**, using the
addSeparator method:

```
a menu .addSeparator()
```

948 Because the JMenu class extends the JMenuItem class, you can treat menus as though they are menu items. Thus, you can construct **hierarchical** or **cascading menus**. Judicious use of the hierarchical-menu concept helps you to avoid overly long menus.

949 Once you have created a menu bar, you attach it to a target, a JApplet instance or a JFrame instance, using setJMenuBar:

```
setJMenuBar( a menubar );
```

950 At this point, you readily can install a menu in the evolving movie-rating application. Because none of the other application instances send information to the menu, you can add the menu by subclassing the MovieApplication class provided in Segment 932.

```
import javax.swing.*;
import java.awt.event.*;
import java.util.*;
public class MovieApplicationWithMenuBar extends MovieApplication {
 // Declare variables
 MovieMenuBar movieMenuBar;
 // Define constructor
 public MovieApplicationWithMenuBar () {
  // Do what MovieApplication does
  super();
  // Install menu bar
  setJMenuBar(new MovieMenuBar(this));
 }
}
```

951 At this point, the revised applet has a menu bar, a menu, and two menu items, but clicking on those display elements produces no results. You have a graphical Potemkin village. Many software vendors use such villages to sell software projects.

952 To put function behind your menu bar, menu, and menu items, you define an inner class that implements the ActionListener interface. That ActionListener interface is the same interface that you used to implement the listener for JTextField and JButton instances in Chapter 49.

953 You could set up separate listeners for both the fileMenuGeneral and fileMenuHorror menu items. Alternatively, you can define one listener and sort out in that listener which menu item has been clicked. Most programmers would define just one listener, on the ground that it is best to keep together all the responses to menu clicks. To determine which menu item has been clicked, the listener uses the getSource method with the event as the argument, as shown in the following preview of the definition of the listener, which is to be an inner class of the MovieMenuBar class:

```
class LocalActionListener implements ActionListener {
 public void actionPerformed (ActionEvent e) {
  JMenuItem jMenuItem = (JMenuItem)(e.getSource());
  if (jMenuItem == fileMenuGeneral) {
   applet.getMovieData().setMovieVector(
    MovieAuxiliaries.readMovieFile("general.movies")
   );
  }
  else if (jMenuItem == fileMenuHorror) {
   applet.getMovieData().setMovieVector(
    MovieAuxiliaries.readMovieFile("horror.movies")
   );
  }
}}}
```

954 Next, you attach a LocalActionListener instance to the appropriate menu items in the MovieApplet initialization method, using addActionListener, as shown in the following definition, which brings together all the previously described program fragments:

```
import java.awt.*;
import java.util.*;
import java.awt.event.*;
import javax.swing.*;
import javax.swing.event.*;
public class MovieMenuBar extends JMenuBar {
 MovieApplication applet;
 private JMenu menu = new JMenu("File");
 private JMenuItem fileMenuGeneral = new JMenuItem("General");
 private JMenuItem fileMenuHorror = new JMenuItem("Horror");
 public MovieMenuBar (MovieApplication a) {
  applet = a;
  add(menu);
  menu.add(fileMenuGeneral);
  menu.add(fileMenuHorror);
  LocalActionListener listener = new LocalActionListener();
  fileMenuGeneral.addActionListener(listener);
  fileMenuHorror.addActionListener(listener);
 }
 class LocalActionListener implements ActionListener {
  public void actionPerformed (ActionEvent e) {
   JMenuItem jMenuItem = (JMenuItem)(e.getSource());
   if (jMenuItem == fileMenuGeneral) {
    applet.getMovieData().setMovieVector(
     MovieAuxiliaries.readMovieFile("general.movies")
    );
   }
```

```
     else if (jMenuItem == fileMenuHorror) {
      applet.getMovieData().setMovieVector(
       MovieAuxiliaries.readMovieFile("horror.movies")
      );
}}}}
```

955   Instead of using a menu bar, you can, if you like, implement a **popup menu** for choosing movie files.

956   You can borrow nearly all you need for a popup menu from what you need for a menu bar. In particular, you can retain the fileMenuGeneral and fileMenuHorror menu items.

Now, however, instead of creating a subclass of the JMenu class, you create a subclass of the JPopupMenu class. You no longer need a JMenu instance variable; the JMenuItem instances connect directly to the MoviePopupMenu instance.

```
import java.awt.*;
import java.util.*;
import java.awt.event.*;
import javax.swing.*;
import javax.swing.event.*;
public class MoviePopupMenu extends JPopupMenu {
 MovieApplication applet;
 private JMenuItem fileMenuGeneral = new JMenuItem("General");
 private JMenuItem fileMenuHorror = new JMenuItem("Horror");
 public MoviePopupMenu (MovieApplication a) {
  applet = a;
  add(fileMenuGeneral);
  add(fileMenuHorror);
  LocalActionListener listener = new LocalActionListener();
  fileMenuGeneral.addActionListener(listener);
  fileMenuHorror.addActionListener(listener);
 }
 class LocalActionListener implements ActionListener {
  public void actionPerformed (ActionEvent e) {
   JMenuItem jMenuItem = (JMenuItem)(e.getSource());
   if (jMenuItem == fileMenuGeneral) {
    applet.getMovieData().setMovieVector(
     MovieAuxiliaries.readMovieFile("general.movies")
    );
   }
   else if (jMenuItem == fileMenuHorror) {
    applet.getMovieData().setMovieVector(
     MovieAuxiliaries.readMovieFile("horror.movies")
    );
}}}}
```

957 Next, you create a listener that pops up the menu when you click the mouse. The listener should implement the MouseListener interface, which insists that you define methods, often empty, for responding to all possible mouse events, as well as to the one of interest. Alternatively, you can implement the interface indirectly, by extending the MouseAdapter class, which implements empty methods for all the methods required by the interface.

The mouse event that is of interest is the mouseClicked event. In response, the show method displays the popup menu at a specified position relative to the clicked component. The getX and getY methods return the coordinates of the mouse pointer at the time the mouse is clicked; thus, the popup menu appears at those coordinates.

```java
import java.awt.event.*;
import javax.swing.*;
public class MovieMouseListener extends MouseAdapter {
 private MovieApplication applet;
 public MovieMouseListener (MovieApplication a) {
  applet = a;
 }
 public void mouseClicked (MouseEvent e) {
  MoviePopupMenu menu = new MoviePopupMenu(applet);
  menu.show((JComponent)(e.getSource()), e.getX(), e.getY());
 }
}
```

958 With the mouse listener in hand, you are ready to attach an instance of the mouse listener to a component using addMouseListener. One option is to attach to the meter. Then, a mouse click in the area occupied by the meter pops up the menu at a point specified by the coordinates used as arguments in the show method, relative to the specified component.

```java
import javax.swing.*;
import java.awt.event.*;
import java.util.*;
public class MovieApplicationWithPopupMenu extends MovieApplication {
 // Define constructor
 public MovieApplicationWithPopupMenu () {
  // Do what MovieApplication does
  super();
  // Install popup menu
  getMeter().addMouseListener(new MovieMouseListener(this));
 }
}
```

959 With the popup menu in use, you see the following:

Welcome to the Movie Applet Demonstration - Netscape 6

Apocalypse Now
The Sting
The Wizard of Oz
Bedtime for Bonzo
The Last House on the Left
Gone with the Wind
Casablanca
The King of Hearts
My Fair Lady

General
Horror

The Sting

Script	8	-	+
Acting	8	-	+
Direction	7	-	+

Applet MovieApplicationWithPopup started

Business ▲ Tech ▲ Fun ▲ Interact ▲

960

SIDE TRIP Advanced techniques allow you to specify displays, created using the `JFileChooser` class, in which you choose a file from a list of files.

961

HIGHLIGHTS

- If you want to make use of a menu bar, **then** create a subclass of the `JMenuBar` class **then** create instances of the `JMenu` and `JMenuItem` classes by instantiating the following patterns:

  ```
  JMenu menu = new JMenu(" label ");
  JMenuItem menu item = new JMenuItem(" label ");
  ```

  then connect together the menu bar, menus, and menu items by instantiating the following pattern:

  ```
  menu or menu bar .add( menu or menu item );
  ```

  and then instantiate the following pattern:

  ```
  setJMenuBar( menu bar );
  ```

- If you want to define a listener to handle the selection of menu items, **then** define an inner class of a `JMenuBar` class:

  ```
  class LocalActionListener implements ActionListener {
  public void actionPerformed(ActionEvent e) {
  JMenuItem jMenuItem = (JMenuItem)(e.getSource());
  // Determine item clicked and react here ...
  }
  }
  ```

  and then add the listener to the menu item:

  ```
  menu item .addActionListener(new LocalActionListener());
  ```

- If you want to open a popup menu, **then** create a subclass of the JPopupMenu class, **and then** connect menu items to the popup menu by instantiating the following pattern:

```
popup menu .add( menu item );
```

- If you want to define a listener to handle the selection of popup menu items, **then** define an inner class of a JPopupMenu class:

```
class LocalActionListener implements ActionListener {
 public void actionPerformed (ActionEvent e) {
  JMenuItem jMenuItem = (JMenuItem)(e.getSource());
  // Determine item clicked and react here ...
 }
}
```

- If you want to define a listener to handle a mouse click, popping up a popup menu, **then** define an inner class inside your applet or frame:

```
class LocalMouseListener extends MouseAdapter {
 parent class parent;
 LocalMouseListener( parent class  p) {parent = p;}
 public void mouseClicked (MouseEvent e) {
  // React to click here ...
 }
}
```

and then add the listener to the appropriate component:

```
component .addMouseListener(new LocalMouseListener(this));
```

51 HOW TO DEVELOP YOUR OWN LAYOUT MANAGER

962   Usually, you can arrange GUI elements as you please using the border layout you learned about in Segment 727, the grid layout you learned about in Segment 919, and the various layouts described in Appendix E. As you learn in this chapter, you also can define your own layout manager to handle especially tricky situations. You may, if you wish, skip to Chapter 52; the apparatus explained in this chapter is not used elsewhere in this book.

963   When arranging components within a container, Java provides position and size knowledge to each component via the setBounds method, as in the following expression, where the upper–left corner of the component is to lie at the position within its container given by x and y, and the width and height are width and height.

```
component .setBounds(x, y, width, height)
```

964   If you wish, you can write programs that use no layout manager, but then you must specify locations and sizes yourself, via your own calls to setBounds. In the following display, each embedded component is a fixed-size square. The surrounding container is too small to contain all four squares:

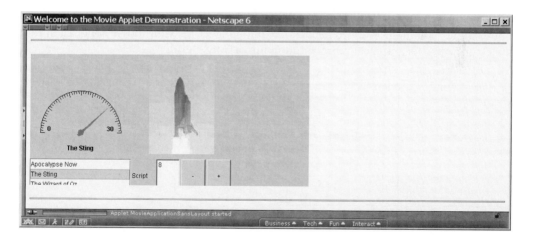

965   To produce the display in Segment 964, you remove the default layout manager via the call to setLayout with a null argument. Then, the components are positioned and sized, in squares, with setBounds expressions. The positions and sizes are fixed; they do not change as the you change the size of their surrounding container.

```
import javax.swing.*;
import java.awt.event.*;
import java.util.*;
public class MovieApplicationSansLayout extends MovieApplication {
 public MovieApplicationSansLayout () {
  super();
  JScrollPane scroller = new JScrollPane(getJList());
  getContentPane().setLayout(null);
  getContentPane().add("Meter", getMeter());
  getContentPane().add("List", scroller);
  getContentPane().add("Form", getForm());
  getContentPane().add("Poster", getPoster());
  getMeter().setBounds(0, 0, 200, 200);
  getPoster().setBounds(200, 0, 200, 200);
  scroller.setBounds(0, 200, 200, 200);
  getForm().setBounds(200, 200, 200, 200);
 }
}
```

966

SIDE TRIP

GUI builders tend to create displays in which the components have fixed, positions and dimensions. That is, GUI builders tend to use no layout manager, but instead to rely on you to establish attractive, yet fixed component positions and sizes.

967 Generally, displays in which the components have fixed positions and dimensions look ugly when the size of the container grows or shrinks. Accordingly, if you anticipate that users will change a container's size, and if none of the layout managers offered in Java's API suit you, you are likely to want to define your own layout manager.

For example, you might want to define a layout manager for your movie application that divides the applet's graphical representation into a 3 by 3 grid:

968 To define MovieApplicationLayout, you can either extend an existing layout manager, shadowing some of its methods, or define a class that implements the LayoutManager interface. That interface requires you to define, either directly or through an implementing class, methods that add named components, remove components, perform the layout operations, and provide minimum and preferred sizes.

```
public interface LayoutManager {
  public void addLayoutComponent(String name, Component component) ;
  public void removeLayoutComponent(Component component) ;
  public void layoutContainer(Container parent) ;
  public Dimension minimumLayoutSize(Container parent) ;
  public Dimension preferredLayoutSize(Container parent) ;
}
```

969　The methods required by the LayoutManager interface are used by Java's machinery for displaying containers. You never include calls to those methods in your programs.

970　To implement the LayoutManager interface, you provide variables that serve as handles for the named components. Then, you can readily implement addLayoutComponent and removeLayoutComponent.

```
import java.awt.*;
public class MovieApplicationLayout implements LayoutManager {
  private Component meter;
  private Component list;
  private Component form;
  private Component poster;
  public void addLayoutComponent(String name, Component  o) {
    if (name.equals("Meter")) {meter = o;}
    else if (name.equals("List")) {list = o;}
    else if (name.equals("Form")) {form = o;}
    else if (name.equals("Poster")) {poster = o;}
    else {System.err.println(name + " argument unrecognized");}
  }
  public void removeLayoutComponent(Component  o) {
    if (meter == o) {meter = null;}
    else if (list == o) {list = null;}
    else if (form == o) {form = null;}
    else if (poster == o) {poster = null;}
  }
  // Other definitions ...
}
```

971　To do the actual layout, you add the layoutContainer method. That method first obtains the dimensions of the container using the instance variables of the Dimension instance returned by getSize. Then, that method positions and sizes all the known components using setBounds expressions:

```
import java.awt.*;
public class MovieApplicationLayout implements LayoutManager {
 private Component meter;
 private Component list;
 private Component form;
 private Component poster;
 // addLayoutComponent and removeLayoutComponent definitions as in Seg-
ment 970 ...
 public void layoutContainer(Container parent) {
  Dimension d = parent.getSize();
  int height = d.height;
  int width = d.width;
  if(meter != null) {
   meter.setBounds(0, 0, (int) (width / 3), (int) (height * 2 / 3));
  }
  if(list != null) {
   list.setBounds((int) (2 * width / 3), 0, (int) (width / 3), height);
  }
  if(form != null) {
   form.setBounds(0, (int) (height * 2 / 3),
                  (int) (2 * width / 3), (int)(height / 3));
  }
  if(poster != null) {
   poster.setBounds((int) (width / 3), 0,
                    (int) (width / 3), (int) (height * 2 / 3));
  }
 }
 // Other definitions ...
}
```

972 Finally, you supply definitions for the methods that return minimum and preferred sizes. In the following example, the sizes are arbitrarily set such that the program displays small squares:

```
import java.awt.*;
public class MovieApplicationLayout implements LayoutManager {
 private Component meter;
 private Component list;
 private Component form;
 private Component poster;
 public void addLayoutComponent(String name, Component  o) {
  if (name.equals("Meter")) {meter = o;}
  else if (name.equals("List")) {list = o;}
  else if (name.equals("Form")) {form = o;}
  else if (name.equals("Poster")) {poster = o;}
  else {System.err.println(name + " argument unrecognized");}
 }
```

```
public void removeLayoutComponent(Component  o) {
  if (meter == o) {meter = null;}
  else if (list == o) {list = null;}
  else if (form == o) {form = null;}
  else if (poster == o) {poster = null;}
}
public void layoutContainer(Container parent) {
 Dimension d = parent.getSize();
 int height = d.height;
 int width = d.width;
 if(meter != null) {
  meter.setBounds(0, 0, (int) (width / 3),
                    (int) (height * 2 / 3)); }
 if(list != null) {
  list.setBounds((int) (2 * width / 3), 0,
                    (int) (width / 3), height); }
 if(form != null) {
  form.setBounds(0, (int) (height * 2 / 3),
                    (int) (2 * width / 3), (int)(height / 3)); }
 if(poster != null) {
  poster.setBounds((int) (width / 3), 0,
                    (int) (width / 3), (int) (height * 2 / 3)); }
}
public Dimension minimumLayoutSize(Container parent) {
 return new Dimension(50, 50);
}
public Dimension preferredLayoutSize(Container parent) {
 return new Dimension(50, 50);
}
}
```

973 Now, you can use the new layout manager in a variant of the definition shown in Segment 965.

```
import javax.swing.*;
import java.awt.event.*;
import java.util.*;
public class MovieApplicationWithLayout extends MovieApplication {
 public MovieApplicationWithLayout () {
  super();
  getContentPane().setLayout(new MovieApplicationLayout());
  getContentPane().add("Meter", getMeter());
  getContentPane().add("List", new JScrollPane(getJList()));
  getContentPane().add("Form", getForm());
  getContentPane().add("Poster", getPoster());
 }
}
```

974   The program in Segment 973 produces the following, well-proportioned display, even as you vary the size of the applet:

975
PRACTICE
The layout manager defined in Segment 972 ignores the dimension instances returned by the `minimumLayoutSize` and `preferredLayoutSize` methods called on the components. Alter the definition such that the layout manager assigns a width to the list component that is the smaller of the currently computed width and the width provided by the dimension instance returned by a call to `preferredLayoutSize` with the list component as its target.

976
HIGHLIGHTS

- The layout manager's `layoutContainer` method uses `getSize` to determine container size.

- The layout manager's `layoutContainer` method uses `setBounds` to position components within containers.

- If you need to define a layout manager, **then** define a class that implements the `LayoutManager` interface, which requires definitions for:

  - `addLayoutComponent`,

  - `removeLayoutComponent`,

  - `layoutContainer`,

  - `minimumLayoutSize`, and

  - `preferredLayoutSize`.

354

52 HOW TO IMPLEMENT DYNAMIC TABLES

977 When a program's user needs information about a collection of objects, such as a collection of movies, you may wish to provide that information in a table in which each row displays the properties of one object, such as a movie instance.

Conveniently, Java makes it easy for you to create, with little effort, simple tables; if your needs are demanding, Java makes it possible for you to create complex tables that have sophisticated characteristics.

You should skim this chapter to learn what tables offer; you should read it more carefully when you need to construct a table of your own.

978 Using the JTable class, you can create a straightforward table by calling the JTable constructor that takes two vector arguments:

- The first vector consists of row-representing vectors. Each row-representing vector consists of instances. Each instance provides data for a cell.

- The second vector consists of instances. Each instance provides a column label.

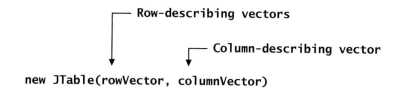

```
new JTable(rowVector, columnVector)
```

979 The following illustrates what you can do with the table constructor shown in Segment 978:

Column 0	Column 1
Cell 0, 0	Cell 0, 1
Cell 1, 0	Cell 1, 1

Table Demonstration

This simple table already demonstrates some of the power of Java's JTable class. By clicking on the boundary between columns, and dragging, you change column widths:

980 The table shown in Segment 979 is produced with the following program. Note that the table must be embedded in a scroll pane; otherwise, the column labels will not appear:

```java
import java.util.*;
import javax.swing.*;
import javax.swing.table.*;
public class TableDemonstration {
 public static void main (String argv []) {
  // Prepare table contents
  Vector columns = new Vector();
  columns.add("Column 0");
  columns.add("Column 1");
  Vector row0 = new Vector();
  row0.add("Cell 0, 0");
  row0.add("Cell 0, 1");
  Vector row1 = new Vector();
  row1.add("Cell 1, 0");
  row1.add("Cell 1, 1");
  Vector rows = new Vector();
  rows.add(row0);
  rows.add(row1);
  // Make the table
  JTable table = new JTable(rows, columns);
  // Show the table
  JFrame frame = new JFrame("Table Demonstration");
  frame.getContentPane().add("Center", new JScrollPane(table));
  frame.setSize(250, 80);
  frame.addWindowListener(new ApplicationClosingWindowListener());
  frame.show();
 }
}
```

981 Internally, an instance of the JTable class contains several class instances that govern a table's look and behavior. Those class instances belong to classes that implement methods, imposed by interfaces, on which JTable instances depend to display data properly.

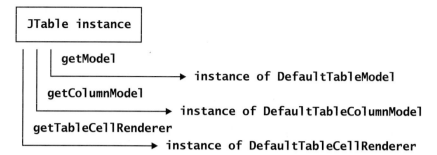

When you create a table using the simple constructor described in Segment 978, that simple constructor provides a default table model, a default table-column model, a default table-cell renderer, and a default list-selection model, hiding from you all the tedious detail involved.

982 The **default table model**, introduced in Segment 985, holds the data that the table displays, provides access to those data for methods defined in JTable, and serves as an anchor point for connecting editing listeners.

The methods that provide access to the default table model are imposed by the TableModel interface. You learn how to modify a table model in Segment 985. You learn how to obtain edited values in Segment 1011.

The **default table-column model** holds information about column labels and column widths. You learn how to modify the default table-column model in Segment 990.

The **default table-cell renderer** determines how data is displayed. You learn why table-cell renderers are important in Segment 996. You learn how to create a table-cell renderer in Segment 997.

983 You alter a table's behavior in one of two ways. You can call a method with a target of the default table model, the default table-column model, or the default table-cell renderer. Or, you can substitute your own table model, table-column model, or table-cell renderer for the defaults supplied automatically.

If you want to substitute your own model or renderer, you use the setters corresponding to the getters—namely setTableModel, setColumnModel, and setTableCellRenderer.

984 The JTable class, together with the DefaultTableModel, DefaultTableColumnModel, and DefaultTableCellRenderer classes, provides a great deal of the behavior required for most tables. Usually, you need to modify only slightly the default behaviors offered by those classes, by calling existing instance methods or by implementing a few shadowing methods in subclasses.

985 For example, the instance of the DefaultTableModel class produced when you construct a JTable instance determines that the cells in the table are editable, but editable cells are not useful unless you connect appropriate listeners to the table; you learn about such listeners later, in Segment 1011.

For the moment, assume that your table's cells are not to be edited. You define a subclass of the DefaultTableModel class in which you define a shadowing version of the isCellEditable method that always returns false. Machinery defined in the JTable class calls that function to decide whether a cell should be editable.

The DefaultTableModel subclass also needs a two-parameter constructor—for a vector of row vectors and for a column vector—that passes both arguments to the corresponding constructor in the DefaultTableModel class.

```
import java.util.*;
import javax.swing.table.*;
public class RatingTableModel extends DefaultTableModel {
 public RatingTableModel (Vector rows, Vector columns) {
  super(rows, columns);
 }
 public boolean isCellEditable(int row, int column) {
  return false;
 }
}
```

986 To make use of the RatingTableModel class defined in Segment 985, you define a subclass of the JTable class. Note that you define in that subclass a constructor that calls the superclass's constructor that takes a table-model argument. That argument is an instance of the RatingTableModel class defined in Segment 985.

```
import java.util.*;
import javax.swing.*;
import javax.swing.table.*;
public class RatingTable extends JTable {
 public RatingTable (Vector rows, Vector columns) {
  super(new RatingTableModel(rows, columns));
 }
}
```

987 Now, with the new table subclass defined in Segment 986, you can create a bare-bones application that displays movie information in a table. The application reuses the data model introduced in Segment 850, and connects the data in that data model to a table by way of a new observer defined in Segment 988. The application and the new observer provide the infrastructure you need to test variations of the table and the table model.

```
import javax.swing.*;
import javax.swing.table.*;
import java.awt.event.*;
import java.util.*;
```

```java
public class MovieTableApplication extends JApplet {
 // Declare instance variables:
 private RatingTable ratingTable;
 private MovieData movieData;
 // Define constructor
 public MovieTableApplication() {
  // Create models
  getMovieData();
  // Create and connect views to application
  getContentPane().add("Center", new JScrollPane(getRatingTable()));
 }
 // Define getters and setters
 public MovieData getMovieData () {
  if(movieData == null) {
   setMovieData(new MovieData());}
  return movieData;
 }
 public void setMovieData (MovieData m) {
  movieData = m;
  movieData.addObserver(new MovieDataObserverForTable(this));
  movieData.changed();
 }
 public RatingTable getRatingTable () {
  if (ratingTable == null) {
   Vector rows = new Vector();
   Vector columns = new Vector();
   // Prepare column labels
   columns.add("Title"); columns.add("Rating"); columns.add("Script");
   columns.add("Acting"); columns.add("Direction");
   // Create and assign new table
   setRatingTable(new RatingTable(rows, columns));
  }
  return ratingTable;
 }
 public void setRatingTable (RatingTable r) {
  ratingTable = r;
 }
 public static void main (String argv []) {
  JFrame frame = new JFrame("Movie Data Table");
  frame.getContentPane().add("Center", new MovieTableApplication());
  frame.setSize(750, 210);
  frame.addWindowListener(new ApplicationClosingWindowListener());
  frame.show();
 }
}
```

988 All that remains is to define the observer class, `MovieDataObserverForTable`, that connects model changes to the table.

The new observer checks all the movies to see which already are recorded in the table; it adds all the movies that it does not find. It checks for movies in the table with a private predicate, `present`. One argument of the private predicate is a vector of row vectors that you obtain using `getDataVector`; the first element of each such row vector is a movie title.

When the observer does add a new row vector, each element in the row vector must be a class instance; thus, `int` values must be wrapped in `Integer` instances. `JTable` procedures know how to deal with both `String` and `Integer` instances, but they are flummoxed by `int` values, because only class instances can be tested for class identity.

```java
import java.util.*;
import javax.swing.*;
import javax.swing.event.*;
import javax.swing.table.*;
public class MovieDataObserverForTable implements Observer {
 MovieTableApplication applet;
 public MovieDataObserverForTable (MovieTableApplication a) {
  applet = a;
 }
 public void update (Observable observable, Object object) {
  Vector movies = applet.getMovieData().getMovieVector();
  RatingTable table = applet.getRatingTable();
  RatingTableModel model = (RatingTableModel)(table.getModel());
  // Check each movie
  for (Iterator i = movies.iterator(); i.hasNext();) {
   Movie movie = (Movie)(i.next());
   String title = movie.getTitle();
   // Ignore movie, if already in the table
   if (!present(title, model.getDataVector())) {
    // Add movie if not already in the table
    Vector row = new Vector();
    row.add(title);
    row.add(new Integer(movie.rating()));
    row.add(new Integer(movie.getScript()));
    row.add(new Integer(movie.getActing()));
    row.add(new Integer(movie.getDirection()));
    // Add new row to the table model
    model.addRow(row);
   }
  }
 }
```

```
// Test title to see if movie is in the data vector
private boolean present (String title, Vector data) {
 // Iterate over all data elements
 for (Iterator i = data.iterator(); i.hasNext();) {
  // Each data element is a row vector
  Vector v = (Vector)(i.next());
  // Title is first element of row vector
  String t = (String)(v.firstElement());
  if (t.equals(title)) {
   return true;
  }
 }
 return false;
 }
}
```

989   Now, you can test the model, the table, the table model, the observer, and the application. The result is a handsome movie table.

Title	Rating	Script	Acting	Directing
Apocalypse Now	14	4	7	3
The Sting	23	8	8	7
The Wizard of Oz	14	4	7	3
Bedtime for Bonzo	17	2	10	5
The Last House on the L...	0	0	0	0
Gone with the Wind	24	8	8	8
Casablanca	30	10	10	10
The King of Hearts	30	10	10	10
My Fair Lady	23	8	8	7
The Sound of Music	17	5	7	5

990   While you are attending to the look and feel of a table, you might also wish to vary the column widths. Your program can extract the column model from your table, using the getColumnModel method, then pick, with the getColumn method, the instance that represents a particular column, and then call the setPreferredWidth method appropriately.

For example, you might decide that your table looks better if you make the title column five times wider than the other columns.

You can arrange for your program to do all the work when the table is constructed. If the total width of the table will be 750 pixels, and the title column will be five times as wide as the four other columns, then the preferred size of the title column is 417, and the preferred size of each of the other columns is 83:

```
import java.util.*;
import javax.swing.*;
import javax.swing.table.*;
public class RatingTable extends JTable {
 public RatingTable (Vector rows, Vector columns) {
  super(new RatingTableModel(rows, columns));
  TableColumnModel model = getColumnModel();
  for (int i = 0; i < columns.size(); ++i) {
   TableColumn column = model.getColumn(i);
   if (i == 0) {
    column.setPreferredWidth(417);
   }
   else {
    column.setPreferredWidth(83);
   }
  }
 }
}
```

991 The `RatingTable` defined in Segment 990 and the application defined in Segment 987 produce the following table:

Title	Rating	Script	Acting	Directing
Apocalypse Now	14	4	7	3
The Sting	23	8	8	7
The Wizard of Oz	14	4	7	3
Bedtime for Bonzo	17	2	10	5
The Last House on the Left	0	0	0	0
Gone with the Wind	24	8	8	8
Casablanca	30	10	10	10
The King of Hearts	30	10	10	10
My Fair Lady	23	8	8	7
The Sound of Music	17	5	7	5

Movie Data Table

992 Next, the `DefaultListSelectionModel` allows row selections; without connected listeners to take note of selections, however, users will be confused. Therefore, you shut off selection. All you need to do is to call the `setRowSelectionAllowed` method defined in the `JTable` class. You learn about selection and listeners later, in Segment 1006.

```
import java.util.*;
import javax.swing.*;
import javax.swing.table.*;
```

```
public class RatingTable extends JTable {
 public RatingTable (Vector rows, Vector columns) {
  super(new RatingTableModel(rows, columns));
  TableColumnModel model = getColumnModel();
  for (int i = 0; i < columns.size(); ++i) {
   TableColumn column = model.getColumn(i);
   if (i == 0) {
    column.setPreferredWidth(417);
   }
   else {
    column.setPreferredWidth(83);
   }
  }
  setRowSelectionAllowed(false);
 }
}
```

993   Now, you learn how to alter the appearance of cells. The JTable machinery obtains the **cell renderer** by calling getTableCellRenderer. Then, machinery defined in the JTable class displays each cell by displaying a component produced by a cell renderer using the data associated with the cell.

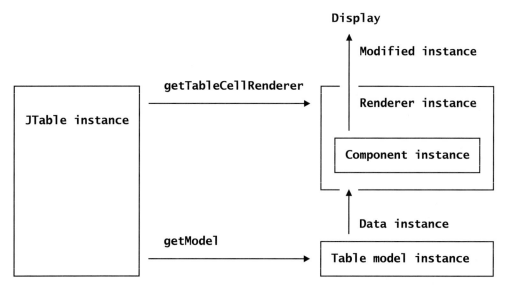

Fundamentally, the cell renderer uses cell data to modify a component held by the renderer; then, the modified component is returned by the cell renderer for display. Because the Component class defines a paint method, the JTable machinery simply calls the paint method using the returned component as the target.

994   To produce a component, cell renderers all contain a getTableCellRendererComponent method. All cell renderers must have that method because existence is imposed by the TableCellRenderer interface.

In the tables that you have seen, the components displayed in table cells are supplied by the getTableCellRendererComponent method in the DefaultTableCellRenderer class, because an instance of the DefaultTableCellRenderer class is used, by default, in JTable instances.

995 The getTableCellRendererComponent method defined for the default table-cell renderer produces left-aligned, opaque, JLabel instances.

More precisely, the getTableCellRendererComponent method returns instances of the DefaultTableCellRenderer class, but these instances are all JLabel instances as well, because DefaultTableCellRenderer extends the JLabel class. If you have selected a cell by clicking on it, the DefaultTableCellRenderer instance returned for that cell has a distinguishing border.

996 In general, the component returned by the getTableCellRenderer method can be any component, in addition too a JLabel instance; the components displayed in table cells can be progress bars, check boxes, tables, or instances any other subclass of the Component class.

The principle virtue of table-cell renderers is that they provide access to the full power of Java's Component classes.

997 The easiest way to change the way that cells are rendered is to create a subclass of a JComponent subclass that implements the TableCellRenderer interface.

The following table-cell renderer, for example, uses and reuses a single, white-background, appropriately right or left-aligned, borderless JLabel instance:

```
import java.awt.*;
import javax.swing.*;
import javax.swing.table.*;

public class MovieTableCellRenderer extends JLabel
                                    implements TableCellRenderer {
  public Component getTableCellRendererComponent(
    JTable table, Object value, boolean isSelected,
    boolean hasFocus, int row, int column) {
   setText(value.toString());
   setOpaque(true);
   setBackground(Color.white);
   if (value instanceof Integer) {
    setHorizontalAlignment(SwingConstants.RIGIIT);
   }
   else if (value instanceof String) {
    setHorizontalAlignment(SwingConstants.LEFT);
   }
   return this;
  }
}
```

998 Note that the getTableCellRendererComponent method defined in Segment 997 returns the same component each time, but possibly with altered properties, in accordance with the arguments supplied.

Reusing the same component, rather than generating a new component for each cell rendering, is relatively efficient.

999 Once you have a new renderer, you can put it to use by connecting it to a table with the setDefaultRenderer method. Note, however, that renderers are associated with **column classes**, which are determined by the getColumnClass method in the table model. The definition of getColumnClass defined by the DefaultTableModel class inconveniently reports every column as having an Object column class.

Accordingly, you need to modify the behavior of the getColumnClass method by having it report the class of the element in the zeroth row; you obtain that class using the getClass method:

```
import java.util.*;
import javax.swing.table.*;
public class RatingTableModel extends DefaultTableModel {
 public RatingTableModel (Vector rows, Vector columns) {
  super(rows, columns);
 }
 public boolean isCellEditable(int row, int column) {
  return false;
 }
 // Define shadowing method
 public Class getColumnClass(int column) {
  return getValueAt(0, column).getClass();
 }
}
```

1000 Once you have ensured that getColumnClass reports the actual class of the elements in each column, you associate your new renderer with the table and classes for which you have prepared that renderer. You can do the association conveniently in a modification of the RatingTable constructor defined in Segment 992.

To handle instances of both the String and Integer classes, you include two calls to setDefaultRenderer, each with an argument that specifies the class for which the renderer is to be used. You specify a class using the class name followed by a dot and then the keyword class.

```java
import java.util.*;
import javax.swing.*;
import javax.swing.table.*;
public class RatingTable extends JTable {
 public RatingTable (Vector rows, Vector columns) {
   super(new RatingTableModel(rows, columns));
   TableColumnModel model = getColumnModel();
   for (int i = 0; i < columns.size(); ++i) {
    TableColumn column = model.getColumn(i);
    if (i == 0) {
     column.setPreferredWidth(417);
    }
    else {
     column.setPreferredWidth(83);
    }
   }
   setRowSelectionAllowed(false);
   MovieTableCellRenderer renderer = new MovieTableCellRenderer();
   setDefaultRenderer(Integer.class, renderer);
   setDefaultRenderer(String.class, renderer);
  }
}
```

1001

SIDE TRIP

You can also associate renderers with particular columns, which gives you column-by-column control. You rarely need such control.

1002 After you define the RatingTable class as shown in Segment 1000, the testing program in Segment 987 produces the following table:

Title	Rating	Script	Acting	Directing
Apocalypse Now	14	4	7	3
The Sting	23	8	8	7
The Wizard of Oz	14	4	7	3
Bedtime for Bonzo	17	2	10	5
The Last House on the Left	0	0	0	0
Gone with the Wind	24	8	8	8
Casablanca	30	10	10	10
The King of Hearts	30	10	10	10
My Fair Lady	23	8	8	7
The Sound of Music	17	5	7	5

Movie Data Table

1003 The parameters in the getTableCellRendererComponent have obvious roles. The table parameter enables you to access the table whose cells are being rendered. The value parameter is assigned to the class instance in the cell. The isSelected parameter is true if the cell has been selected with a mouse click. The hasFocus parameter is true if the cell is the component currently receiving mouse clicks. And the row and column parameters indicate the location of the cell in the table, with the upper-left corner being row 0 and column 0.

1004 The following is a renderer that checks the rating associated with the row in which a cell lies; if that rating is equal to or greater than a specified reference value, it renders the entire row in green to attract attention.

```java
import java.awt.*;
import javax.swing.*;
import javax.swing.table.*;
public class MovieTableCellRenderer extends JLabel
                                 implements TableCellRenderer {
 private static int REFERENCE_VALUE = 25;
 public Component getTableCellRendererComponent(
   JTable table, Object value, boolean isSelected,
   boolean hasFocus, int row, int column) {
  setText(value.toString());
  setOpaque(true);
  setBackground(Color.white);
  if (value instanceof Integer) {
   setHorizontalAlignment(SwingConstants.RIGHT);
  }
  else if (value instanceof String) {
   setHorizontalAlignment(SwingConstants.LEFT);
  }
  Integer i = (Integer)(table.getModel().getValueAt(row, 1));
  if (i.intValue() >= REFERENCE_VALUE) {
   setBackground(Color.green);
  }
  else {
   setBackground(Color.white);
  }
  return this;
 }
}
```

1005 After you define the `MovieTableCellRenderer` class as shown in Segment 1004, the testing program in Segment 987 produces the following table:

Title	Rating	Script	Acting	Directing
Apocalypse Now	14	4	7	3
The Sting	23	8	8	7
The Wizard of Oz	14	4	7	3
Bedtime for Bonzo	17	2	10	5
The Last House on the Left	0	0	0	0
Gone with the Wind	24	8	8	8
Casablanca	30	10	10	10
The King of Hearts	30	10	10	10
My Fair Lady	23	8	8	7
The Sound of Music	17	5	7	5

1006 If you wish to allow row selection, you have three options: You can allow to be selected only single rows; only contiguous rows; or any rows. You specify your choice by calling the setSelectionMode method with one of three values stored as static variable values in the ListSelectionModel interface, such as SINGLE_INTERVAL_SELECTION. You drop the statement that calls the setRowSelectionAllowed method with false as the argument.

```java
import java.util.*;
import javax.swing.*;
import javax.swing.table.*;
public class RatingTable extends JTable {
 public RatingTable (Vector rows, Vector columns) {
  super(new RatingTableModel(rows, columns));
  TableColumnModel model = getColumnModel();
  for (int i = 0; i < columns.size(); ++i) {
   TableColumn column = model.getColumn(i);
   if (i == 0) {
    column.setPreferredWidth(417);
   }
   else {
    column.setPreferredWidth(83);
   }
  }
  setSelectionMode(ListSelectionModel.SINGLE_INTERVAL_SELECTION);
  MovieTableCellRenderer renderer = new MovieTableCellRenderer();
  setDefaultRenderer(Integer.class, renderer);
  setDefaultRenderer(String.class, renderer);
 }
}
```

Other argument choices are MULTIPLE_INTERVAL_SELECTION and SINGLE_SELECTION.

1007 Of course, if you specify a selection mode, you presumably want a listener to take note of selection events. The following illustrates the view side of such a listener. Nothing happens on the model side; the listener only prints the range of the selected rows. Such a method—which extends part way, but not all the way, toward useful work—is called a **stub.**

The listener implements ListSelectionListener, which requires a valueChanged definition, which is called by the machinery that watches for list-selection events. The **list-selection model** supplies information about the selected range. The getValueIsAdjusting call ensures that nothing happens until you have completed your selection operation by releasing your mouse button.

```
import javax.swing.*;
import javax.swing.event.*;
public class MovieRowSelectionListener implements ListSelectionListener
{
 private MovieTableApplication application;
 public MovieRowSelectionListener (MovieTableApplication a) {
  application = a;
 }
 public void valueChanged (ListSelectionEvent e) {
  if (!(e.getValueIsAdjusting())) {
   ListSelectionModel lsm
    = application.getRatingTable().getSelectionModel();
   System.out.println("Selected range boundaries are "
                    + lsm.getMinSelectionIndex()
                    + " and "
                    + lsm.getMaxSelectionIndex());
  }
 }
}
```

1008 Listeners, such as the one defined in Segment 1007, are connected to list-selection model inside the table, which you obtain using the getSelectionModel method, as illustrated in the following, RowMovieTableApplication subclass of the MovieTableApplication class. All that the subclass definition does is to define a zero-parameter constructor that connects the table to an instance of the MovieRowSelectionListener class defined in Segment 1007.

```
import javax.swing.*;
public class RowMovieTableApplication extends MovieTableApplication {
 public RowMovieTableApplication () {
  ListSelectionModel lsm = getRatingTable().getSelectionModel();
  lsm.addListSelectionListener(new MovieRowSelectionListener(this));
 }
 public static void main (String argv []) {
  JFrame frame = new JFrame("Movie Data Table");
  frame.getContentPane().add("Center",
                            new RowMovieTableApplication());
  frame.setSize(750, 210);
  frame.addWindowListener(new ApplicationClosingWindowListener());
  frame.show();
 }
}
```

1009 Alternatively, you may wish to combine the listener defined in Segment 1007 with the demonstration application defined in Segment 1008, by defining the listener as an inner class.

1010 If you wish to allow selective cell editing, you must change the table model's call to the isCellEditable method. For example, the following allows editing of all the columns, except those devoted to the title and rating.

```java
import java.util.*;
import javax.swing.table.*;
public class RatingTableModel extends DefaultTableModel {
  public RatingTableModel (Vector rows, Vector columns) {
    super(rows, columns);
  }
  public boolean isCellEditable(int row, int column) {
    if (column >= 2) {return true;}
    return false;
  }
  public Class getColumnClass(int column) {
    return getValueAt(0, column).getClass();
  }
}
```

1011 Of course, if you allow cell editing, you presumably want a listener to take note of that editing. The following illustrates the view side of such a listener. Nothing happens on the model side; the listener only prints edited value. The listener is a stub, just as the listener defined in Segment 1007 is a stub.

The listener implements the TableModelListener interface, which imposes the definition of tableChanged, which is called by the machinery that watches for editing events. The table-model event supplies information about the change, identified by the getFirstRow and getColumn methods. There is also a getLastRow method, but when you edit individual cells, the first row and the last row are the same.

```java
import javax.swing.event.*;
import javax.swing.table.*;
public class MovieTableCellListener implements TableModelListener {
  MovieTableApplication application;
  public MovieTableCellListener (MovieTableApplication a) {
    application = a;
  }

  public void tableChanged (TableModelEvent e) {
    int row = e.getFirstRow();
    int column = e.getColumn();
    if (row < 0 || column < 0) {return;}
    TableModel model = application.getRatingTable().getModel();
    Object o = model.getValueAt(row, column);
    System.out.println("Edited value is " + o + " of " + o.getClass());
  }
}
```

1012 In a subclass of the MovieTableApplication class, you connect your new listener to the rating-table model. All the subclass definition does is to call addListSelectionListener on the appropriate target with an instance of the MovieTableCellListener class defined in Segment 1011 as an ordinary argument.

Note that you must not have row selection turned on, as row selection would interfere with cell editing. Accordingly, you should use the RatingTable definition provided in Segment 1000.

```
import javax.swing.*;
import javax.swing.table.*;
public class CellMovieTableApplication extends MovieTableApplication {
 public CellMovieTableApplication () {
  TableModel tm = getRatingTable().getModel();
  tm.addTableModelListener(new MovieTableCellListener(this));
 }
 public static void main (String argv []) {
  JFrame frame = new JFrame("Movie Data Table");
  frame.getContentPane().add("Center",
                             new CellMovieTableApplication());
  frame.setSize(750, 210);
  frame.addWindowListener(new ApplicationClosingWindowListener());
  frame.show();
 }
}
```

1013
SIDE TRIP
You can make many other refinements by harnessing the power and rich variety offered by the JTable class.

1014
HIGHLIGHTS

- If you want to create a simple table, **then** call the JTable constructor with row and column vectors as arguments.

- If you want to shut off editing, **then** implement a shadowing isCellEditable method in a subclass of the default table model, **and then** install an instance of that subclass in the table.

- If you want to change the width of columns, **then** call the setPreferredWidth method, with a target that you obtain by extracting a particular column-describing instance from the column model that you obtain from the table.

- If you want to change the way that a cell is rendered, **then** define a a cell renderer, **and then** install an instance of that new renderer in the table.

- If you want to shut off row selection, **then** call the setRowSelectionAllowed method with the table as the target and **false** as the argument.

- **If** you want to set up a selection listener, **then** connect that selection listener to the list-selection model, that you obtain from the table.

- **If** you want to set up an editor listener, **then** connect that editor listener to the table model that you obtain from the table.

53 HOW TO ACTIVATE REMOTE COMPUTATIONS

1015 Prior to Chapter 43, you learned how to write standalone applications; such applications are stored and run on your computer.

Commencing with Chapter 43, you learned how to write applets; those applications are stored on a server computer, but run inside a web browser on your client computer.

In this chapter, you learn about RMI, an acronym for remote method invocation; RMI enables a client computer to run a method on a server computer when requested by the client computer. A server-computer class instance is the method target, and a client-computer class instances are ordinary arguments.

1016 The reasons why you might want your computer, a client, to run a method on another computer, a server, include the following:

- The method requires a great deal of computation, and the server is a faster computer.

- The method requires a great deal of computation, and you have managed to break up the computation into multiple pieces, which you can ship off to multiple server computers.

- The method is maintained by someone else; rather than enduring reinstallations, you simply run the method remotely, on the server, where the method is maintained.

- The method makes use of information that is available on a server, but is not available on your computer.

1017 To understand how remote method invocation works, you first imagine that there is a class, the `RatingServer` class, which defines a magical method for computing movie ratings, superior to all other known methods. Suspending disbelief, you learn that the magical method merely finds the best of the individual ratings; evidently, the method is for positive-attitude movie watchers.

```
public class RatingServer {
 public int serverRating (Movie m) {
  System.out.println("RatingServer asked for a rating");
  int s = m.getScript();
  int a = m.getActing();
  int d = m.getDirection();
  return 3 * Math.max(Math.max(s, a), d);
 }
}
```

1018 With the `RatingServer` class defined, if only you had access to an instance of that class, and did not mind running `serverRating` on your own computer, you could substitute `serverRating` wherever your program would otherwise use the `rating` method defined in the `Movie` class.

For example, the observer defined in Segment 988 uses the `rating` method, so you could make the following substitution, with `serverRating` replacing `rating`.

```
// Replaced
// row.add(new Integer(movie.rating()));
// Substituted in
row.add(new Integer((new RatingServer()).serverRating(movie)));
```

1019 Of course, while you are testing the `RatingServer` class, you probably want to avoid the complexity of a complete application, so you might define just a stub, such as `ClientStub`:

```
import java.rmi.*;
import java.math.*;
public class ClientStub {
 public static void main(String args[]) {
   // Construct a movie for testing
   Movie movie = new Movie(2, 3, 8, "Psycho");
   // Construct a rating server for testing
   RatingServer ratingServer = new RatingServer();
   // Test and print
   int rating = ratingServer.serverRating(movie);
   System.out.println("The server returned a rating of " + rating);
 }
}
————————————————— Result —————————————————
RatingServer asked for a rating
The server returned a rating of 24
```

1020 Now, suppose that you want to move the `RatingServer` instance to another computer—a server. You need answers to several questions:

- How do you inform the server that a particular class instance is to be made available remotely; how does the client find an instance that has been made available remotely?

- How does the client find an instance that has been made available remotely?

- How much do the client and server computers need to know about each other's classes at compile time? How do you supply that information?

- How much do the client and server computers need to know about each other's classes at run time? How is that information exchanged?

- How do you supply to the client and server information about each other's classes at compile time and at run time?

1021 At the time that the `RatingServer` class is compiled, on the server computer, all that the compiler needs to know about the `Movie` class is that there are various methods with various signatures, and obtaining that knowledge requires access to only a modified version of the MovieInterface defined in Segment 765.

The modification specifies that implementers, such as the Movie class, are serializable, as explained in Chapter 34. The reason for introducing serializability is that the server needs access to the actual compiled definitions of Movie methods, at run time, rather than to just definition signatures, because the RatingServer method, serverRating, calls Movie methods. To enable that access, the compiled Movie class is shipped off to the server, from the client, at run time, in serialized form, and we say that the client and server, at this point, are **tightly coupled**.

```
import java.io.*;
public interface MovieInterface extends Serializable {
 // Setters
 public abstract void setScript (int i) ;
 public abstract void setActing (int i) ;
 public abstract void setDirection (int i) ;
 // Getters
 public abstract int getScript () ;
 public abstract int getActing () ;
 public abstract int getDirection () ;
 public abstract String getTitle () ;
 public abstract String getPoster () ;
 // Miscellaneous methods
 public abstract int rating () ;
 public abstract void changed () ;
}
```

1022 Similarly, at the time that the MovieDataObserverForTable or ClientStub class are compiled, on the client computer, all the compiler needs to know about the RatingServer class is that there is a serverRating method, with a particular signature, which is provided adequately by an interface, RatingServerInterface.

Note that the RatingServerInterface not only specifies the serverRating method, but also extends the Remote interface, which informs the compiler that not only must implementing classes implement the specified method, but also that the method is to be called by a client and run on a server.

```
import java.io.*;
import java.rmi.*;
public interface RatingServerInterface extends Remote {
 public abstract int serverRating(MovieInterface m)
   throws RemoteException ;
}
```

1023 The serverRating method defined in Segment 1022 throws a RemoteException, recognizing that a remote method invocation can produce errors that occur because a network is involved, and that the invocation is, in fact, remote.

1024 With RatingServerInterface defined in Segment 1022, and MovieInterface defined in Segment 1021, you can make the following changes in the evolving RatingServer and ClientStub classes. Note that both a parameter and a variable are typed by interface names, rather than by class names:

```
import java.rmi.*;
public class RatingServer implements RatingServerInterface {
  public int serverRating (MovieInterface m) throws RemoteException {
    System.out.println("RatingServer asked for a rating");
    int s = m.getScript();
    int a = m.getActing();
    int d = m.getDirection();
    return 3 * Math.max(Math.max(s, a), d);
  }
}
```

```
import java.rmi.*;
import java.math.*;
public class ClientStub {
  public static void main(String args[]) throws RemoteException {
    // Construct a movie for testing
    Movie movie = new Movie(2, 3, 8, "Psycho");
    // Construct a rating server for testing
    RatingServerInterface ratingServer = new RatingServer();
    // Test and print
    int rating = ratingServer.serverRating(movie);
    System.out.println("The server returned " + rating);
  }
}
```

1025 You need to do more work to prepare the RatingServer for remote method invocation. For example, RatingServer must extend UnicastRemoteObject, rather than extending Object, because the constructors and methods of UnicastRemoteObject perform all sorts of wizardry that enable remote activation. RatingServer must also implement the Serializable interface.

Also, you now must define a zero-argument constructor that calls the zero-argument UnicastRemoteObject constructor and throws the RemoteException exception.

The definition is required because the zero-argument constructor in `UnicastRemoteObject` happens to throw the `RemoteException` exception.

```java
import java.rmi.*;
import java.rmi.server.*;
public class RatingServer extends UnicastRemoteObject
        implements RatingServerInterface, Serializable {
 public RatingServer () throws RemoteException {
  super();
 }
 public int serverRating (MovieInterface m) throws RemoteException {
  System.out.println("RatingServer asked for a rating");
  int s = m.getScript();
  int a = m.getActing();
  int d = m.getDirection();
  return 3 * Math.max(Math.max(s, a), d);
 }
}
```

1026 Clients and servers communicate with each other via a **registry** running on the server computer.

The registry needs to be informed about instance that are to be accessed by clients. Thus, to create a `RatingServer` instance that is ready to receive method calls from a client computer, you must establish a connection with the server computer's running registry program.

The connection is done via a class method, `rebind`, of the `Naming` class, which connects a name with a remotely accessible instance. The `rebind` method takes two arguments: one is a **host identifier**, combined with a name of your choice. The second is the remotely accessible instance.

The host identifier is a specification, such as `whitney.ai.mit.edu`, that specifies the computer on which the registry runs. Typically, this computer is the same one on which the server runs, in which case the host identifier is `localhost`. The client uses a name of your choice—such as `ratingService`—to tell the registry what the client seeks.

Because both `rebind` and the `RatingServer` constructor throw exceptions, both the `rebind` call and the `RatingServer` construction must appear in a `try–catch` combination.

```
import java.rmi.*;
import java.rmi.server.*;
public class RatingServer extends UnicastRemoteObject
                          implements RatingServerInterface {
 public RatingServer () throws RemoteException {
  super();
 }
 public int serverRating (MovieInterface m) throws RemoteException {
  System.out.println("RatingServer asked for a rating");
  int s = m.getScript();
  int a = m.getActing();
  int d = m.getDirection();
  return 3 * Math.max(Math.max(s, a), d);
 }
 public static void main(String[] args) {
  try {
   Naming.rebind("//localhost/ratingService", new RatingServer());
   System.out.println("Rating server connected to server");
  }
  catch (Exception e) {
   System.err.println("RatingServer exception: " + e.getMessage());
   e.printStackTrace();
  }
 }
}
```

1027 You compile the server program shown in Segment 1026 with the Java compiler, `javac`, as explained in Segment 51:

```
javac RatingServer.java
```

In addition, once you have compiled the server program, you must perform a second compilation step, using `rmic`, the remote method invocation compiler.

```
rmic RatingServer
```

1028 Now that you have completed the definition of the server-side `RatingServer` class, you move back to the client side to modify the `ClientStub` class to access a remote—rather than local—instance of the `RatingServer` class.

Another class method, `lookup`, of the `Naming` class provides the required access using a host identifier, such as `whitney.ai.mit.edu`, and the name with which you have chosen to identify the remote instance.

As you did on the server side, you need a `try–catch` combination to deal with thrown exceptions.

```java
import java.rmi.*;
import java.math.*;
public class ClientStub {
 public static void main(String args[]) {
  // Construct a movie for testing
  Movie movie = new Movie(2, 3, 8, "Psycho");
  // Construct a rating server for testing
  try {
   String computer = "whitney.ai.mit.edu";
   System.out.println("The client is asking server, "
                      + computer + ", for a rating");
   RatingServerInterface ratingServer
    = (RatingServerInterface)
      (Naming.lookup("//" + computer +"/ratingService"));
   int rating = ratingServer.serverRating(movie);
   System.out.println("The server, "
                      + computer + ", returned " + rating);
  }
  catch (Exception e) {
   System.err.println("Rating client exception: " + e.getMessage());
   e.printStackTrace();
  }
 }
}
```

1029 Now you have server defined in Segment 1026, compiled with javac and rmic, and the client defined in Segment 1028, compiled with javac; you are ready to test both.

First, on the server computer you open a window in which you start the registry. If you use the code-testing registry program supplied by Sun Microsystems, Inc., then you use the rmiregistry command:

```
rmiregistry
```

Next, on the server computer, you start the server program in another window:

```
java RatingServer
Rating server connected to server
```

Then, with the server started, you can start the client stub in a window on the client computer:

```
java ClientStub
The client is asking server, whitney.ai.mit.edu, for a rating
The server, whitney.ai.mit.edu, returned 24
```

Plainly, the server has returned a result. Returning to the server window, you see that the client has come calling.

```
java RatingServer
Rating server connected to server
Rating server asked for rating
```

1030 To run the client and server on the same computer, for testing, you need only to replace a full internet address with `localhost` in the client stub defined in Segment 1028:

```
...
// Replaced
// String computer = "whitney.ai.mit.edu";
String computer = "localhost";
...
```

Everything on the server side is unchanged.

- **If** you want to run a program on a server computer, **then** you should use Java's client–server remote-method-invocation mechanism.

- Equip both the client and the server with interfaces that provide signatures for methods to be run on the other side.

- Have the server implement `UnicastRemoteObject` and a zero-argument constructor that calls `super`.

- Be sure that all client code to be run on the server is serialized.

- Use the `Naming` class to bind on the server side and to perform lookup on the client side.

- Compile the client class with the `javac` command, and compile the server class with the `javac` command and then the `rmic` command.

- Start the RMI registry using the `rmiregistry` command.

- Start the server with the `java` command. At this point, clients can call methods to be run on the server.

54 HOW TO COLLECT INFORMATION USING SERVLETS

1032 An **applet** is a program that is shipped from a server to a client browser and run in that browser. A **servlet** is a program that activated by a client browser and run on a servlet server.

In this chapter, you learn how browser forms call and send arguments to servlets, and you learn how servlets receive arguments from and deliver results back to browsers.

The word *servlet* is derived from *server + applet*; thus, a servlet is a little server-side application. Nothing prevents you from writing large servlets, however.

1033 There are two primary ways to communicate with a servlet from a browser. One way is to specify the name of the servlet in an HTML link, as explained in Segment 1034.

Another way, using HTML forms, is introduced in Segment 1044.

Thus, you see examples of both kinds of communicaion. The result of the first example is the display of a rating form that makes you the critic. The result of the second is a file update that reflects your opinion, as expressed via the displayed form.

1034 The following steps lead to the actuation of a servlet instance from an HTML link.

- You click on the link, in which the address tag supplies the location and name of a servlet, as in the following example:

  You can <a href="//whitney.ai.mit.edu/servlet/startcritic">vote</a> on movies yourself, if you wish.

- The servlet server looks up the servlet name, `startcritic`, in a table described in Segment 1037; it finds a class name, `GetCriticFormServlet`.

- Unless a `GetCriticFormServlet` instance has been constructed already, the servlet server constructs a `GetCriticFormServlet` instance, and calls the class's `init` method with the instance as the target.

- The servlet server, by convention, calls the `GetCriticFormServlet` class's `doGet` method with the instance as the target.

- The `doGet` method prepares HTML-decorated text to be sent back to the browser for display.

1035
SIDE TRIP
Because the `doGet` method runs entirely on the servlet server, Java's security mechanism allows you full access to all the servlet server's resources, including file reading and writing.

If the servlet server should be shut down, it shuts down active servlets by calling the destroy method, and then garbage collects storage allocated to those servlets. Some servlet servers shut down servlets that have been conspicuously inactive.

1037 A file—named **servlets.properties** by default—contains the table that relates servlet names to class names. That file resides on the servlet server computer, and the servlet server uses that file to respond to servlet-naming URLs.

Suppose, for example, that you have two names, startcritic and processcritic, which identify two classes, GetCriticFormServlet and ProcessCriticFormServlet. Then, the servlets properties table contains the following lines.

```
# This file contains name-class pairs for the example servlets
# Lines beginning with # are comments
# Returns an HTML page containing a form
startcritic.code=GetCriticFormServlet
# Processes completed form
processcritic.code=ProcessCriticFormServlet
```

1038 You learn how to define a servlet in Segment 1041. Once you have written a collection of servlets and have written or augmented a servlets.properties file, you need to know where to put them. Unfortunately, the place will depend on the servlet server that you happen to use. If you happen to use a servlet server supplied by Sun Microsystems, Inc., then the servlets.properties file belongs in a directory named WEB-INF, a subdirectory of the servlet server directory, and all your servlets belong in a directory named servlets, a subdirectory of the WEB-INF directory. If you have divided your servlets into packages, however, then servlets acts as though it were on your CLASSPATH, as described in Chapter 35, and your servlets belong in subdirectories of the servlets directory corresponding to your package names.

Of course, you can tell the servlet server to look in a place other than the default place for servlets; In general, however, you would be wise to run your servlet server with the default location, inasmuch as software developers tend to test software mostly with the defaults.

1039 The ritual that you use to start up a servlet server will depend on the servlet server that you happen to use. If you happen to use a servlet server supplied by Sun Microsystems, Inc., running on a Windows computer, then you open a command window, change to the servlet server directory, and type the following:

```
startserver
```

Similarly, if you want to stop the servlet server, you open another window and type the following:

```
stopserver
```

1040 The following shows the elements involved in servlet communication and servlet use.

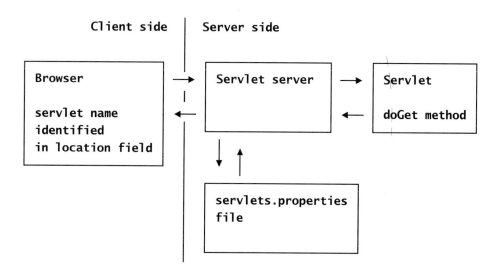

Client side | Server side

Browser

servlet name
identified
in location field

Servlet server

servlets.properties
file

Servlet

doGet method

1041 The easiest way to define a servlet is to extend the HttpServlet class, shadowing the doGet method. That method has two parameters: the request parameter's value is a class instance that contains information about the request (ignored in the following example); the response parameter's value is a class instance that your program uses to convey information back to the browser from which the request originated.

The setContentType method prepares the response instance to receive the text of an HTML page. The getWriter method obtains an output stream on which to write text, which happens to be an instance of the PrintWriter class.

Once doGet completes, the servlet server returns the information contained within the response instance to the client, to be displayed by the browser as a new HTML page. Evidently, doGet is so named because it *gets* a new HTML page.

```
import java.io.*;
import javax.servlet.*;
import javax.servlet.http.*;
public class GetCriticFormServlet extends HttpServlet {
 public void doGet (HttpServletRequest request, HttpServletResponse re-
sponse)
           throws ServletException, IOException {
  response.setContentType("text/html");
  PrintWriter output = response.getWriter();
  output.println("<HTML><HEAD><TITLE>");
  output.println("You be the critic!");
  output.println("</TITLE></HEAD><BODY>");
  // HTML content, such as the form shown in Segment 1043, ...
  // printed to output stream here using println ...
  output.println("</BODY></HTML>");
  output.flush();
 }
}
```

1042 Servlets often return HTML forms, such as the following. From such a form, you are expected make a selection from a **pull-down list** or to press various **radio buttons**. When you have finished, you are expected to transmit your choices to a servlet server by pressing the Vote button.

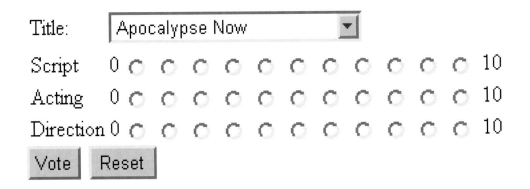

1043 To create the form shown in Segment 1042, you can write HTML code. Alternatively, you can have a servlet—such as the servlet defined in Segment 1041—write HTML code for you. That HTML code will feature the <form> tag. Working in tandem with the <form> tag, you find <select>, <option>, and <input> tags. All are explained in Segment 1044.

The HTML code includes <table>, <tr>, and <td> tags because they produce a pleasing layout. The <tr> tag signals the start of a table row; the <td> tag signals the start of a table datum.

```
<pre>
<form method=get
      action="http://whitney.ai.mit.edu/servlet/processcritic">
<table><tr><td>Title: <td>
<select name=title size=1>
<option>Apocalypse Now
<option>The Sting
<option>The Wizard of Oz
<option>Bedtime for Bonzo
<option>The Last House on the Left
<option>Gone with the Wind
<option>Casablanca
<option>The King of Hearts
<option>My Fair Lady
<option>The Sound of Music
</select>
```

```
<tr><td>Script<td>
0 <input type=radio name=script value=0>
<input type=radio name=script value=1>
<input type=radio name=script value=2>
<input type=radio name=script value=3>
<input type=radio name=script value=4>
<input type=radio name=script value=5>
<input type=radio name=script value=6>
<input type=radio name=script value=7>
<input type=radio name=script value=8>
<input type=radio name=script value=9>
<input type=radio name=script value=10> 10
// Repeat for acting and direction ...
</table>
<input type=submit value="Vote"> <input type=reset value="Reset">
</form>
</pre>
```

1044 In Segment 1043, the <form> tag exhibits two parts. The first combination, method=get, specifies that the communication between the browser and the servlet is to follow the **get protocol**, rather than the **post protocol**, as explained in Segment 1062.

The second combination specifies the name of a servlet to be run, processcritic, located by way of the URL, http://whitney.ai.mit.edu/servlet/processcritic. This URL may target a computer different from the one on which the form is located.

1045 Information is supplied to the servlet specified in the <form> tag by the pull-down menu and radio buttons. For example, if you select an item from a pull-down menu—bracketed by <select> and </select> tags, and punctuated by <option> tags—then the name identified in the <select> tag and a string prefixed by an <option> tag are supplied to the target servlet.

Thus, if you select Casablanca, then the title–Casablanca name–value combination is supplied to the target servlet.

```
<form ···>
...
<select name=title ···>
...
<option>Casablanca
...
</select>
</form>
```

1046 Similarly, if you press a radio button, then the name–value combination identified in the radio-button tag is supplied to the target servlet.

Thus, if you press the radio button associated with <input type=radio name=script value=9>, then the script–9 name–value combination is supplied to the target servlet.

```
<form ···>
...
<input type=radio name=script value=9>
...
</form>
```

1047 To send off all name–value pairs to the servlet server, you press the submit button, labeled Vote. If you want to start over, you can use the reset button, which clears all selections.

```
<input type=submit value="Vote">  <input type=reset value="Reset">
```

1048 To make use of name–value pairs, you deploy the getParameter method, with the request as the target. In the following definition of ProcessCriticFormServlet, the doGet is a stub. It merely constructs a table that echos the arguments back to the browser.

```
import java.io.*;
import javax.servlet.*;
import javax.servlet.http.*;
public class ProcessCriticFormServlet extends HttpServlet {
 public void doGet (HttpServletRequest request,
                    HttpServletResponse response)
             throws ServletException, IOException {
  // Process arguments
  String title = request.getParameter("title");
  String script = request.getParameter("script");
  String acting = request.getParameter("acting");
  String direction = request.getParameter("direction");
  // Writing preparation
  response.setContentType("text/html");
  PrintWriter webWriter = response.getWriter();
  // Writing HTML page
  webWriter.println("<HTML><HEAD><TITLE>");
  webWriter.println("You were the critic!");
  webWriter.println("</TITLE></HEAD><BODY>");
  webWriter.println("<h1>You have voted as follows for <u>"
                    + title
                    + "</u></h1>");
  webWriter.println("<table cellpadding=5 border=1 >");
  webWriter.println("<tr><td>Script<td>" + script);
  webWriter.println("<tr><td>Acting<td>" + acting);
  webWriter.println("<tr><td>Direction<td>" + direction);
  webWriter.println("</table><p>");
  webWriter.println(
    "<a href=\""
    + response.encodeRedirectURL("/servlet/startcritic")
    + "\">"
  );
```

```
webWriter.println("Click here</a> to vote again.");
webWriter.println("</BODY></HTML>");
webWriter.flush();
// Real work goes here ...
}}
```

1049 You can enhance the servlet introduced in Segment 1048 by adding statements that write information to a file. Note that the new version implements the `SingleThreadModel` interface, as explained in Segment 1050.

```java
import java.io.*;
import javax.servlet.*;
import javax.servlet.http.*;
public class ProcessCriticFormServlet extends HttpServlet
                                implements SingleThreadModel {
 public void doGet (HttpServletRequest request, HttpServletResponse response)
                 throws ServletException, IOException {
  // Process arguments
  String title = request.getParameter("title");
  String script = request.getParameter("script");
  String acting = request.getParameter("acting");
  String direction = request.getParameter("direction");
  // Writing preparation
  response.setContentType("text/html");
  PrintWriter webWriter = response.getWriter();
  // Writing HTML page goes here ...
  // File output
  String user = request.getRemoteUser();
  String host = request.getRemoteHost();
  FileOutputStream stream
   = new FileOutputStream("VotingData.txt", true);
  PrintWriter fileWriter = new PrintWriter(stream);
  if (user != null) {
   fileWriter.println("Voter: " + user + " at " + host);
  }
  else {fileWriter.println("Voter at " + host);}
  fileWriter.println("Evaluated \"" + title + "\" stipulating:");
  if(script != null) {fileWriter.println("Script: " + script);}
  if(acting != null) {fileWriter.println("Acting: " + acting);}
  if(direction != null) {
   fileWriter.println("Direction: " + direction);
  }
  fileWriter.println("");
  fileWriter.flush();
  stream.close();
}}
```

1050 Ordinarily, servlet servers are content to handle multiple requests simultaneously, by wrapping each in its own thread. Accordingly, if your servlets write information to a file, you need to worry about what happens if one client's work is underway when another client's request arrives. Otherwise, you risk having one client step on another's toes, as explained in Segment 902.

The easiest way to avoid multiple-thread toe stomping is to have your servlets implement the `SingleThreadModel` interface, as does the servlet defined in Segment 1049, which shuts off multithreading. Otherwise, you need to use Java's synchronization mechanism to protect state-retaining files, as explained in Segment 903.

1051
SIDE TRIP
Ordinarily, if your website has many users, you need to use a relational database product to store information, rather than using ordinary files. Such products provide robust data handling and easy data access.

1052 Eventually, you may want your servlets to store information on the client computer. For example, to provide a more informative interaction, you might want to keep track of the number of times that a client has voted, or you might want to store the client user's name, or you might want to prevent a client from voting for the same movie more than once.

To achieve such objectives, you have your servlet establish **cookies** on the client computer.

1053 Cookies have names and values, both of which are strings. You need to supply both when you construct a cookie, as in the following statement, in which you name the `Cookie` instance `votes` and provide a string, 0, as the cookie's value:

```
Cookie cookie= new Cookie("votes", "0");
```

1054 To send a cookie to a client, you add it to the response using `addCookie`, as in the following statement, where the variable `response` is an instance of the `HttpServletResponse` class.

```
response.addCookie(cookie);
```

1055 Note that you must add cookies to the response class instance before you access the response's writer, because cookies become part of the header of the information sent back to the client. Once you access the response's writer, you are not allowed to alter the header.

1056 Note that the volume of data that can be stored in a cookie is limited to a small number of kilobytes.

1057 To get a cookie that has been stored on a client, you first collect all the available cookies using the `getCookies` method. Then, you look for the name of the cookie you want in the returned array of cookies. You deploy the `getName` method to find the cookie, once you find the cookie, you deploy the `getValue` method.

```
Cookies [] cookies = request.getCookies();
for (int i = 0; i < cookies.length; ++i) {
 if("votes".equals(cookies[i].getName())) {
  ··· cookies[i].getValue() ···
}}
```

1058 What you have learned about cookies is put to use in the following revision of the servlet, ProcessCriticFormServlet, defined previously in Segment 1049. Note that, because cookie values are always strings, you must convert them to int values.

```
import java.io.*;
import javax.servlet.*;
import javax.servlet.http.*;
public class ProcessCriticFormServlet extends HttpServlet {
 public void doGet (HttpServletRequest request, HttpServletResponse response)
            throws ServletException, IOException {
  // Process arguments
  String title = request.getParameter("title");
  String script = request.getParameter("script");
  String acting = request.getParameter("acting");
  String direction = request.getParameter("direction");
  // Cookie processing
  int voteCount = 0;
  Cookie [] cookies = request.getCookies();
  System.out.println("There are " + cookies.length + " cookies");
  // Look for existing cookie
  for (int i = 0; i < cookies.length; ++i) {
   if("votes".equals(cookies[i].getName())) {
    voteCount = Integer.parseInt(cookies[i].getValue());
   }
  }
  // Write new cookie
  ++voteCount;
  Cookie cookie = new Cookie("votes", String.valueOf(voteCount));
  response.addCookie(cookie);
  // Writing preparation
  response.setContentType("text/html");
  PrintWriter webWriter = response.getWriter();
  // Writing HTML page goes here ...
  // New line informing users of the vote count
  webWriter.println("You have cast "
            + voteCount
            + (voteCount == 1 ? " vote" : " votes")
            + " so far<p>");
  // Rest of writing HTML page goes here ...
  // File output goes here ...
}}
```

1059 Cookies are URL specific; there is no danger that cookies placed by servlets executing in the servlet server or servlet servers associated with one URL will interfere with cookies placed by servlets executing in the servlet server or servlet servers associated with another URL.

Cookies are not servlet specific, however; cookies placed by one servlet on one servlet server are provided to all servlets that work with the client's browser. Thus, you can use cookies to communicate among servlets.

1060 You can create multiple cookies that have the same name, as long as you have not exhausted the memory limit placed on cookies. You can use identical names if, for example, you want to keep track of the movies that a given user has evaluated. For each, you might construct a cookie such as the following:

```
Cookie cookie= new Cookie("evaluated", "title of movie");
```

Note, however, that browsers are not obligated to maintain an indefinite number of cookies. You should not count on storing more than 10 cookies, to be on the safe side.

1061 Ordinary cookies stay on the client there until they become too old. It is up to you to decide what *too old* means. If you do nothing, a cookie is *too old* as soon as the client browser shuts down. Otherwise, you can set the lifetime of a cookie, specifying it in seconds. For example, the following destroys a cookie immediately:

```
cookie.setMaxAge(0);
```

The following causes a cookie to persist for 1 year:

```
cookie.setMaxAge(60 * 60 * 24 * 365);
```

1062 The servlets explained in this chapter follow the **get protocol**, rather than the **post protocol**. The server connection and data transmission take place in one step, rather than in two. Generally, the get protocol is good for smaller volume, faster communication, and the post protocol is good for larger volume, more secure communication. Servlets use `doGet` to handle the get protocol, and `doPost` to handle the post protocol.

1063

HIGHLIGHTS

- A servlet is a program that runs on a remote computer when activated by a browser click on a link or form element.

- Servlet servers locate servlets by way of a `servlets.properties` file.

- **If** you want to implement a servlet, **then** define a subclass of the `HttpServlet` class with a `doGet` method. You can define the `doGet` method to do any of the following.

  - Analyze forms.

  - Write information to a local file.

  - Prepare HTML text to be returned to the servlet-initiating browser.

- **If** you want a servlet to store information on a client computer, **then** have the servlet create and return a cookie.

55 HOW TO CONSTRUCT JAR FILES FOR PROGRAM DISTRIBUTION

1064   In previous chapters, you have learned how to write standalone programs, applets, servlets, and remotely invoked programs. In this chapter, you learn how to combine multiple-file programs into a single compressed file called a JAR file, where JAR is an acronym for Java Archive.

1065   The Java JAR file has an unfortunate name, inasmuch as archiving is but one of several reasons why you should gather together all your application files into a JAR file. Other reasons include the following:

- JAR files simplify program distribution. You have only one file to move about, rather than a whole directory, or directory hierarchy, full of files.

- JAR files save space and time. You have only one compressed JAR file to store or to ship over the web.

- JAR files provide version management. Each time you reach a stable point in your program, you can create a JAR file.

- JAR files enable security. You can add a digital signature to a JAR file that lessens the chance that a manipulated version will get into the hands of an innocent user.

1066   Before you create a JAR file, you need to create an application-describing **manifest file**. Minimally, your manifest file needs just one line that identifies the application class that starts your application. For example, if the MovieApplicationTestor class starts your application, then the manifest file must contain the following line:

```
Main-Class: MovieApplicationTestor
```

1067   Once you have a manifest file, say manifest.txt, then you can create a JAR file using the command-line jar program. Suppose, for example, that your current directory contains all the class files needed by your movie application program. Then, you can create a JAR file by typing the following:

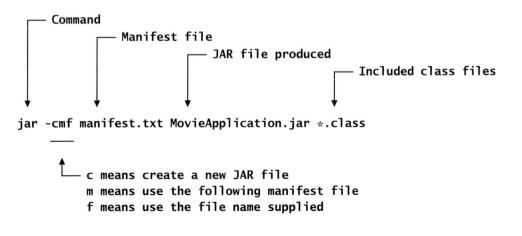

```
jar -cmf manifest.txt MovieApplication.jar *.class
```

c means create a new JAR file
m means use the following manifest file
f means use the file name supplied

You can use wildcards to identify a collection of files, as shown. Alternatively, you can supply a list of explicit file names, separated by spaces.

1068 If you have divided your application into packages—such as the `application`, `model`, and `view` packages—then your directory structure will include a directory with `application`, `model`, and `view` subdirectories. To combine all the class files in those subdirectories into a JAR file, you type the following, once you have made the current directory be the parent directory of the `application`, `model`, and `view` directories.

```
jar -cmf manifest.txt MovieApplication.jar application model view
```

If you want only the class files in those directories, you use a wildcard—by typing, for example, `application/*.class`, instead of `application`.

1069 If your application includes all the images in an image directory, you can include those images in the JAR file as follows:

```
jar -cmf manifest.txt MovieApplication.jar application model view images
```

Alternatively, if your applications includes all the images in the current directory, in files with a `jpg` extension, you type the following:

```
jar -cmf manifest.txt MovieApplication.jar application model view *.jpg
```

1070 Once you have a JAR file, running a standalone application is straightforward. You are accustomed to typing the following to start an application from a class file:

```
java MovieApplicationTestor
```

To start an application from a JAR file, you type the following:

```
java -jar MovieApplication.jar
```

Note that, for the JAR version to work, you must have created the JAR file using a manifest file, as explained in Segment 1066, that identifies the `MovieApplicationTestor` class as the application-starting class.

1071 Certain applications use previously prepared JAR files. If your application uses such a previously prepared JAR file—say, the `Entertainment.jar` file—you would include a reference to it file in your JAR file's manifest, as shown in the following expansion of the manifest file introduced in Segment 1066.

```
Main-Class: MovieApplicationTestor
Class-Path: Entertainment.jar
```

1072 If you like, you can include useful descriptive information in the manifest file. For example, you can describe each package by a section that begins with its relative path name, including the trailing slash. Then, you can specify, for example, version details:

```
Main-Class: MovieApplicationTestor
Class-Path: Entertainment.jar
Name: application/
Specification-Title: "Application specifications"
Specification-Version: "3.141"
Specification-Vendor: "XYZ, Inc."
Implementation-Title: "Application implementation"
Implementation-Version: "Build 2.718"
Implementation-Vendor: "XYZ, Inc."
Name: model
...
Name: view
...
```

- If you want to distribute a program, **then** prepare a manifest file by instantiating the following pattern:

  Main-Class: `name of application-starting class`

  and then prepare a JAR file by instantiating the following pattern:

  jar -cmf `name of manifest file` `name of JAR file` *.class

- If your program contains resources, then include those resources in your JAR file by instantiating the following pattern when you create that JAR file:

  jar -cmf `manifest file` `JAR file` *.class `resource file`

APPENDIX A: OPERATOR PRECEDENCE

1074 The following table lists Java's precedence and associativity characteristics. Each box contains operators that have equal precedence. The top box contains the highest-precedence operators:

Operator level	Associativity
( ) [ ] .	left to right
! ++ -- + (unary) - (negation) new (data type)	right to left
* / %	left to right
+ -	left to right
<<= >>=	left to right
== !=	left to right
&	left to right
^	left to right
|	left to right
&&	left to right
||	left to right
?:	right to left
= += -= *= /= %= &= ^= |= <<= >>=	right to left

Note that the name of each data type, when surrounded by parentheses, is considered a casting operator. Also, the parentheses following a method name are considered to be the function-call operator.

The & and | operators, as well as the exclusive-or operator, ^, are bitwise operations, rather than Boolean operators.

APPENDIX B: THE METER CANVAS

1075 The following Meter class is used in examples in this book. The definition includes statements that illustrate how you draw elements, such as lines, arcs, and triangles:

```java
import java.lang.*;
import java.awt.*;
import javax.swing.*;
import java.util.*;
public class Meter extends JComponent implements MeterInterface {
 String title = "Title to Be Supplied"; // Title string for the meter
 int minimum, maximum;          // Minimum and maximum values displayed
 int value;                     // Currently displayed value
 static int border = 10;        // Minimum space between dial and frame
 int yOffset;                   // Gap at the bottom
 int xCenter;                   // Center of pointer
 int yCenter;                   // Center of pointer
 int radius;                    // Radius of dial circle
 // Two-parameter constructor takes arguments specifying the
 // the minimum and maximum values that the meter displays:
 public Meter (int x, int y) {
  minimum = x;
  maximum = y;
  value = (x + y) / 2;
 }
 // Title setter:
 public void setTitle(String s) {title = s; repaint();}
 // Value setter:
 public void setValue(int v) {
  // If the value is less than the minimum, set to minimum:
  if (v < minimum) {value = minimum;}
  // If the value is greater than the maximum, set to maximum:
  else if (v > maximum) {value = maximum;}
  else {value = v;}
  repaint();
 }
 public int getValueAtCoordinates (int x, int y) {
  Dimension d = getSize();
  xCenter = (int)(d.width / 2);
  yOffset = (int)(d.height / 4);
  yCenter = (int)(d.height - yOffset);
  double angle = Math.atan2(x - xCenter, yCenter - y) + (Math.PI / 2);
  double fraction = angle / Math.PI;
  return (int)Math.round(fraction * (maximum - minimum) + minimum);
 }
```

```java
// Draw the tick marks associated with the meter:
// Write the title associated with the meter, centered at bottom:
// Paint, by calling other methods:
public void paint(Graphics g) {
 computeKeyValues();
 Dimension d = getSize();
 drawTics(g);
 drawText(g);
 drawPointer(g);
}
// Perform miscellaneous chores
private void computeKeyValues () {
 Dimension d = getSize();
 xCenter = (int)(d.width / 2);
 yOffset = (int)(d.height / 4);
 yCenter = (int)(d.height - yOffset);
 radius = Math.min(xCenter, yCenter) - (2 * border);
}
private void drawTics(Graphics g) {
 double angleDelta = Math.PI / 50.0;
 double angle = 0.0;
 int innerRadius = (int)(radius - (radius / 10));
 int middleRadius = (int)(radius - (radius / 20));
 // Draw an arc on which to draw the tics:
 g.drawArc(xCenter - radius,
           yCenter - radius,
           radius * 2,
           radius * 2, 0, 180);
 // Draw about 50 tick marks with about 10 major ticks
 for (int i=0; i<=50; i++, angle += angleDelta) {
  double cosAngle = Math.cos(angle);
  double sinAngle = Math.sin(angle);
  int x1, x2, y1, y2;
  x1 = (int)(radius * cosAngle) + xCenter;
  y1 = yCenter - (int)(radius * sinAngle);
  if (i%5 == 0) {
   x2 = (int)(innerRadius * cosAngle) + xCenter;
   y2 = yCenter - (int)(innerRadius * sinAngle);
  }
  else {
   x2 = (int)(middleRadius * cosAngle) + xCenter;
   y2 = yCenter - (int)(middleRadius * sinAngle);
  }
  g.drawLine(x1, y1, x2, y2);
 }
}
```

```
private void drawText(Graphics g) {
 Dimension d = getSize();
 // Prepare font
 int fontSize = Math.max(12, d.width / 30);
 g.setFont(new Font("Helvetica", Font.BOLD, fontSize));
 // Write title:
 FontMetrics f = g.getFontMetrics();
 int stringWidth = f.stringWidth(title);
 int textXOffset = (d.width - stringWidth) / 2;
 int textYOffset = (3 * d.height / 4) + (2 * f.getHeight());
 g.drawString(title, textXOffset, textYOffset);
 // Set minimum and maximum values
 int fontHeight = f.getHeight();
 int fontDescent = f.getDescent();
 int middleRadius = (int)(radius - (radius / 20));
 String sval = String.valueOf(minimum);
 stringWidth = f.stringWidth(sval);
 // Draw the minimum-value string:
 g.drawString(sval,
              xCenter - middleRadius + 10,
              yCenter - fontDescent);
 sval = String.valueOf(maximum);
 stringWidth = f.stringWidth(sval);
 // Draw the maximum-value string:
 g.drawString(sval,
              xCenter + middleRadius - stringWidth - 10,
              yCenter - fontDescent);
}
private void drawPointer(Graphics g) {
 // Compute the angle dictated by the value;
 // Increase the angle from left to right:
 double angle = ((double)(value - minimum)
                / (double)(maximum - minimum)) * Math.PI;
 // Measure from left to right
 angle = Math.PI - angle;
 double cosAngle = Math.cos(angle);
 double sinAngle = Math.sin(angle);
 // Compute coordinates of pointer's point
 int xPoint = (int)(radius * cosAngle);
 int yPoint = (int)(radius * sinAngle);
 // Compute miscellaneous values
 int pointerLength = (int) (1.1 * radius);
 int pointerHalfWidth = (int) (pointerLength / 20);
 int ovalRadius = (int) (pointerHalfWidth * 1.5);
 // Obtain current Color instance:
 Color colorHandle = g.getColor();
```

```java
// Reset color temporarily:
g.setColor(Color.gray);
// Draw the circle
g.fillOval(xCenter - ovalRadius,
           yCenter - ovalRadius,
           2 * ovalRadius,
           2 * ovalRadius);
// Compute the points on the pointer border;
// note that y increases downward
int xpoints[] = new int[3];
int ypoints[] = new int[3];
xpoints[0] = xPoint + xCenter;
ypoints[0] = yCenter - yPoint;
xpoints[1] = xPoint
             - (int)(pointerLength * cosAngle)
             - (int)(pointerHalfWidth * sinAngle) + xCenter;
ypoints[1] = yCenter
             - (yPoint - (int )(pointerLength * sinAngle)
             + (int)(pointerHalfWidth * cosAngle));
xpoints[2] = xPoint
             - (int)(pointerLength * cosAngle)
             + (int)(pointerHalfWidth * sinAngle) + xCenter;
ypoints[2] = yCenter
             - (yPoint - (int)(pointerLength * sinAngle)
             - (int)(pointerHalfWidth * cosAngle));
// Draw the pointer
g.fillPolygon(xpoints, ypoints, 3);
// Restore color:
g.setColor(colorHandle);
}
// Assist in sizing:
public Dimension getMinimumSize() {return new Dimension(200, 200);}
public Dimension getPreferredSize() {return new Dimension(200, 200);}
}
```

APPENDIX C: APPLET PARAMETERS

1076

This appendix explains how you can specify a value for an applet parameter in an HTML file.

1077 To create a value for, say, a parameter named `file`, you specify the parameter name and the value, a string, in an HTML file as follows:

```
                        ┌── Name
                        │
                     ───▼──
<param name=file value="general.movies">
                      ────────────────
                               ▲
                               └── Value
```

Such parameter specifications lie between an `<applet ··· >`—`</applet>` pair, as illustrated by the following example:

```
<html>
<head><title>Welcome to the Movies!</title></head>
<body>
<hr>
In the following display, click on a movie to see its rating.
<hr>
<applet code="MovieApplet.class" width=400 height=150>
<param name=file value="general.movies">
</applet>
<hr>
</body>
</html>
```

1078 To get the value specified in an HTML file, you use the `getParameter` method defined for the `JApplet` class:

```
                        ┌── Parameter name
                        │
                     ───▼──
getParameter("file");
```

1079

In the version of the `MovieApplication` class defined in Chapter 43, the movie file name was wired into the class definition:

```
setMovieVector(MovieAuxiliaries.readMovieFile("general.movies"));
```

Instead, you can use a file name wired into an HTML file by using the parameter mechansim:

```
setMovieVector(MovieAuxiliaries.readMovieFile(getParameter("file")));
```

APPENDIX D: THE SWING CLASSES

1080 This appendix shows how the JFrame, JApplet, JPanel, and other related classes fit together in the class hierarchy, and explains why there are other classes with similar names.

The diagram shows how the JFrame, JApplet, JComponent, and JPanel fit in a hierarchy that also contains the Frame, Applet, and Panel classes:

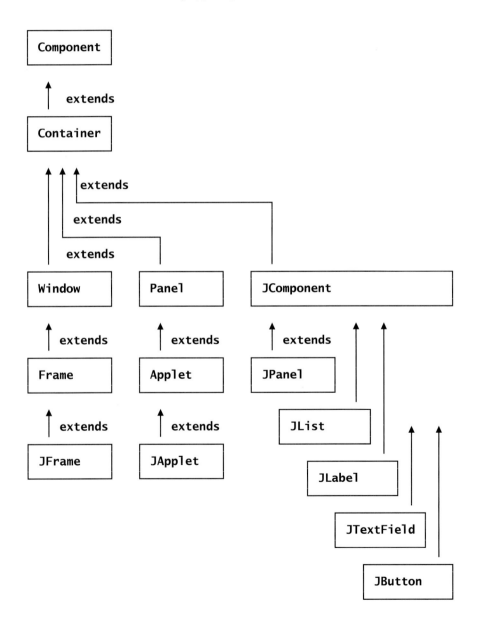

1081   The `JPanel`, `JList`, `JLabel`, `JTextField`, and `JButton` classes all extend the `JComponent` class; only the `JPanel`, `JList`, and `JLabel` classes are direct subclasses of the `JComponent` class.

1082   When we use the terms **frame, applet, panel, component, label, text field**, and **button**, we refer to instances of the `JFrame`, `JApplet`, `JPanel`, `JComponent`, `JLabel`, `JTextField`, and `JButton` classes. The older, less capable classes, which have names such as `Frame` and `Applet`, and their arrangement in the hierarchy, were retained in `Java` for backward compatibility.

APPENDIX E: LAYOUT MANAGERS

1083 If you use a layout manager, the relative sizes of all the components in a panel are governed by a complex arbitration process. Each type of layout manager handles the size-arbitration process in its own way.

You may, if you wish, avoid layout managers, but then you must fix the sizes of your components and their positions, as described in Segment 964.

1084 As they arbitrate among components, layout managers work with information provided as follows:

- If the component is an applet viewed via an HTML file, then that HTML file specifies a window into which all the applet's components must fit.

When you include a reference to an applet in an HTML file, you must supply window dimensions, and your applet will have to work itself into those dimensions, however Procrustean they may be:

- If the component is a frame with a `setSize` method called, then that `setSize` method specifies a window into which all components must fit.

If you do not supply a `setSize` method in a frame, Java will work with the operating system to choose a frame-window size:

- If the component is neither an applet nor a frame, then the `getMinimumSize` method and a `getPreferredSize` method help to determine component size.

If you do not supply `getMinimumSize` and `getPreferredSize` methods in your components, Java works with defaults.

1085 If you do not include a call to the `setSize` method in your frames, and you do not include definitions for `getMinimumSize` and `getPreferredSize` in your components, then the choices negotiated may lead to unintelligible layout results, and certain of your components may not appear at all.

1086 Layout managers often seem to have mysterious minds of their own. Accordingly, to get a feel for what sorts of layouts are possible, you see, in the following segments, a variety of layout managers in action, in a variety of circumstances.

1087 To assist in your experiments with layout managers, you need to define a component with appropriate `getMinimumSize` and `getPreferredSize` methods defined. One convenient way to define such a component is to extend the `JButton` class, shadowing the `getMinimumSize` and `getPreferredSize` methods:

```
import java.awt.*;
import javax.swing.*;
public class TestButton extends JButton {
 public TestButton (String t) {
  super(t);
 }
 public Dimension getMinimumSize() {return new Dimension(50, 30);}
 public Dimension getPreferredSize() {return new Dimension(50, 30);}
}
```

1088 Having defined the TestButton class, you can use instances of that class to experiment with, for example, the border-layout manager. The following, for example, defines a test panel:

```
import java.awt.*;
import javax.swing.*;
public class TestPanel extends JPanel {
 public TestPanel() {
  setLayout(new BorderLayout());
  add("North", new TestButton("N"));
  add("East", new TestButton("E"));
  add("South", new TestButton("S"));
  add("West", new TestButton("W"));
  add("Center", new TestButton("C"));
 }
}
```

1089 You can run the program shown in Segment 1088 using the following test program:

```
import javax.swing.*;
import java.awt.event.*;
public class TestFrame extends JFrame {
 public static void main (String argv []) {
  new TestFrame("Layout Window");
 }
 TestPanel testPanel = new TestPanel();
 public TestFrame(String title) {
  super(title);
  getContentPane().add("Center", testPanel);
  setSize(260, 150);
  addWindowListener(new LocalWindowListener());
  show();
 }
// Definition of LocalWindowListener as in Segment 702 ...
}
```

When you run the test program, you see the following display:

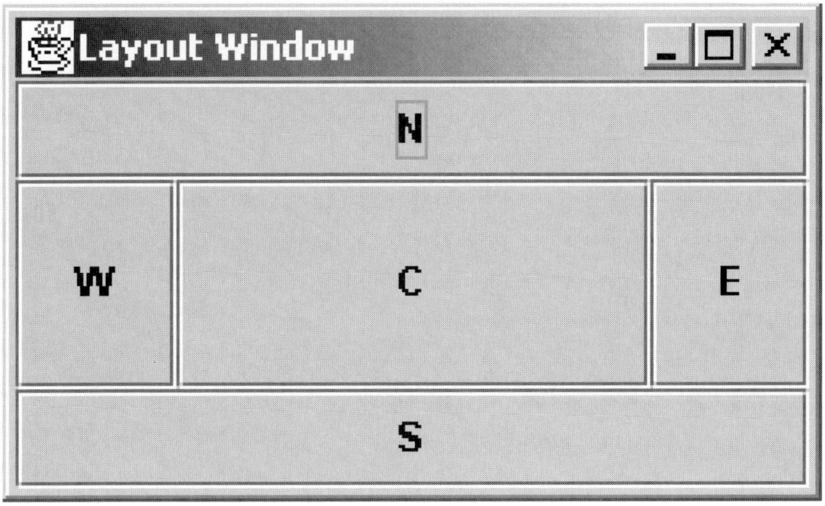

1090 Of course, you do not need to place a component in any particular position. The following shows the border layout with the south component omitted. The west, center, and east components expand southward to take up the vacated space:

1091 Similarly, the following shows the border layout with the east component omitted. The center component expands eastward to take up the vacated space:

1092 Finally, the following shows the border layout with the center component omitted. A hole appears in the space vacated by the center component:

1093 As you learned in Segment 919, the grid-layout manager lays out components on a regular grid. The following grid layout places components in two rows and three columns:

```
import java.awt.*;
import javax.swing.*;
public class TestPanel extends JPanel {
 public TestPanel () {
  setLayout(new GridLayout(2, 3));
  add(new TestButton("A"));
  add(new TestButton("B"));
  add(new TestButton("C"));
  add(new TestButton("D"));
  add(new TestButton("E"));
  add(new TestButton("F"));
 }
}
```

1094 When you use the definition shown in Segment 1093, you produce the following display:

1095 You can separate the components by supplying the GridLayout class constructor with row- and column-spacing arguments:

— Spacing between row elements

— Spacing between column elements

setLayout(new GridLayout(2, 3, 15, 10));

When you use such spacing, you see the following:

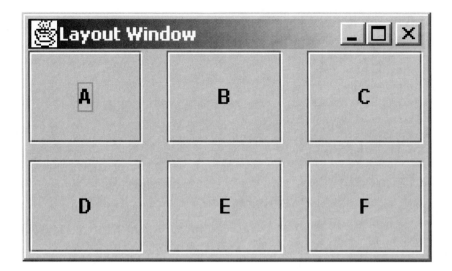

1096 You can use the grid layout manager to place components in a single row or column. All you need to do is to use arguments of 0 and 1. If you use 1 as the first argument, you get a row:

And if you use 1 as the second argument, you get a column:

1097 The flow-layout manager lays out components from left to right, top to bottom, placing as many components in a row as the space allows. The following flow layout places four components in the first row and two in the second:

```java
import javax.swing.*;
import java.awt.*;
public class TestPanel extends JPanel {
 public TestPanel () {
  setLayout(new FlowLayout());
  add(new TestButton("A"));
  add(new TestButton("B"));
  add(new TestButton("C"));
  add(new TestButton("D"));
  add(new TestButton("E"));
  add(new TestButton("F"));
 }
}
```

1098 When you use the definition shown in Segment 1097, you produce the following display:

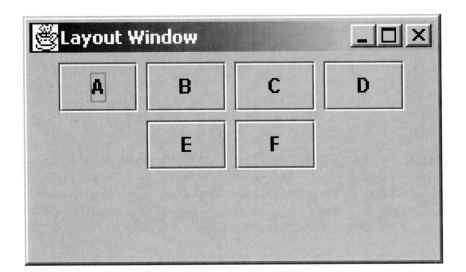

1099 The most complex layout manager, the gridbag-layout manager, provides fine control over component layout. Conceptually, the gridbag-layout manager divides your display into rows and columns, and any component can span any number of rows and any number of columns.

1100 Note that the numbering of rows and columns is zero based, with the origin in the upper-left corner:

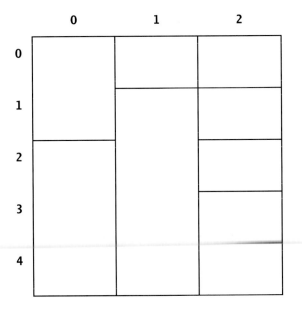

1101 To specify a gridbag layout, you create an instance of the GridBagLayout class, which you then associate with the surrounding applet using the setLayout method:

```
GridBagLayout gbl = new GridBagLayout();
setLayout(gbl);
```

1102 The allocation of checkerboard squares into components is governed by an instance of the GridBagConstraints class:

```
GridBagConstraints gbc = new GridBagConstraints();
```

1103 Among the many ways that you can condition the instance of GridBagConstraints, two deserve special mention. First, you arrange for particular components to expand by setting the weightx or weighty instance variables, or both, of the gridbag constraint:

```
gbc.weightx = 1.0; ←— Spread out horizontally
gbc.weighty = 1.0; ←— Spread out vertically
```

Second, you arrange for the expandable component to fill the available space by setting the fill instance variable to the value of the BOTH class variable:

```
gbc.fill = GridBagConstraints.BOTH; ←— Fill space
```

If you want to fill one way, but not the other, you use the HORIZONTAL or VERTICAL class-variable values, rather than the BOTH class variable value.

1104 Once you have set the weightx, weighty, and fill instance variables, you can place individual components.

First, you condition the placement of the next component by making adjustments to gridx and gridy instance variables of the GridBagConstraints instance:

```
gbc.gridx = 1; ←— Upper-left corner of component is in the second row
gbc.gridy = 2; ←— and third column
```

Second, you specify the number of rows and columns that the component is to span by adjusting gridwidth and gridheight instance variables:

```
gbc.gridwidth = 2;  ←— Component spans two columns
gbc.gridheight = 1; ←— and one row
```

Third, you associate the constraint with a component using setConstraints, an instance method of the GridBagLayout class:

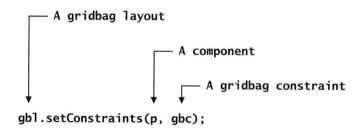

```
gbl.setConstraints(p, gbc);
```

Fourth, and finally, you add the component to the layout using add:

```
add(p);
```

1105 You do not need to create a fresh instance of GridBagConstraints for every component; you need only one instance, as long as you adjust the instance-variable values that change before each component placement.

1106 All the key gridbag-layout machinery is exhibited in the following example, in which the repetitive part of component placement is done in the placeComponent method, keeping clutter controlled:

```
import java.awt.*;
import javax.swing.*;
public class TestPanel extends JPanel {
 public TestPanel () {
  GridBagLayout gbl = new GridBagLayout();
  setLayout(gbl);
  GridBagConstraints gbc = new GridBagConstraints();
  // Fill both ways and allow expansion of all components:
  gbc.fill = GridBagConstraints.BOTH;
  gbc.weightx = 1.0;
  gbc.weighty = 1.0;
  // Place components:
  placeComponent(0, 0, 1, 2, "A", gbl, gbc);
  placeComponent(1, 0, 1, 1, "B", gbl, gbc);
  placeComponent(0, 2, 1, 3, "C", gbl, gbc);
  placeComponent(1, 1, 1, 4, "D", gbl, gbc);
  placeComponent(2, 0, 1, 1, "E", gbl, gbc);
  placeComponent(2, 1, 1, 1, "F", gbl, gbc);
  placeComponent(2, 2, 1, 1, "G", gbl, gbc);
  placeComponent(2, 3, 1, 1, "H", gbl, gbc);
  placeComponent(2, 4, 1, 1, "I", gbl, gbc);
 }
 // Handle placement details:
 public void placeComponent
   (int x, int y, int w, int h,
    String s, GridBagLayout l, GridBagConstraints c) {
   c.gridx = x;          c.gridwidth = w;
   c.gridy = y;          c.gridheight = h;
   TestButton p = new TestButton(s);
   l.setConstraints(p, c);   add(p);
 }
}
```

1107 Using the gridbag layout shown in Segment 1106, you produce the following display:

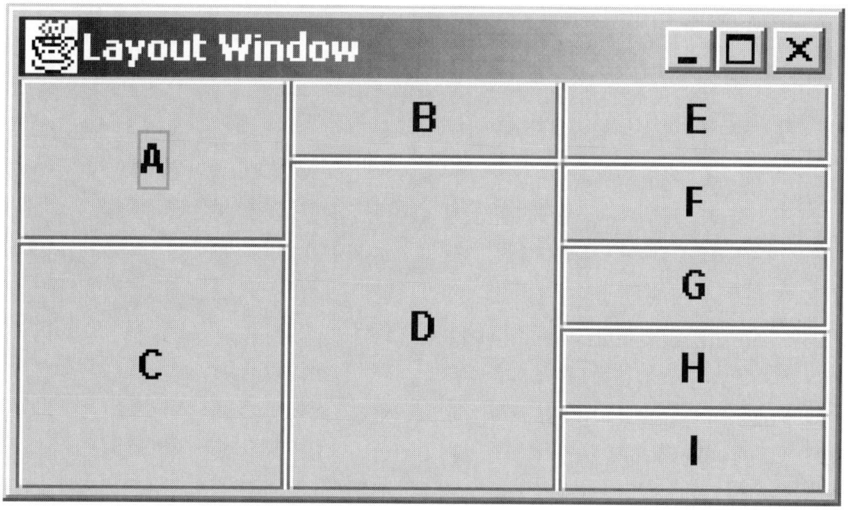

1108 The rows do not all need to have the same height, and the columns do not all need to have the same width. For example, you can arrange for column widths to be in the ratio 2:1:3, and for row heights to be in the ratio 1:1:2:1:1:, as follows:

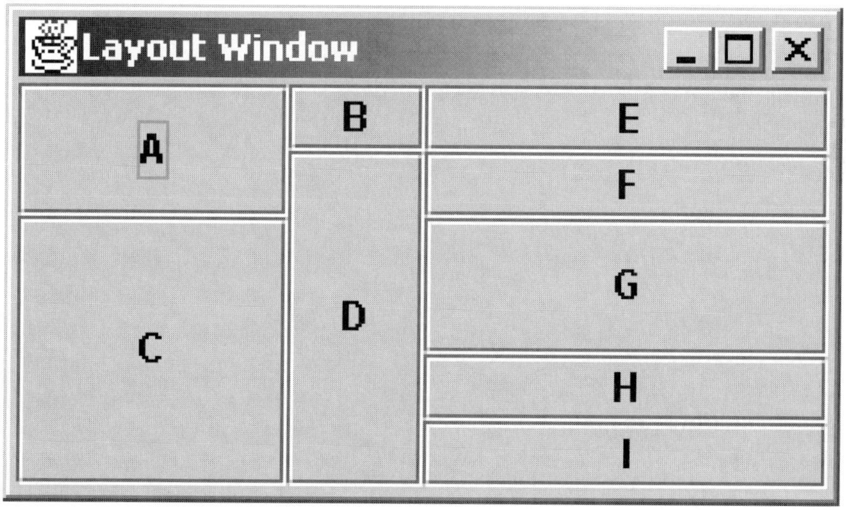

1109 To produce the display shown in Segment 1108, you first set the minimum and preferred sizes to 0 in the definition of the IndifferentButton button component:

```
import java.awt.*;
import javax.swing.*;
public class IndifferentButton extends JButton {
 public IndifferentButton (String t) {
  super(t);
 }
 public Dimension getMinimumSize() {return new Dimension(0, 0);}
 public Dimension getPreferredSize() {return new Dimension(0, 0);}
}
```

Then, you insert adjustments to the `gridx` and `gridy` parameters:

```
import java.awt.*;
import javax.swing.*;
public class TestPanel extends JPanel {
 public TestPanel () {
  GridBagLayout gbl = new GridBagLayout();
  setLayout(gbl);
  GridBagConstraints gbc = new GridBagConstraints();
  // Fill both ways:
  gbc.fill = GridBagConstraints.BOTH;
  // Allow expansion of all components:
  gbc.weightx = 2.0;
  gbc.weighty = 1.0;
  // Place components:
  placeComponent(0, 0, 1, 2, "A", gbl, gbc);
  placeComponent(0, 2, 1, 3, "C", gbl, gbc);
  gbc.weightx = 1.0;
  placeComponent(1, 0, 1, 1, "B", gbl, gbc);
  placeComponent(1, 1, 1, 4, "D", gbl, gbc);
  gbc.weightx = 3.0;
  placeComponent(2, 0, 1, 1, "E", gbl, gbc);
  placeComponent(2, 1, 1, 1, "F", gbl, gbc);

  gbc.weighty = 2.0;
  placeComponent(2, 2, 1, 1, "G", gbl, gbc);
  gbc.weighty = 1.0;
  placeComponent(2, 3, 1, 1, "H", gbl, gbc);
  placeComponent(2, 4, 1, 1, "I", gbl, gbc);
 }
// Definition of placeComponent as in Segment 1106 ...
}
```

1110   You can, of course, arrange complex layouts by embedding component-containing containers in surrounding containers. In the following, for example, border-layout components are embedded, at all positions, in another border-layout component:

1111 You might think that you would have to worry about the possibility that a user might make your GUI ugly by scaling that interface's window in an odd or extreme way. In practice, you do not have to worry at all when you are working with applets, because an applet's size is fixed, once and for all, in the HTML file. And you do not have to worry much, even when you are working with standalone applications, because few users change window sizes.

APPENDIX F: THE GRAPHICS2D PACKAGE

In Chapter 39 and Chapter 40, you learned to use a graphics context to perform basic display operations. In early versions of Java, all drawing was done via a graphics context, an instance of the Graphics class, but because the Graphics class enabled only straightforward drawing, Java's custodians added the more sophisticated Graphics2D class.

1113 It is easy to adapt an existing program, such as the meter program shown in Segment 748, to work with the Graphics2D class, instead of with the Graphics class. Because the Graphics2D class is a subclass of the Graphics class, all the methods in the Graphics class still work. All you need to do is to cast the Graphics instance supplied as the paint method's argument into an instance of the Graphics2D class, and then to work with that instance of the Graphics2D class.

```
import java.awt.*;
import javax.swing.*;
public class Meter extends JComponent implements MeterInterface {
 String title = "Title to Be Supplied";
 int minValue, maxValue, value;
 public Meter (int x, int y) {
  minValue = x; maxValue = y; value = (y + x) / 2;
 }
 public void setValue(int v) {value = v; repaint();}
 public void setTitle(String t) {title = t; repaint();}
 public void paint(Graphics x) {
  Graphics2D g = (Graphics2D) x;
// Rest of paint as in Segment 748 ...
 }
 public Dimension getMinimumSize() {return new Dimension(150, 100);}
 public Dimension getPreferredSize() {return new Dimension(150, 100);}
}
```

Note that there is no getValueAtCoordinates method, as defined in Segment 748, as that method is not relevent to the explanation of the methods of the Graphics2D clas.

1114 The methods supplied by the Graphics class expect you to supply coordinate values as int instances that define screen locations. The methods supplied by the Graphics2D class itself expect you to supply coordinates in a **user coordinate space** in which the coordinates are specified by float instances. Instances of the Graphics2D class translate those float instances into a **display coordinate space**, in which the coordinates are specified in whatever form is natural to the display device.

1115 A Graphics graphics context allows you to draw straight lines using drawLine with integer coordinates.

A `Graphics2D` graphics context allows you to draw not only straight lines, but also **quadratic curves** and **Bezier curves**.

1116 To draw a line using the `Graphics2D` graphics context, you first construct a **path**, an instance of the `GeneralPath` class, such as `path` in the following illustration:

```
GeneralPath path = new GeneralPath();
```

1117 Once you have constructed a path, you specify the shape of that path using **path-defining methods**. The two most commonly used path-defining methods in the `GeneralPath` class are `moveTo` and `lineTo`. The `moveTo` method specifies a virtual pen move from the current position to a specified position without leaving a track; the `lineTo` method specifies a virtual pen move from the current position to a specified position with a track.

Thus, to specify the straight lines required by the meter, you use the following `moveTo` and `lineTo` operations, once you have converted the `int` variables of Segment 1113 to `float` variables.

```
path.moveTo(lineXOffset, lineYOffset);
path.lineTo(lineXOffset + meterWidth, lineYOffset);
path.moveTo(lineXOffset + pointerPosition, lineYOffset);
path.lineTo(lineXOffset + pointerPosition, lineYOffset - meterHeight);
```

1118 Occasionally, you may wish to complete a closed figure by drawing a line from the current position to the place specified by the most recent `moveTo` method. You use the `closePath` method, with no arguments.

1119
SIDE TRIP

The `quadTo` and `curveTo` methods draw **quadratic curves** and **Bezier curves**. The `quadTo` method takes four `float` arguments, which define two points. The second point is the destination; the first is a quadratic **control point**. The `curveTo` method takes six `float` arguments, which define three points. The third point is the destination; the first two are Bezier control points.

1120 Once you have defined a path's shape, you use the `draw` method to draw that path on an instance of `Graphics2D`, `g`:

```
g.draw(path);
```

1121 Doing path-oriented drawing requires including the `java.awt.geom` package, as shown in the following adaptation of the `Meter` definition given in Segment 1113. Note also that `moveTo` and `lineTo` require `float` arguments, rather than `int` arguments. Also, the `Graphics2D` class defines a `drawString` method that takes `float` arguments, so the following definition uses `float` variables for drawing the text. Thus, both line drawing and text drawing are done in user coordinates.

```java
import java.awt.*;
import javax.swing.*;
import java.awt.geom.*;
public class Meter extends JComponent implements MeterInterface {
 String title = "Title to Be Supplied";
 int minValue, maxValue, value;
 public Meter (int x, int y) {
  minValue = x; maxValue = y; value = (y + x) / 2;
 }
 public void setValue(int v) {value = v; repaint();}
 public void setTitle(String t) {title = t; repaint();}
 public void paint(Graphics x) {
  Graphics2D g = (Graphics2D) x;
  // Obtain Dimension instance:
  Dimension d = getSize();
  // Draw:
  float meterWidth = d.width * 3 / 4;
  float meterHeight = meterWidth / 20;
  float pointerPosition
   = meterWidth * (value - minValue) / (maxValue - minValue);
  float lineXOffset = (d.width - meterWidth) / 2;
  float lineYOffset = d.height / 2;
  GeneralPath path = new GeneralPath();
  path.moveTo(lineXOffset, lineYOffset);
  path.lineTo(lineXOffset + meterWidth, lineYOffset);
  path.moveTo(lineXOffset + pointerPosition, lineYOffset);
  path.lineTo(lineXOffset + pointerPosition,
              lineYOffset - meterHeight);
  g.draw(path);
  // Prepare font
  int fontSize = d.width / 30;
  g.setFont(new Font("Helvetica", Font.BOLD, fontSize));
  // Write title:
  FontMetrics f = g.getFontMetrics();
  float stringWidth = f.stringWidth(title);
  float textXOffset = (d.width - stringWidth) / 2;
  float textYOffset = (d.height / 2) + (2 * f.getHeight());
  g.drawString(title, textXOffset, textYOffset);
 }
 public Dimension getMinimumSize() {return new Dimension(150, 100);}
 public Dimension getPreferredSize() {return new Dimension(150, 100);}
}
```

1122 So far, the Graphics2D graphics context—the one used in Segment 1121—exhibits no special advantage relative to the Graphics graphics context used in Segment 1113. However, an advantage emerges immediately if you wish to transform a drawing, because

Graphics2D instances can be told to apply one or more of the transformations known in mathematics as the **affine transformations**.

The affine transformations include, as special cases, all translations, rotations, flips, and changes of scale.

1123
SIDE TRIP Mathematically, an affine transformation translates image coordinates, x, y, to new coordinates, x', y', as follows:

$$x' = m_{11}x + m_{12}y + m_{13}$$
$$y' = m_{21}x + m_{22}y + m_{23}$$

For a pure rotation by an angle, θ,

$$m_{11} = \cos(\theta)$$
$$m_{11} = -\sin(\theta)$$
$$m_{21} = \sin(\theta)$$
$$m_{22} = -\cos(\theta)$$

and $m_{13} = m_{23} = 0$.

For a pure translation by Δ_x, Δ_y, $m_{13} = \Delta_x$ and $m_{23} = \Delta_y$.

Other combinations provide flips, changes of scale, and even shears.

1124 To create an affine transformation for translation, you first define an AffineTransform class. Then, you use the translate method.

For example, to create an affine transform, transform, that translates by one-half of the width and height of a dimension, d, you write the following statements:

```
AffineTransform transform = new AffineTransform();
transform.translate(d.width / 2, d.height / 2);
```

1125 You use the setTransform method to attach the affine transform to a Graphics2D graphics context, g:

```
g.setTransform(transform);
```

1126 Incorporating a transformation into the definition of the Meter's paint method enables you to write simpler arithmetic expressions.

For example, in the following, you see expressions specialized to realizing the meter's shape and other expressions specialized to centering the meter in the component. With that separation, you can easily, for example, add short vertical lines at the end of the meter's horizontal line. The shape expressions presume a coordinate system centered at the midpoint of the meter's horizontal line:

```java
import java.awt.*;
import javax.swing.*;
import java.awt.geom.*;
public class Meter extends JComponent implements MeterInterface {
 String title = "Title to Be Supplied";
 int minValue, maxValue, value;
 public Meter (int x, int y) {
  minValue = x; maxValue = y; value = (y + x) / 2;
 }
 public void setValue(int v) {value = v; repaint();}
 public void setTitle(String t) {title = t; repaint();}
 public void paint(Graphics x) {
  Graphics2D g = (Graphics2D) x;
  // Obtain Dimension instance:
  Dimension d = getSize();
  // Draw:
  float meterWidth = d.width * 3 / 4;
  float meterHeight = meterWidth / 20;
  float pointerPosition
   = meterWidth * (value - minValue) / (maxValue - minValue);
  // Offset to new origin:
  pointerPosition = pointerPosition - (meterWidth / 2);
  GeneralPath path = new GeneralPath();
  path.moveTo(- meterWidth / 2, - meterHeight);
  path.lineTo(- meterWidth / 2, 0);
  path.lineTo(meterWidth / 2, 0);
  path.lineTo(meterWidth / 2, - meterHeight);
  path.moveTo(pointerPosition, 0);
  path.lineTo(pointerPosition, - meterHeight);
  AffineTransform transform = new AffineTransform();
  transform.translate(d.width / 2, d.height / 2);
  g.setTransform(transform);
  g.draw(path);
  // Prepare font
  int fontSize = d.width / 30;
  g.setFont(new Font("Helvetica", Font.BOLD, fontSize));
  // Write title:
  FontMetrics f = g.getFontMetrics();
  float stringWidth = f.stringWidth(title);
  float textXOffset = - stringWidth / 2;
  float textYOffset = 2 * f.getHeight();
  g.drawString(title, textXOffset, textYOffset);
 }
 public Dimension getMinimumSize() {return new Dimension(150, 100);}
 public Dimension getPreferredSize() {return new Dimension(150, 100);}
}
```

1127 Using the `rotate` method, you can produce an affine transform that rotates by an angle expressed in radians. For example, if you wish to rotate by 90°, counterclockwise, you rotate by $-\pi/2$ radians.

Conveniently, the `Math` class provides a value for π as the value of a class variable, `PI`. Thus, to create an affine transform for a 90° counterclockwise rotation, you write the following statements:

```
AffineTransform transform = new AffineTransform();
transform.rotate(- Math.PI / 2);
```

1128 Java applies transformations in the order dictated by mathematical convention. Thus, if the `translate` transform appears before the `rotate` transform, then Java applies the rotation transform first, followed by the translation transform.

1129 Thus, for example, if you wish to rotate, then translate, you write the following:

```
AffineTransform transform = new AffineTransform();
transform.translate(d.width / 2, d.height / 2);
transform.rotate(- Math.PI / 2);
```

On the other hand, if you wish to translate, then rotate, you write the following:

```
AffineTransform transform = new AffineTransform();
transform.rotate(- Math.PI / 2);
transform.translate(d.width / 2, d.height / 2);
```

1130 The following produces a rotated meter.

```
import java.awt.*;
import java.awt.geom.*;
import javax.swing.*;
public class Meter extends JComponent implements MeterInterface {
 String title = "Title to Be Supplied";
 int minValue, maxValue, value;
 public Meter (int x, int y) {
  minValue = x; maxValue = y; value = (y + x) / 2;
 }
 public void setValue(int v) {value = v; repaint();}
 public void setTitle(String t) {title = t; repaint();}
```

```
public void paint(Graphics x) {
 Graphics2D g = (Graphics2D) x;
 // Obtain Dimension instance:
 Dimension d = getSize();
 // Draw:
 float meterWidth = d.width * 3 / 4;
 float meterHeight = meterWidth / 20;
 float pointerPosition
  = meterWidth * (value - minValue) / (maxValue - minValue);
 // Offset to new origin:
 pointerPosition = pointerPosition - (meterWidth / 2);
 GeneralPath path = new GeneralPath();
 path.moveTo(- meterWidth / 2, - meterHeight);
 path.lineTo(- meterWidth / 2, 0);
 path.lineTo(meterWidth / 2, 0);
 path.lineTo(meterWidth / 2, - meterHeight);
 path.moveTo(pointerPosition, 0);
 path.lineTo(pointerPosition, - meterHeight);
 AffineTransform transform = new AffineTransform();
 transform.translate(d.width / 2, d.height / 2);
 transform.rotate(- Math.PI / 2);
 g.setTransform(transform);
 g.draw(path);
 // Prepare font
 int fontSize = d.width / 30;
 g.setFont(new Font("Helvetica", Font.BOLD, fontSize));
 // Write title:
 FontMetrics f = g.getFontMetrics();
 float stringWidth = f.stringWidth(title);
 float textXOffset = - stringWidth / 2;
 float textYOffset = 2 * f.getHeight();
 g.drawString(title, textXOffset, textYOffset);
 }
 public Dimension getMinimumSize() {return new Dimension(150, 100);}
 public Dimension getPreferredSize() {return new Dimension(150, 100);}
}
```

1131 If you do not supply an affine transform using the setTransform method, Java uses by default the identity transform, which leaves your drawing unchanged.

1132 You can supply a Graphics2D graphics context not only with an AffineTransform instance, which alters position, but also with a BasicStroke instance, which alters appearance. You use **strokes** to make lines thick or thin and plain or dashed. You also use strokes to determine how lines are capped and joined.

For example, to create a stroke, stroke, that draws lines 10 units wide, capped with butt ends, and joined to other lines with mitered corners, you write the following statement, using two class variables in the BasicStroke package to control caps and joins:

```
BasicStroke stroke
  = new BasicStroke(10, BasicStroke.CAP_BUTT,
                        BasicStroke.JOIN_MITER);
```

Then, to attach the stroke to a Graphics2D graphics context, g, you use the setStroke method:

```
g.setStroke(stroke);
```

1133 The following range of options is available for capping and joining:

- JOIN.MITER: Extend outside edges until they meet at a point.

- JOIN.BEVEL: Extend outside edges, but trim off point.

- JOIN.ROUND: Round off outside edges smoothly.

- CAP.ROUND: Terminate with round end.

- CAP.BUTT: Terminate with square end.

- CAP.SQUARE: Terminate with square end that projects one-half of the width of the line beyond the terminal coordinates.

1134 If you do not supply a stroke using the setStroke method, Java uses CAP_SQUARE and JOIN_MITER by default.

1135 If you like, you can use setColor with Graphics2D graphics contexts, just as you can use setColor with ordinary Graphics graphics contexts. Alternatively, you can create an instance of the Paint class, to produce fancy effects. For example, the following creates an instance of the GradientPaint subclass of the Paint class, for which the color changes continuously from one point to another:

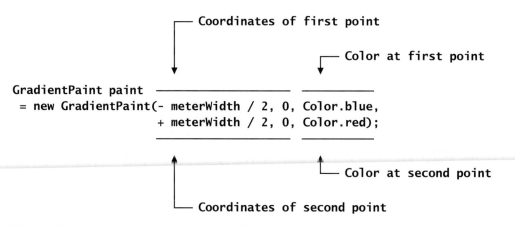

```
GradientPaint paint
  = new GradientPaint(- meterWidth / 2, 0, Color.blue,
                      + meterWidth / 2, 0, Color.red);
```

To attach the paint to a Graphics2D graphics context, g, you use the setPaint method:

```
g.setPaint(paint);
```

1136 The following version of the paint method in Meter illustrates the use of stroke and paint refinements:

```java
import java.awt.*;
import javax.swing.*;
import java.awt.geom.*;
public class Meter extends JComponent implements MeterInterface {
 String title = "Title to Be Supplied";
 int minValue, maxValue, value;
 public Meter (int x, int y) {
  minValue = x; maxValue = y; value = (y + x) / 2;
 }
 public void setValue(int v) {value = v; repaint();}
 public void setTitle(String t) {title = t; repaint();}
 public void paint(Graphics x) {
  Graphics2D g = (Graphics2D) x;
  // Obtain Dimension instance:
  Dimension d = getSize();
  // Draw:
  float meterWidth = d.width * 3 / 4;
  float meterHeight = meterWidth / 20;
  float pointerPosition
   = meterWidth * (value - minValue) / (maxValue - minValue);
  // Offset to new origin:
  pointerPosition = pointerPosition - (meterWidth / 2);
  GeneralPath path = new GeneralPath();
  path.moveTo(- meterWidth / 2, - meterHeight);
  path.lineTo(- meterWidth / 2, 0);
  path.lineTo(meterWidth / 2, 0);
  path.lineTo(meterWidth / 2, - meterHeight);
  path.moveTo(pointerPosition, 0);
  path.lineTo(pointerPosition, - meterHeight);
  AffineTransform transform = new AffineTransform();
  transform.translate(d.width / 2, d.height / 2);
  g.setTransform(transform);
  BasicStroke stroke
    = new BasicStroke(10, BasicStroke.CAP_BUTT,
                         BasicStroke.JOIN_BEVEL);
  g.setStroke(stroke);
  GradientPaint paint
    = new GradientPaint(- meterWidth / 2, 0, Color.blue,
                        + meterWidth / 2, 0, Color.red);
  g.setPaint(paint);
  g.draw(path);
```

```
  // Prepare font
  int fontSize = d.width / 30;
  g.setFont(new Font("Helvetica", Font.BOLD, fontSize));
  // Write title:
  FontMetrics f = g.getFontMetrics();
  float stringWidth = f.stringWidth(title);
  float textXOffset = - stringWidth / 2;
  float textYOffset = 2 * f.getHeight();
  g.drawString(title, textXOffset, textYOffset);
 }
 public Dimension getMinimumSize() {return new Dimension(150, 100);}
 public Dimension getPreferredSize() {return new Dimension(150, 100);}
}
```

1137 If you use MovieApplication, as defined in Segment 726, to display an instance of Meter, as defined in Segment 1136, you see the following—but in glorious color, rather than in black and white:

INDEX

COLOPHON

The authors produced camera-ready copy for this book using TEX/, which is Donald E. Knuth's computer typesetting language.

We transformed source text into PostScript files using the products of Y&Y, of Concord, Massachusetts.

The text was set primarily in 10-point Sabon Roman. The page numbers, chapter headings, and segment headings were set in Frutiger Ultra Black. The computer programs were set in 9-point Lucida Sans bold.

The authors tested all programs using the compiler produced by Sun Microsystems, Inc.

SOFTWARE

The programs in this book are available via the browser-based version of this book, accessible via the URL provided on the back cover of this book. You simply use the view-source mechanism in your browser and copy from the display presented.

Also, unless someone has loaded Java software on your computer, you will need to download various tools, such as those available via the following links. Keep in mind that such links tend to become obsolete quickly, so you may need to find more current links by rummaging around on the Internet yourself, starting, perhaps at the Java URL, `http://java.sun.com/`.

- `http://java.sun.com/j2se/`: download a Java development kit and documentation from Sun Microsystems, Inc. The company also supplies general documentation via `http://developer.java.sun.com/developer/infodocs/`, which includes the language specification.
- `ftp://ftp.javasoft.com/pub/jdk1.1/rmi/class-server.zip`: download a registry maintaining program, suitable for RMI testing, from Sun Microsystems, Inc.
- `http://java.sun.com/products/servlet/`: download a servlet development kit, which includes the servlet server described in Chapter 54, from Sun Microsystems, Inc.
- `http://java.sun.com/products/plugin/`: download an HTML applet translator, from Sun Microsystems, Inc., which directs the popular browsers to use the latest plug-in Java, rather than their built-in versions.

BOOKS

Other Books in this Series

On To C, by Patrick Henry Winston

On To C++, by Patrick Henry Winston

On To Smalltalk, by Patrick Henry Winston

The *On To* series stands on the idea that the best way to learn a new programming language is to follow an example that answers natural questions in a natural order. Then, once you understand how to express a complete, albeit simple program, you extend your understanding by learning about features that make you more efficient, flexible, and sophisticated.

Thus, you learn a new programming language in much the same way you learned your native tongue—you learn essentials first, then you build on those essentials as situations arise that require you to know more.

Other Books by Patrick Henry Winston

Artificial Intelligence (Third Edition), by Patrick Henry Winston

Lisp (Third Edition), by Patrick Henry Winston and Berthold Klaus Paul Horn